MW00563592

EVEREST, INC.

EVEREST, INC.

The RENEGADES *and* ROGUES

who BUILT AN INDUSTRY *at*

the TOP OF THE WORLD

WILL COCKRELL

G

GALLERY BOOKS

New York London Toronto Sydney New Delhi

G

Gallery Books
An Imprint of Simon & Schuster, LLC
1230 Avenue of the Americas
New York, NY 10020

First Gallery Books hardcover edition April 2024

GALLERY BOOKS and colophon are registered trademarks of Simon & Schuster, LLC

Simon & Schuster: Celebrating 100 Years of Publishing in 2024

For information about special discounts for bulk purchases, please contact Simon & Schuster Special Sales at 1-866-506-1949 or business@simonandschuster.com.

The Simon & Schuster Speakers Bureau can bring authors to your live event. For more information or to book an event, contact the Simon & Schuster Speakers Bureau at 1-866-248-3049 or visit our website at www.simonspeakers.com.

Interior design by Jaime Putorti

Manufactured in the United States of America

10 9 8 7 6 5 4 3 2 1

Library of Congress Cataloging-in-Publication Data has been applied for.

ISBN 978-1-9821-9045-3
ISBN 978-1-9821-9047-7 (ebook)

CONTENTS

INTRODUCTION

B etween 1953, when Edmund Hillary and Tenzing Norgay Sherpa became the first people to summit Mount Everest, and 1992, when the first paying clients were successfully guided up it, only 394 climbers reached the top. Between 1992 and 2024, more than 11,500 others accomplished this same feat. The vast majority of them—more than 90 percent—were the clients and employees of a small number of mountain-guiding companies.

How did a peak that was at first deemed unclimbable, then downgraded to simply suicidal, become one that thousands of people could scale? In *Everest, Inc.*, I answer that question. Doing so necessitated reporting what is perhaps one of the most thrilling untold tales in mountaineering history, if not the history of entrepreneurialism writ large.

While there have been plenty of other written works and films about Everest, they've typically been focused on one specific tragedy or triumph. As a result, they've added up to a skewed view of the mountain, especially of what it's like today. *Everest, Inc.* links together the most influential moments of the last four decades of the mountain's history and shows that they've really been twists and turns on the same wild ride. It reveals that the modern history of Everest is, fundamentally, the history of the *guiding industry* on Everest. And in taking us to the present moment, it shows how the relationship Nepalis have to their national treasure—Sagarmatha, as the Sherpa people refer to the mountain—as well as their feelings of ownership over it have evolved, going from rock bottom to historic heights in the space of a decade.

The misconceptions about Everest guiding run deep, dating back to that first ascent in 1953 and the false notion that Tenzing Norgay guided Edmund Hillary to the summit, or sometimes that it was the other way around. The majority of the stickiest Everest myths, however, were seeded by *Into Thin Air*, Jon Krakauer's brilliant first-person account of an unusually heart-wrenching day. It remains *the* book about guiding on high peaks, and the lens through which just about all Everest stories continue to be viewed. But Krakauer's scorching indictment of overcrowding, dangerously smug guides, and bumbling client climbers was written in 1996, only *four* years after guides first cracked the code on Everest. The mountain's place in popular culture is seemingly frozen in time, so it's no wonder that whenever concerns are aired about Everest in the press, someone warns that "it'll be 1996 all over again." The notion is as outdated as the plastic-shelled boots climbers used in Krakauer's day.

Year after year, stories aimed at grabbing the attention of the morbidly curious still hijack the Everest narrative. And when there isn't tragedy to report on, the mountain is either depicted as a circus, with amateurs who don't belong buying their way to the top, or a soap opera, with greedy guides and inept clients as the villains, and Sherpas as the victims. Each overly simplified story pushes the myth of what the guiding industry truly is further and further from the more complicated and interesting truth. The time has come for a recalibration of our understanding of who the clients and guides are on the iconic mountain, and why they're drawn to it.

Before the first successful guided expedition, only about 10 percent of climbers reached the summit. Today, the number is roughly 70 percent. Less than 0.5 percent die while trying. No one knows the story of how we got here better than the Western guides and client climbers, the Sherpa guides and high-altitude workers, and the entrepreneurs and industry watchers who have played a role in the industry over the last forty years. I interviewed more than 120 of those people for this book.

Admittedly, before I began doing my research, I thought I knew a lot about Everest. Once I scratched the surface and then as I continued to dig, however, the surprises were endless. I've been writing and reporting about climbing and mountaineering for more than twenty years, including several years as a senior editor at *Men's Journal* magazine, which frequently ran Everest stories. In fact, *Men's Journal* was the first to publish a feature about the 1996 disaster, written by Peter Wilkinson (Krakauer's article in *Outside* magazine that was the basis for his book came out two months later). I worked as a senior editor at *Men's Journal* between 2009 and 2014, and went on to write for *Outside* often, as well as many other national publications about Everest, and mountaineering in general. And I've been an avid but amateur climber and mountaineer for my whole life. I hiked to Everest base camp in Nepal in the spring of 2022. I felt like I'd been run over by a bus at that altitude but my inadequacy as a high-altitude climber gave me an enormous appreciation for how impressive it is to merely attempt to climb Everest, let alone summit—and how downright superhuman it is that guides get so many inexperienced people to the summit, safely, year after year.

On my base camp visit and in reporting this book, I came into contact with an army of journeymen and -women who are intoxicated with guiding others through one of the biggest challenges of their lives, and have made a dream come true for people from all over the world. I also gained a deep understanding of the transformative effect the Everest guiding industry is having on the country of Nepal and on the livelihoods of the Sherpa people.

While I have attempted to bring the rumors into balance with a less pessimistic truth in this book, no one gets a free pass. Dysfunction has indeed plagued the guiding industry at times. Mistakes have been made. Lives have been lost, and things remain as complex as ever. Telling the complete story of the industry requires acknowledging uncomfortable facts and inconvenient truths, sometimes about people and companies whom climbers, clients, or guiding industry insiders have long put on a pedestal. I believe it's necessary to unpack these stories in order to have the standing to also give full credence to the industry's accomplishments. Because, while it has its issues to account for, there are many positive things about the guiding industry that deserve to be acknowledged.

When it comes to the mountain that looms largest in our collective consciousness, rumor has always outrun the truth. My hope is that *Everest, Inc.* is an entertaining and thought-provoking step toward rectifying that—because in the case of the guiding industry on Everest, the truth really is more fascinating than fiction.

EVEREST, INC.

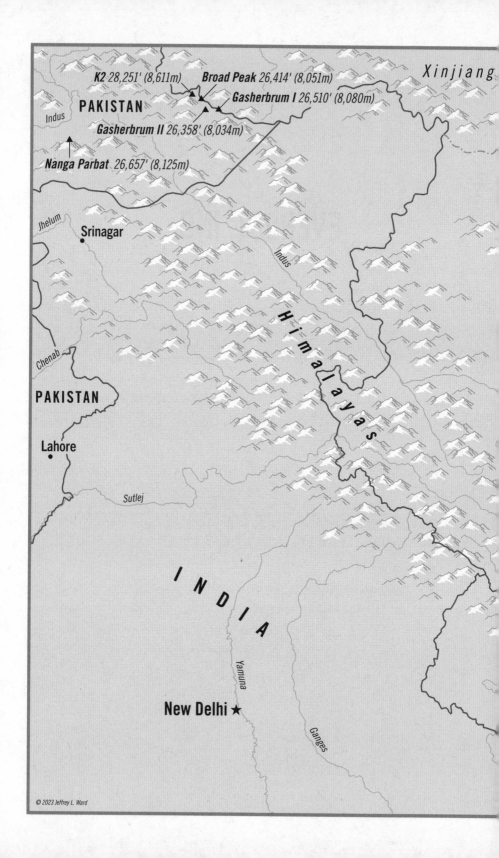

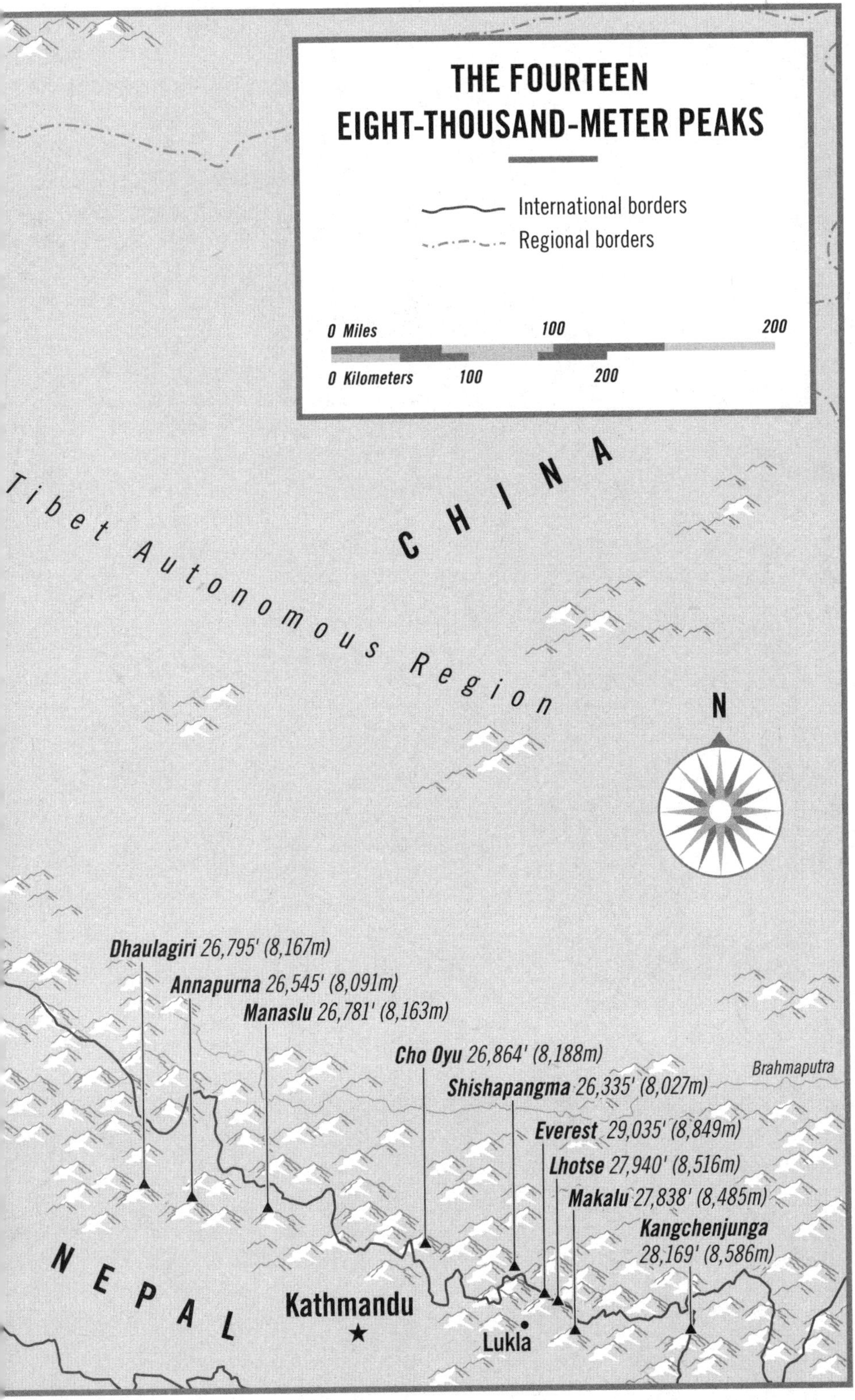

THE FOURTEEN
EIGHT-THOUSAND-METER PEAKS

—————— International borders

·—·—·—· Regional borders

| 0 Miles | | 100 | | 200 |

| 0 Kilometers | 100 | | 200 | |

CHINA

Tibet Autonomous Region

N

Dhaulagiri 26,795' (8,167m)

Annapurna 26,545' (8,091m)
Manaslu 26,781' (8,163m)

Cho Oyu 26,864' (8,188m)
Shishapangma 26,335' (8,027m)

Brahmaputra

Everest 29,035' (8,849m)
Lhotse 27,940' (8,516m)
Makalu 27,838' (8,485m)

*Kangchenjunga
28,169' (8,586m)*

NEPAL

Kathmandu
★

Lukla

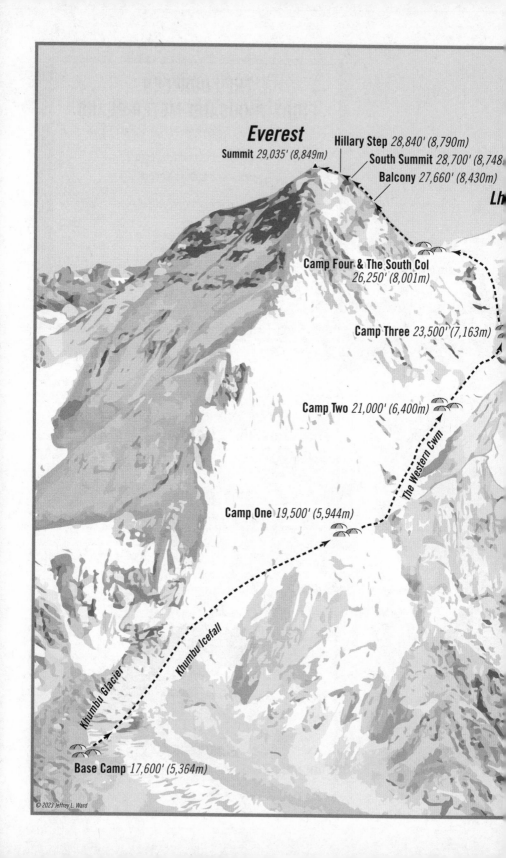

Everest
Summit *29,035' (8,849m)*

Hillary Step *28,840' (8,790m)*
South Summit *28,700' (8,748*
Balcony *27,660' (8,430m)*

Lh

Camp Four & The South Col
26,250' (8,001m)

Camp Three *23,500' (7,163m)*

Camp Two *21,000' (6,400m)*

The Western Cwm

Camp One *19,500' (5,944m)*

Khumbu Icefall

Khumbu Glacier

Base Camp *17,600' (5,364m)*

© 2023 Jeffrey L. Ward

Nuptse

TYPICAL TIMELINE *of a* GUIDED EVEREST CLIMB *in* SPRING *Via* THE SOUTH COL ROUTE

Total length of trip: six to eight weeks

LATE MARCH: ARRIVE IN NEPAL

Day 1-2: Gather in Kathmandu

APRIL: TREK TO BASE CAMP AND ACCLIMATIZE

Day 3: Fly by small plane or helicopter to Lukla in the Khumbu Valley

Day 4-13: Trek for approximately ten days to Base Camp

Day 14-16: Begin acclimatizing to Base Camp elevation and refreshing climbing skills

Day 16-35: Continue acclimatizing at Base Camp and by climbing nearby peaks; travel through the Khumbu Icefall on rotations to Camp One and Camp Two, returning to Base Camp

EARLY MAY: FINAL ACCLIMATIZATION ROTATION

Day 36-40: Make a rotation from Base Camp to Camp Three and back

MID-MAY: SUMMIT PUSH

Expedition leaders identify a suitable two-to-three-day weather window for summiting, then set a date to leave Base Camp four to five days before that

Day 41: Climb from Base Camp to Camp Two

Day 42: Rest at Camp Two

Day 43: Climb from Camp Two to Camp Three

Day 44: Climb from Camp Three to Camp Four

Day 45: Climb from Camp Four to the summit and back (some climbers will descend all the way to Camp Two)

Day 45-46: Descend to lower camps and rest

Day 47-48: Return to Base Camp and rest

LATE MAY: RETURN TRIP

Day 48-53: Trek for three to five days to Lukla, then fly to Kathmandu

PROLOGUE

The summit of Mount Everest is split right down the middle by the border between Nepal and the Tibet Autonomous Region of China, but the vast majority of climbers make their attempt from the Nepal side. If they're clients of a guiding company, as almost all Everest climbers are today, they do so via the South Col Route–the same one that Edmund Hillary and Tenzing Norgay Sherpa used during their first ascent. On their way to the 29,035 foot summit, clients pass through five well-stocked camps, from the relatively flat and balmy base camp, at 17,600 feet, to the head-spinning and frigid Camp Four, at 26,250 feet. Camp Four sits on the South Col—a saddle-shaped pass between Everest and the adjacent peak Lhotse, the fourth-highest mountain in the world.

Trekkers and climbers reach base camp by first taking one of a dozen daily flights from Nepal's capital city, Kathmandu, to Tenzing-Hillary Airport in the small village of Lukla, at 9,400 feet. From there, they spend ten days ascending and descending narrow switchbacks and rough staircases hand-built out of local granite, crossing swaying cable bridges over churning glacier-fed rivers, and admiring pink rhododen-drons in full spring bloom during the most popular climbing season. They bed down each evening in cozy stone teahouses heated by yak-dung furnaces in increasingly small villages with centuries-old Bud-dhist temples. As base camp nears, the landscape of variegated earth tones becomes monochromatic, all black rock, white snow, and blue ice. While the Khumbu Glacier on which base camp sits looks like a vast rock garden, it is really the surface of a constantly shifting frozen river that has chewed its way through the surrounding metamorphic rock and deposited the crushed-up debris on the surface. When trekkers crest the final moraine before base camp, at last they see the hundreds of brightly colored, dome-shaped tents stretching across nearly a mile of the glacier.

Many of those who will be attempting the summit as part of a guided expedition will arrive in base camp to incongruous comforts for such a remote outpost, including carpeted lounges with beanbag chairs, high-speed internet access, masseuses, full bars, baristas, and movie screens. The diversions are meant to help fill the ample downtime, as climb-ers and their guides spend up to eight weeks on their expedition. It's often said that Everest expeditions are two weeks of climbing crammed into two months. Climbers spend approximately a week, cumulatively, ascending to Camps Two and Three, and up nearby peaks to acclimatize to the crippling altitude. Then, when it's time to go for the summit—which usually isn't until about day thirty-five of the expedition, if all is going smoothly—it takes less than a week to climb from base camp to the peak. Coming back down takes only about three days.

Getting from base camp to Camp One requires navigating the mountain's most treacherous section, where the Khumbu Glacier makes a sudden 2,000-foot climb in the span of about a mile and a half. This landscape of slick ice, enormous blocks of teetering snow, and gaping crevasses is known as the Khumbu Icefall. Camp One is more of a supply depot for oxygen bottles and other gear than an overnight pitstop, so climbers typically push on to Camp Two. Perched at 21,000 feet, in a seemingly benign valley called the Western Cwm (pronounced "koom"), Camp Two has fifty or so tents tucked into sheltered nooks of rock and ice. Surrounding the tents is a towering horseshoe-shaped amphitheater of jagged peaks and ridges consisting of Everest, Lhotse, and a rarely climbed, slightly lower, but more technical subpeak called Nuptse. Frayed, faded Buddhist prayer flags flap in the near-constant breeze as climbers hide out from the elements and sip lemon ginger tea in cramped mess tents that double as command centers—or ERs when disasters strike.

The terrain of Camp Two must be treated with great respect. Routine storms blow in, and avalanches, even distant ones, can push blasts of air and an apocalyptic cloud of white powder into the camp with such force that it rips tents apart or blows them away. Complacent newbies have been swallowed by cracks in the ice while fetching water for an afternoon tea. Even elite mountaineers have been lost. A beloved and skilled Nepalese climber named Babu Chiri Sherpa died in 2001 after falling into a crevasse while taking photos near Camp Two.

Bottom line: in the thin air of Camp Two, it is hard enough to walk a few feet away from your tent to relieve yourself, let alone run for your life. This is why on a now-infamous day in late April 2013, professional climbers Ueli Steck and Simone Moro, and their companion and cameraman Jonathan Griffith, were sick with dread as they fled down the mountain from Camp Two without time to consider the safest route. They had no choice. They were being chased.

Steck and Moro represented an increasingly small slice of Everest society: elite mountaineers who neither paid others to guide them nor took money to guide others. They were sponsored climbers, who received

a salary from huge outdoor companies including the North Face and
Mountain Hardwear to beguile and inspire amateurs with their daring
first ascents and pioneering records.

Steck, thirty-seven at the time, was one of the most famous climbers
on earth—a national hero of Switzerland, where they treat professional
mountaineers like Americans treat NBA players. His nickname: "the
Swiss Machine." Moro, forty-six, was an Italian who had been coming to Everest since he was twenty-one years old and had summited
four times already. He also worked as a pilot for an elite high-altitude
helicopter rescue operation in the Himalayas. At thirty-three, Jonathan
Griffith, an Englishman, was less experienced, there primarily to film
Steck and Moro's groundbreaking climb for as long as he could keep
up with them.

By 2013, there were only a couple of routes left on the mountain that had either never or only rarely been climbed before, and the
Europeans were set to attempt one of them. Not only did Steck and
Moro intend to summit Everest via this extremely dangerous route,
they wanted to continue on in a single twenty-hour push to then summit Lhotse, also via a new route. They planned to do all of this without
supplemental oxygen.

The pro climbers, however, were operating on the fringes of a jug-
gernaut that can justly be described as the Everest-industrial complex.
On any given day in April and May (Everest's spring climbing season) there are approximately 1,500 people at base camp. Only a small
fraction are independent climbers like Steck and Moro. The rest are
clients or employees of the booming commercial guiding businesses,
in which amateur climbers—or even complete novices—pay as much
as $300,000 for a heavily assisted shot at the summit. The South Col
Route is like a two-lane freeway, with a 75-miles-per-hour speed limit,
and no shoulder to pull off on. Though they hoped to ultimately attempt
a new route, the elite climbers were using the South Col Route up to

Camp Three for acclimatization climbs and gear-shuttling purposes in preparation for their big day.

Put another way, Steck and Moro were attempting something akin to looking for an Amazon butterfly species that lives in the path of a one-hundred-ton scorched-earth logging operation.

April 27, 2013, was a day of rest for the Western mountain guides and their clients. Some would be taking it easy in base camp; others would do the same at Camp Two on an acclimatization rotation. Steck, Moro, and Griffith saw this particular rest day as an opportunity to move more freely on the mountain at a time when less-experienced climbers would not be crowding the route. That morning, they set off from their tents in Camp Two for Camp Three on an acclimatization foray.

After Camp Two, the horizontal world ends and a vertical world begins. Climbers must spend a hard day scaling a section of an imposing and often icy slope known as the Lhotse Face. Camp Three is hacked into the side of the face at 23,500 feet, with man-made terraces just wide enough to fit a few tents.

By midday, the Europeans were halfway to Camp Three. Also on the face that day was a small group of Sherpa climbers, working for the guiding companies. Sherpas—an ethnic group native to the Solu-Khumbu region of the Himalayas, where Everest sits—had always played a significant role in the guiding industry, but by 2013 they were beginning to take increasing ownership of it, and thus were becoming more protective of it than ever before. Poverty was once crippling for the Sherpas of the Solu-Khumbu, even by Nepali standards. The Everest business had changed that.

The half dozen or so Sherpas working on the Lhotse Face were installing a three-thousand-foot rope safety line. This and the rest of the approximately twelve miles of "fixed rope" that is installed on Everest each season would essentially act as a limp handrail for the benefit of less-experienced client climbers, who would need the safety net during their trudge toward the top. (The ropes are left in place and remain on the mountain until they are buried by the snow, fall apart naturally, or are cut loose because they're in the way.) Among the team were Mingma Tenzing Sherpa, a well-liked and very experienced sirdar (a management position held by Sherpas), who worked for the American guiding company International Mountain Guides (IMG), and Tashi Riten Sherpa, a young IMG employee. The rest were employees of other Western guiding companies.

The job the Sherpas were doing was particularly delicate, involving hundreds of pounds of rope and climbing hardware such as razor-sharp ice screws and carabiners. Installing the fixed ropes often takes several days, and there are well-understood rules among the guiding companies about steering clear of the Sherpas until they're finished. All the commercial teams had met and explicitly agreed to avoid the face for several days. Steck, Moro, and Griffith were not at that meeting. As a small, noncommercial team, they did not feel obliged to clear their movements with other expedition leaders.

Still, aware of the dangers of the task the Sherpas had in front of them, the three had purposely plotted a route up the face that was a good 150 feet away from the rope-fixing team. They would also be climbing without ropes—"alpine style"—which would allow them to give the Sherpas a wide berth and move past them quickly. Griffith's footage from the day shows Steck plunging his ax into the snow, ascending quickly and playfully like a child climbing a tree. The alpinists were clearly enjoying themselves.

In order to reach Camp Three, however, they needed to eventually traverse across the face and over the Sherpas' ropes. The Sherpas were stacked in a long line as they worked at various elevations. The Europeans understood the importance of treading lightly and moving quickly. The two crews slowly merged, with Steck, Moro, and Griffith moving laterally, passing above some Sherpas and below others. As the climbers from both teams drove the spikes of their crampons and axes into the face for purchase, chunks of ice and snow rained onto those below. Mingma Tenzing rappelled down to confront Steck and Moro, yelling. Tension grew. Insults flew. Soon there was grabbing and shoving among the men clinging to the icy mountainside.

A fall seemed imminent—until a single word ended everything.

In a panic, Moro called one of the Sherpas a *machikne*. "Motherfucker" is the direct translation from Nepali, but the insult is considered far worse to the Nepalese. Moro had long worked side by side with Sherpas in his job as a helicopter rescue pilot, and he says he knew the word from late-night card games with some of his many Sherpa friends. In that moment, he believed his Swiss friend was about to be pulled off the face and killed. The shock of the insult stopped everything. As it turned out, one of the Sherpas' radios happened to be stuck in the Talk position, and the entire exchange was being broadcast into every mess tent on the mountain. Expedition leaders in the camps below listened raptly, helpless to intervene.

Then, with eerie calm, the Sherpas gathered their gear and began descending back toward Camp Two. It was only one p.m., and there was still much rope to fix. The three Europeans decided to stay behind and continue some of the rope work themselves as an act of goodwill. They knew there would be a reckoning when they returned to camp, though nothing that couldn't be settled over a cup of tea and a handshake, they thought—especially after letting the Sherpas know they'd helped with the ropes.

By late afternoon, most Western climbers and Sherpas at Camp Two are making small talk while sipping tea—or something stronger—in one of the heated mess tents. Entering Camp Two around three p.m., Steck, Moro, and Griffith planned on addressing what had happened on the Lhotse Face right away. They were eager to put the conflict behind them. They would just drop their climbing equipment at their tents, then continue straight on to the communal tents of the guide services to talk to the Sherpas and hash things out with the help of the guiding company expedition leaders. They knew the Sherpa climbers would likely already have recounted the incident to their bosses.

Before the Europeans even had time to reach the guide company camps, they were intercepted by Greg Vernovage, the IMG expedition leader. Vernovage had overheard the entire incident on the radio. "We asked everyone to just stay in their camps while we worked things out," he recalls. But while he was eager to smooth things over and was willing to be the middleman, there was no question about who he felt was to blame. "We had asked everyone in Camp Two to steer clear of the face that day, while the Sherpas worked," he says.

Vernovage walked with the three European climbers back to one of their tents. They were all discussing the best way to move forward when Melissa Arnot, a twenty-nine-year-old American guide, burst in, panicked. "You guys need to get out of here," she warned. "They're coming."

Arnot hastily explained that dozens of Sherpas were marching toward them, banded together from separate expeditions, many wearing scarves to cover their faces and some clutching baseball-size rocks.

Steck, Moro, and Griffith realized that there was no hope of calmly hashing things out. The angry voices drew near too quickly for them to get their gear together and escape. "We were trapped," Steck recalls. "I'm pretty used to dealing with dangerous situations. But people are different from mountains." As he cowered in his tent, Steck couldn't help but consider the irony that this might be the way his life came to an end. "I was thinking about how I've climbed so many cool mountains, without oxygen, without ropes—'I can't believe this is how I'll die. I'm so stupid for coming to Everest.'"

Rocks began to fly at the Europeans' tent. One struck Steck in the head, unleashing a stream of blood down his face. Vernovage and Arnot attempted to hold the line, standing firm with their arms linked between the tent and the Sherpas. Vernovage was staring down many of his own trusted employees. "I lost the ability to calm them down," he said in a documentary about the incident. "Many were young and I didn't know that was in them until I saw it." Another guide, Marty Schmidt, joined the standoff and knocked a rock from a Sherpa's hands.

Amid the chaos, Steck, Moro, and Griffith managed to split up to hide in separate tents. Steck's head was still gushing with blood when he heard Sherpas nearby saying, "Get that guy out. First we kill him, then we look for the other two." Moro too says he heard Sherpas saying that they deserved to die.

Many Sherpas dispute this, including the young Tashi Riten. He admits to stoking the violent confrontation, but not that far. "If Sherpas had really wanted to kill them, would they be alive now?" he asks. Tashi Riten also acknowledges that he ignored some of the more senior Sherpas who were trying to calm the situation, as he and some of the other younger men rallied for a fight. Dawa Steven Sherpa, the owner of the guiding company Asian Trekking and something of an elder statesman on Everest by that point, says, "We asked our senior Sherpas at Camp Two to try and go talk sense into the young rope-fixing Sherpas."

Tashi Riten did not back down. He stood in front of Moro's tent and demanded an apology. "I had once heard that in Italy, having to kneel is the worst thing," he says. Cell phone footage shows Moro emerging from a tent and immediately dropping to his knees in deference, asking for forgiveness. Arnot, in tears, pleaded for calm and mercy. Rocks continued to fly. One Sherpa reached past Arnot and Vernovage and slapped Moro across the face. Another kicked him with a heavy mountaineering boot. Arnot and Vernovage continued to stand their ground. Many who were there later said that the presence of a strong woman was likely the only thing that staved off an all-out attack.

With the European climbers essentially cornered, the Sherpas offered what felt like a draconian compromise. "They told us that if we were not gone in an hour they would kill all three of us," remembers Griffith. The men gathered a few necessities. As they set off in the fading light, they paused just long enough to notice the silhouettes of some Sherpas on the ridgeline, watching them flee.

Thirty minutes later, they reached the top of the Khumbu Icefall. They were so scared that they decided to avoid the standard, safer route, and make it more difficult for the Sherpas to follow them. This was an especially risky choice given the fact that they were traveling soon after the hottest part of the day, when melting ice and snow makes the glacier even more unpredictable.

As the Europeans danced through the gantlet of crevasses and kept a lookout for falling ice, the expedition leaders in base camp—Westerners and Sherpas alike—were having heated conversations over radio about how to handle the situation. For many, the priority was saving the season from an all-out mutiny. The guiding business was livelihood and lifeblood for them all, and this incident felt like an existential threat. Blame was being meted out on both sides. "Some company owners were already calling for us to be jailed," says Tashi Riten. "They requested an armed police force to come and get us." No such force materialized.

Eventually, the Europeans made it safely to base camp. Steck was truly shaken and insisted they leave immediately. Griffith agreed. "Ueli and Jonathan wanted to get the fuck out of there," says Moro. But Moro wanted to stay, still hoping to work out a truce. He loved Everest, called the place home for a good part of the year, and felt a deep connection to the Sherpas who had become his friends. He hated the idea of damaging the place and its people.

Moro's argument won out, and with the help of Dawa Steven and a New Zealander guide company owner named Russell Brice, among others, a meeting was organized. "I was pushing for the outcome of the meeting to be put in writing," Tashi Riten says. "It wasn't enough to just have an oral agreement. Otherwise, in coming generations, there will always be shame about this event, and we were just defending our pride."

A peace treaty of sorts was drawn up, agreed to, and signed. But the two main things it stipulated were reiterations of the norm as it already stood: Sherpas would be the ones to fix ropes, and their work would be undisturbed. It seems the settlement was less about the specific incident between the Europeans and Sherpas than an expression of the feeling among Sherpas that they deserved more control and respect. They deserved to be heard.

With the incident smoothed over, the Europeans abandoned their climb and left the Khumbu (though Moro did continue to fly rescue helicopters the rest of the season). Tashi Riten was let go by IMG, though he was rehired by a Nepali company to finish out the season. He has always regretted that the conflict turned physical, but he also says "there were some people that thanked me," pointing to what he saw as a reduction in the disrespect aimed at Sherpas after they'd stood up for themselves.

Meanwhile, the 2013 spring guiding season resumed. Roughly eight hundred people had their sights set on the summit that season. Six hundred and eighty-four people were successful and eight died—unremarkable statistics for an Everest season. To a typical client, it might have seemed as if nothing much had happened. In fact, everything had changed. The fuse that had been slowly burning for decades, ever since a Texan named Dick Bass had inadvertently kicked off the Everest guiding industry twenty-seven years earlier, had at last reached the powder keg.

1

LARGE MOUTH BASS

It was a sunny Wednesday in Burbank, California, 535 feet above sea level. By late afternoon, fifty-foot palm trees were casting long, skinny shadows across the boulevards, soon to be clogged with Angelenos waiting their turn to get on a freeway. Inside the vast soundstages of NBC Studios, however, time and place faded away as contestants bought vowels on the set of *Wheel of Fortune* and soap stars rehearsed dialogue for *Days of Our Lives*.

In Studio 1, Doc Severinsen and his band played through a commercial break as host Johnny Carson prepared to bring out his final guest for the May 15, 1985, episode of *The Tonight Show*. The guest didn't have the star power of Roger Moore, who would be stopping by later in the week to promote his turn as 007 in *A View to a Kill*. Nonetheless, there was about to be a *Tonight Show* first.

An applause sign flashed above the studio audience, cameras rolled into position, and Carson locked eyes with the ten million Americans watching at home. "OK, let me tell you a little bit about my next guest. Richard Bass is a businessman—spent most of his life sitting behind a desk. He's fifty-five years old and he's achieved the remarkable feat of climbing the highest mountain on each of the seven continents of the world.

"Two weeks ago, believe it or not, he was on top of Mount Everest—would you welcome Richard Bass."

The man who emerged from behind the light blue curtain was a couple of inches shy of six feet and wore an expensive-looking dark navy suit with a black tie. Lean, with weathered good looks, a warm smile, and a movie-star squint, he could be mistaken for *The Rockford Files'* leading man, James Garner. Yet a movie star Bass was not. Clearly new to this showbiz thing, the Texan glanced down at the floor and headed straight for Carson. After a handshake, Richard Bass—or Dick, to his friends—took his seat beside the comedian Robert Klein and Carson's sidekick, Ed McMahon. Bass crossed his legs, revealing a shiny black cowboy boot, and smiled.

"Obviously, the chapped lips are from being on top of Mount Everest, right?" Carson asked.

"Very definitely," Bass said in his thick drawl, chuckling.

Carson asked a couple of questions about the seven mountains he'd summited—such as how he went about choosing which to climb first—but there was a palpable sense that both host and guest were eager to talk about one in particular. Carson cut to the chase. "So, this was your fourth attempt to climb Mount Everest."

"That's right," Bass said. "We started in eighty-two. It was four years in a row."

"And how many people have been to the top of Mount Everest?"

"Oh, approximately one hundred and seventy or so." (Bass was the 174th.) "About one in ten are successful." While those were impressively low odds, Carson had invited Bass onto his show because Bass's accomplishment had an extra layer of improbability. Bass was known for sayings like "The only exercise I ever get is running through airports to catch a plane," and he'd stated that the only climbing he did was "getting up and out of bed." Throughout his life, Bass had embraced the idea of succeeding at things with as little preparation as possible, his Seven Summits endeavor included.

"Now, most mountain climbers, as I know it, spend a lot of time on the training to do something like that," Carson probed. "And you went out in a relatively short amount of time and did it."

"That's true," Bass replied. "I found that I have a really slow-beating heart, naturally, and a low blood pressure." He had a way of recounting his adventures, whether in business or in the mountains, as though they were a lucky accident. He smiled again, looked up at the studio audience, and with a characteristic dash of self-deprecation, landed a punch line he used often: "And I talk a lot, so I keep my lungs in good shape—I'm physically made for it."

Carson then cued footage of Bass on Everest, filmed just a few weeks earlier, while Bass narrated. Scenes of him plunging his ax into icy walls and tiptoeing over gaping crevasses did have a fish-out-of-water feel, but it was clear he knew the mountain intimately. When the defining image appeared—Bass on the summit, shrouded in cloud, unrecognizable behind layers of goose down, Gore-Tex, goggles, and an oxygen mask—words escaped him.

"Summit day is a real ordeal," was all Bass could muster for Carson.

Carson went fishing for more, though he seemed to realize that the right words were beyond his own reach as well: "The exhilaration must be incredible at that moment, thinking about this for years and years, and all of a sudden realizing . . . you're on top of Mount Everest."

Bass beamed, not adding a word.

"It's a remarkable achievement—congratulations," Carson told him before turning to the camera.

"We'll take a break, we'll be right back."

●   ●   ●

Climbing Everest was by no means Dick Bass's first preposterous idea.

Raised in Dallas, he was the second son of Harry W. Bass Sr., one of the richest and most influential men in the natural gas industry. In 1949, at the age of nineteen while on a summer vacation in Europe, he visited Zermatt, Switzerland, where he first laid eyes on what many say is the most perfectly shaped mountain in the world: the Matterhorn. In the Alps, mountain guides are as common as dairy farmers, and for them, climbing the Matterhorn is just another day at the office. Bass hired one to help him climb it, and he soon stood on the summit, smitten with the idea that he'd been able to scale one of the world's most famous mountains with this person's help.

Well aware that his path to success in life was about as short and straight as a drag strip if he just paid a few dues, Bass graduated from Yale in 1950 with a degree in geology and then served two years in the navy, stationed in Korea, once sneaking off to Japan to hike to the top of Mount Fuji. Upon his return to the States, he began to learn his way around the family business. He married his first wife, Rita, and had four children, but never stopped daydreaming or searching for challenges that he could sink his teeth into. Indeed, Bass was heir to an oil empire that had set him up for life, yet it was never his money that defined him, it was the surprising ways in which he chose to spend it.

In 1965, an opportunity came up to invest in a small ski resort project in Colorado, today known as Vail. He had a home built on a prime lot near the main chairlift and spent the next six years traveling between Vail and Dallas, juggling family life with his gnawing desire to be in thin air, surrounded by mountains. He was determined to instill a sense of adventure in his children—and an appreciation for suffering—with predawn hikes and hunting trips in subzero temperatures.

One night at a party in Vail, Bass met an out-of-towner named Ted Johnson, who told him about a piece of paradise just outside Salt Lake

City, Utah, called Little Cottonwood Canyon. Johnson was on the hunt for a partner to help develop a new ski resort. "The first time he saw that glaciated valley, he couldn't believe something so Alpine existed in the United States," his eldest son, Jim Bass, who was there with him on that initial trip, remembers. "It was a cathedral experience for my dad." In 1970, Johnson and Bass broke ground on Snowbird Ski Resort.

Unsurprisingly, the ever-social Dick Bass found that his favorite part of ski resort ownership was guest relations. Bass would shake hands, tell stories on the chairlift, and ski with anyone he could, thus living up to the fond nickname he'd been given: "Large Mouth Bass." But he would also return from winter trips in Europe with grand ambitions to create the biggest and best ski resort in the world. In Jim's words, his father was "a dreamer—not an execution guy."

Johnson sold his stake in Snowbird to Bass in 1974, and while it was on its way to becoming one of the biggest ski resorts in the country, it was struggling financially. By the end of 1980, Bass was fifty-one years old and $4 million in debt. The bank was breathing down his neck. Mountains had always brought him solace during times like these, and right about then, Bass would have climbed just about anything to clear his head.

"My dad was under unbelievable pressure at all times, keeping Snowbird going," says Jim. "Another one of his lines was that going climbing allowed him to run away from his debtors. That guy had nine lives, financially—he'd be flat on his back and then some miracle would happen."

One afternoon in the winter of 1981, he found himself mingling with his ski and safety patrol employees during their daily après-ski ritual at Snowbird's Tram Club. Skiers and resort staff swapped stories over a few beers while marveling at the mechanics of the mountain's main gondola, which were on display behind giant windows that faced the engine room. Among the Snowbird staff present was the ski patrol manager, Bob Bonar, and a senior patroller named Marty Hoey.

When she wasn't at Snowbird, Hoey was one of the only woman guides on Mount Rainier in Washington, and the only one on North America's tallest peak, Denali, in Alaska. (Formerly known as Mount McKinley, its indigenous name of Denali was officially restored by the federal government in 2015.)

"Will you guide me up Denali?" Bass asked Hoey, sensing he might have found his escape.

At twenty-nine, Hoey had already gained a reputation as one of the strongest mountain guides in the country. Her five-foot-six frame and delicate features were paired with a stoic disposition and tireless work ethic. She was employed in a world where she was either underestimated or overscrutinized because of her gender. In response to Bass's question, she joked her way out of having to say no. "Bass, your hot air won't get you up that mountain," she said. It was a rebuke so good, Bass would retell it for the rest of his life.

While Bass took the jab in stride, he wasn't about to take no for an answer. After weeks of his wearing her down and charming her into thinking he was up to the challenge, Hoey eventually agreed to guide Bass and his four kids to the top of Denali that spring. But she also did her best to explain that, on a mountain like Denali, there is little margin for error. She knew how much Bass hated to train. "I don't think you can make it," she told him, matter-of-factly.

A few months later, in the spring of 1981, a bush plane dropped Bass, his four children, Hoey, Bob Bonar, and a couple of other guides Hoey knew, along with a thousand pounds' worth of gear and food, on the Kahiltna Glacier. They were sixteen miles and 13,000 feet below Denali's 20,310-foot summit.

Even for someone who spent his life leaping before looking, Bass seemed to be in way over his head. He had taken only a few strides on his cross-country skis when the sixty-plus pounds on his back, and fifty more in the sled he was towing, overwhelmed him. He couldn't go more than ten feet without gasping for air, and he was pouring sweat beneath the unforgiving Arctic sun. Bass tried to hide it but his kids could tell he was struggling. Jim remembers his dad declaring on day one that Hoey was right—he wasn't going to make it. But Bass started quietly reciting poems to himself in order to find a rhythm that would carry him to their first camp, and he eventually made it.

It was during his days on Denali that Bass learned something about his body that would change the course of his life. The higher he climbed, the stronger he felt. At altitudes that were so dizzying his daughters, Barbara and Bonnie, finally decided they wouldn't be going any higher, Bass felt energized. His legs grew stronger and his heart slowed. He reveled in the fact that he was having no problem at all keeping pace with Hoey.

On summit day, he felt unstoppable. He reached the roof of North America in the late afternoon and, despite it being 37 degrees below zero, waved his ice ax and let out a cry of joy. "The altitude didn't seem to affect him at all," remembers Bonar. Hoey was impressed.

Bonar says that, during the descent, it was as if Bass's subconscious suddenly became aware of what pushing himself to his physical limits in the mountains meant to him—how necessary it was to his psyche, how it shaped his perspective on everything from fatherhood to friendship to financial stress. Climbing the highest peak in North America felt like the beginning of something. But of what?

Bass began thinking about one of his childhood heroes, Richard Halliburton. The early twentieth-century adventurer and writer had often mentioned wanting to sail the seven seas. What about climbing the highest mountain on each of the seven continents? Bass wondered. In addition to Denali, those would be Aconcagua in Argentina, Kilimanjaro in Tanzania, Elbrus in the Soviet Union, Vinson in Antarctica, Kosciuszko in Australia, and, of course, Everest in Nepal. As he later recounted in a book about his adventures, he thought, *Christ, I've only got six to go.*

When Bass mentioned his Seven Summits idea to Hoey, her response showed just how much the Denali climb had changed her opinion of him. "That's a fantastic idea," she said. "In fact, I'd like to come with you."

Bass's quest to climb the highest mountain on each of the seven continents began much as it ended: on a Hollywood studio back lot. In the summer of 1981, just a few weeks after he had summited Denali, he found himself in Los Angeles on the Warner Bros. lot, watching the studio president, Frank Wells, pace the boardroom. "We've got a lot to talk about," Wells began.

It turned out that Wells also wanted to climb the Seven Summits, and he was looking into the logistics. Through his friend, the actor Clint Eastwood, Wells had hired a man named Jack Wheeler to assist with the planning. Wheeler was a sort of professional adventurer who had been hired by Eastwood to scout film locations in the Arctic that could double as the Soviet Union for the spy thriller *Firefox*.

By chance, Wheeler had then met Bass at a party in Dallas. They struck up a conversation about mountain climbing, and when Wheeler mentioned Wells and his ambitions, Bass could hardly believe what he was hearing. They'd had the same dream. Wells and Bass decided to meet to talk about teaming up.

"I've checked into it—no one has climbed all Seven Summits. We would be the first," Wells said. This was true, though they were unaware that a handful of others were already trying. For the next twenty minutes, as Wells ranted like a man possessed, Bass found himself in the rare position of not being able to get a word in edgewise. Only a year younger than Bass, Wells, a Rhodes scholar and Stanford Law graduate, was from a similar ilk. At six feet four, he had the physique of an athlete and the glow of a man who felt at home in the elements.

As Bass sat listening to Wells put the horse way before the cart, he wasn't sure what to make of him. Wells had even less climbing experience than he did, and a similar disdain for training. Given the debt Snowbird was in, Bass knew he really shouldn't be spending money and time away from work for such an expedition. But Wells's enthusiasm got Bass's imagination running wild. Bass genuinely felt he had met a kindred spirit.

Never one to let reality get in the way of a big dream, Bass followed his instincts and the two shook on it that day: they'd attempt the Seven Summits together. Swept up in the moment, he even agreed to meet Wells in the Soviet Union the very next month to climb Europe's highest peak. Just three weeks after their initial meeting, in the fall of 1981, Bass and Wells arrived in the Caucasus Mountains and stood at the foot of the 18,510-foot Mount Elbrus.

The climb turned out to be more of a reality check than the start of something special. Wells and Bass dutifully followed their Russian guides up the seemingly endless snow ramp that led to the summit. Yet as Bass tapped into his reserves of stamina and recited poetry to propel him forward, Wells ran out of gas at 17,000 feet. When Bass stepped onto the summit, Wells was lying flat on his back lower down the mountain while his guide put crampons on his boots for him. After Wells took just a few more steps, his guide told him it was time to turn around. Wells didn't argue.

2

PEAK XV

In the 1980s, ambitious mountaineers would tell you that you don't wait until you're ready to climb Mount Everest; you climb it when the opportunity presents itself.

Shortly after Bass summited Elbrus, he got a call from Hoey. She said that some guides she knew from Rainier Mountaineering Inc (RMI), the company she worked for when not at Snowbird, were planning a personal trip in the spring of 1982 to attempt Everest from the Tibet side. Lou Whittaker, an ox of a man and the founder of RMI, was leading the climb. Since funding was always one of the biggest challenges in putting together an Everest expedition, Hoey suggested to Bass and Wells that a hefty financial contribution might just be enough to get their names added to the climbing permit. Both China (which since 1951 had controlled Tibet) and Nepal operated on a strict one-climbing-permit-per-route policy on Everest at the time, and to be offered an opportunity to join an expedition in the 1980s was like getting accepted to Harvard—Bass and Wells knew better than to pass it up.

Whittaker had his eyes on a horrifying line up Everest that required climbing ten thousand feet of steep ice, snow, and rock called the North Wall. This rather direct ascent up the face led to the same ridge where the famed British climber George Mallory had died sixty years prior. Mallory's petrified body still remained on the mountain, face down in the scree, his preserved naked back exposed, white and inert like a fallen marble statue.

Whittaker was one of the few climbers in the world with the credentials for such an undertaking. He was not only the twin brother of Jim Whittaker, the first American to summit Everest, in 1963, but also quite possibly the most experienced mountain guide in the United States. Perhaps Whittaker believed that summiting Everest via such a challenging route as the North Wall would be enough to allow him to step out from the shadow cast by his brother.

In putting together his team, Whittaker plucked the best and the brightest from his RMI guide staff. In addition to Hoey, he brought the six-foot-four, two-hundred-pound Eric Simonson; the soft-spoken but unshakable Phil Ershler; and the notoriously loyal and hardworking George "Geo" Dunn. The three young men were the backbone of RMI at the time. Whittaker also added a few seasoned big-mountain vets to the team, such as his longtime friend Jim Wickwire, the first American to summit the notoriously deadly second-highest peak in the world, K2.

Whittaker had been scrounging for any sponsorship or donation he could find, including one from a local beer company that chipped in $5,000 in return for footage of him cracking open a can at the top. It was a fraction of what they needed. So at Hoey's suggestion, he agreed to meet with Bass and Wells to talk money. At the Gateway Inn diner, at the Mount Rainier National Park entrance, Wells asked Whittaker how much he needed. "All of it," Whittaker answered matter-of-factly. "One hundred and eighty thousand dollars." Wells was unfazed. Bass's denial about his own financial situation at the time was powerful. They agreed right away to put up the cash.

At the time, it was the unlikeliest of alliances. No mountain guide had ever brought someone to Everest before, bearing explicit responsibility for that person's success and safety. The mere idea of guiding on Everest hadn't even really been discussed within the climbing community. This was exactly why Whittaker was relieved when Bass and Wells went to great lengths to insist that they be considered regular members of the expedition—not clients. Everest was still chewing up elite climbers and spitting them out—throwing them off 7,000-foot icy faces to their death or entombing them in 150-foot-deep crevasses. One hundred and seventeen people had summited by then—nearly a hundred Western climbers and about two dozen Nepali Sherpa climbers—but sixty-three people had also died trying. It was no place for amateurs. Bass and Wells's chances of summiting and making it back down alive seemed slim to none. But that was explicitly understood to be their problem, not Whittaker's.

In January 1982, a few months before they were due to leave for Tibet, Wells had a shot at redemption and a much-needed boost in confidence when he and Bass headed to Argentina to attempt South America's highest peak, Aconcagua. At 22,837 feet, Aconcagua is a popular stepping stone to the thin air of the Himalayas. They invited some of the same guides and experienced climbers that would be part of their upcoming Everest expedition, including Hoey, Dunn, and Wickwire.

Unfortunately for Wells, the expedition had worryingly similar results to the one on Elbrus. What Bass lacked in ice ax technique he more than made up for in stamina and good cheer, and he made it to the top—Bass had now climbed three of the Seven Summits himself. Meanwhile, the higher up they got, the bigger a liability Wells became and, once again, he flamed out.

Nevertheless, in April 1982, Bass, Wells, and a dozen of America's best mountain guides and climbers were riding a train across the Tibetan Plateau, headed for the Rongbuk Glacier. It was a monthlong overland journey just to get to base camp. For mountaineers like Whittaker, and for mountain fanatics like Bass and Wells, it made them feel as though they were following in hallowed footsteps. The early mountaineering history of Everest had unfolded primarily on the unforgiving ridges and rock faces of the mountain's north side.

The people living in the foothills around Everest had always known that the mountain was something special. Those to the north called it Chomolungma, or "Holy Mother of the Universe"; those to the south called it Sagarmatha, "Goddess of the Sky." But when British surveyors "discovered" the mountain in the middle of the nineteenth century, they were unaware of any local names and simply called it Peak XV.

The British had already made themselves at home next door in India, and everyone from botanists to geologists were making expeditions into the "unexplored" wilds of Nepal in search of new discoveries to add to Britain's trophy case. Surveyors, in particular, were falling over themselves to measure the highest peaks of the world.

In 1852, an Indian mathematician named Radhanath Sikdar, who worked for the British survey office, declared he had discovered the world's highest mountain. Peak XV, by his measurement, was 29,002 feet. (Impressively, Sikdar's calculation—which he did from afar and possibly without having ever seen the mountain, but through compiling data from other sightings—was just 26 feet short of the updated computation made a century later with modern surveying technology.) The British renamed the mountain in honor of the previous surveyor general of Britain, George Everest.

As soon as a British team of mountaineers reached the Rongbuk

Glacier in 1921 and deemed Everest climbable, the Brits became fixated on winning the race to the summit. George Mallory was the driving force in this obsessive march toward the top. He made multiple attempts, all from the north side, until his most famous in 1924, when he and his climbing partner, Sandy Irvine, went missing. The two were last seen alive on the northeast ridge, just below 28,000 feet. Thus launched one of Everest's most enduring mysteries: whether they summited and then died on the descent, or perished before reaching their goal.

Political bickering between Tibet and Britain, paired with the increasing isolationism of a Nepalese king who wanted foreigners out of his country, kept all Westerners off Everest for nine years following Mallory's death. When climbing resumed from Tibet in the 1930s and 1940s, the attempts remained unsuccessful, but they did bring about a major development in Himalayan mountaineering. Many Nepalese men from the Sherpa ethnic group were migrating to the British base of Darjeeling in India, looking for work as porters. They were also becoming more skilled as climbers. This meant British teams could count on recruiting the same experienced men they had worked with year after year.

One such porter was Ang Tharkay Sherpa, who in 1935 recommended his friend Tenzing Norgay Sherpa for expedition work. Tenzing Norgay, just twenty-one at the time, was born in a small Tibetan border village near Makalu, raised in Thamey in the Khumbu Valley, and had settled in India. Despite his slight frame, Tenzing Norgay quickly distinguished himself for his agility on the snow, as well as his stamina, strength, and loyalty.

The 1950 invasion and subsequent occupation of Tibet by China was a wake-up call for the Nepalese. Isolationism wasn't in their best security interest, as it would leave them vulnerable to attack from China, so they began forging international relationships and allowing more foreigners into the country. In 1950, a British mountaineer named Bill Tillman, who had participated in Everest expeditions on the Tibet side in the 1930s, teamed up with Charles Houston, an American doctor, to explore the Nepal side. They were the very first Westerners to travel all the way up to the foot of Everest from the south. From previous vantage points, the Khumbu Icefall spilling off Everest's south side looked far too dangerous to cross. On closer exploration, Tillman and Houston decided it wasn't so impassable after all. In fact, the route they could just about make out—to the low point between Everest and Lhotse, a saddle-shaped feature known as the South Col, and then up the windswept southeast ridge—looked rather inviting.

But while Nepal had opened its borders, climbing permits remained a bottleneck, with just one permit per route being granted each year. And in 1952, it was the Swiss who got permission to make the first serious attempt of Everest from the Nepal side, via the southeast ridge. The Swiss climber Raymond Lambert and Tenzing Norgay reached 28,200 feet on the expedition, the highest verified point to date, before they were forced to retreat when bad weather enshrouded the peak. Upon hearing the news that the Swiss had not succeeded, the British rejoiced, for it was they who had permission the following year. The Swiss had essentially loosened the lid of the jar. Sure enough, on May 29, 1953, it popped.

The 1953 British expedition had a sense of destiny about it. It was well organized, militaristic in its discipline, and included some extremely ambitious mountaineers who were not afraid to jockey for position on summit attempts. In the end, it was the New Zealander Edmund Hillary who outmaneuvered the others and set off in clear weather with Tenzing Norgay, who had now spent more time high on Everest than any other climber.

The second Kiwi in history to climb Everest, Nick Banks, who summited in 1979, knew Hillary well. "The fascinating thing about Hillary is that he's often portrayed as the bumbling happy-go-lucky beekeeper, which is complete rubbish," says Banks today. "He was the most striving, ambitious man you'd ever meet."

When Hillary and Tenzing Norgay stepped onto the top of the world together, their tears were hidden behind goggles, oxygen masks, hoods, and hats. Hillary extended his arm to shake Norgay's hand; Norgay instead pulled Hillary close and embraced him. It cemented a lifelong bond.

The popularity of Nepal's South Col route took off in the wake of Hillary and Norgay's history-making moment. With Tibet still closed to Westerners in the wake of the Chinese invasion, it wasn't until 1960 that Everest was finally summited from the north side, by a mixed Chinese and Tibetan team. In 1979 Tibet reopened to Western climbers, but by 1982, when Whittaker, Bass, and Wells arrived, there had still been only three successful expeditions from the north side, which had put sixteen people on top of Everest, in contrast to the one hundred or so who had summited from the Nepal side.

The Whittaker expedition took a Chinese rail line to Lhasa on the Tibetan Plateau, where they enjoyed one last night in a decent hotel. Late that evening, Bass and Wells dropped in on Hoey to say goodnight.

One of the people Hoey was bunking with had some big band music from the 1940s on the radio. Bass perked up. He later recounted the moment wistfully in his book.

"My kind of dance music," Bass remarked.

"Wish I knew how to dance to this," Hoey replied.

Bass extended his hand, and within minutes, he had Hoey doing the foxtrot. It was a poignant father-daughter-like moment, with an embarrassed but jovial Hoey, wearing earrings Bass had bought for her when they were in South America, laughing each time she got her footwork wrong. As Hoey had been so instrumental in Bass's being able to pursue his Seven Summits dreams, and had taught him such a great deal along the way, he now basked in the feeling of teaching her something—leading, even.

The following four days were spent aboard old military trucks on atrociously rutted, muddy roads, which, on the north side, take you right up to base camp itself. This was a part of the world seemingly trapped in time. Expedition members recounted shoeless locals emerging from mud huts to stare and tug at the thick hair growing from their legs. After the teeth-rattling drive, and a couple of days at base camp sorting gear, Whittaker and the others covered the final distance to the advanced base camp at 21,000 feet atop the Rongbuk Glacier with a train of shaggy-haired yaks that carried their supplies. As they trekked, they got the thrilling experience of seeing Everest rise from the Tibetan Plateau completely unobstructed, punctuating the grandeur of the Himalayan Range—earth's most impressive example of uplift.

Including the western spur where Pakistan, China, and India converge, called the Karakoram, the Himalaya region covers about 230,000 square miles—about the same area as the state of Texas and more than twice the size of the United Kingdom. There are fourteen Himalayan summits that rise above 8,000 meters (26,247 feet), which are commonly referred to as the "eight-thousanders." The Karakoram is home to four of them: Broad Peak, Gasherbrum I, Gasherbrum II, and K2. Sitting nearby in Pakistan is Nanga Parbat. At the far opposite end of the Himalayas, on the border between India and Nepal, is the world's third-highest mountain, Kangchenjunga. The remaining eight-thousanders—Everest, Lhotse, Makalu, Cho Oyu, Dhaulagiri, Manaslu, Annapurna, and Shishapangma (in descending order of height)—are all more or less clustered in the middle, around the Nepal-Tibet border.

In Whittaker's group there were seventeen climbers and two and a half tons of gear and food. It would be one of a tiny handful of Everest expeditions in history to date to not use any hired Sherpa help, and the climb itself would take eight weeks, largely due to the monumental task of shuttling gear and food up the mountain.

After three weeks of living at the advanced base camp and doing laps to set up the higher camps, even Bass and Wells were carrying impressive loads, earning respect from the team. Whittaker gave them his blessing to make a trip up the steep section above Camp Three.

But it was clear long before the trip ended that neither of them would be going any farther than Camp Four, at 23,500 feet. The terrain was simply too technical. And based on the condition the other climbers were in, noticeable to all as they staggered into camp, Bass and Wells made peace with this decision pretty quickly.

Once Camp Five was set up at 25,000 feet, the team felt it was time to select the strongest members to try for the summit. Whittaker chose Hoey, Wickwire, Dave Mahre, and Larry Nielson to be the ones to go for it. At the end of a long day, Mahre and Nielson were about 150 feet above Hoey and Wickwire, scouting for a place to make their Camp Six. In the deteriorating weather, Mahre and Nielson shouted down for more rope. Wickwire and Hoey, who were taking a break, stood up and scrambled to help. Wickwire then watched in horror as Hoey began falling backward. As she slid headfirst down the face, she rolled to one side and made a lunge for the rope, but couldn't grab it. She disappeared. Wickwire was stunned as he looked down to see Hoey's harness splayed open, still attached to the rope. The waistbelt was undone. It is believed that for some unknown reason, she undid it during the break.

When Bass heard the news on the radio, he dropped his oatmeal. He and Wells were devastated. Whittaker later sent a team to look for her body, but all they found was one of her crampons and some blood on the rocks. Had Hoey summited Everest, she would have been the first American woman to do so. Alas, no one from Whittaker's team summited that year.

Before leaving the Rongbuk Glacier, the team built a rock cairn as a memorial to Hoey and carved her name into a stone plaque that they placed on top. They held a service for her before somberly beginning the arduous process of returning to civilization.

While Bass had spent most of his time on Everest's north side portering gear, without any realistic shot at the summit, he left having experienced a sad but intrinsic truth about mountaineering: people die. Even friends. It's a reality that seemed to be baked into the very planning of an Everest expedition, as after Hoey's death, Whittaker still sent one more team toward the summit, with Nielson ultimately making a brave push by himself to 27,500 feet, before returning to base camp with severe frostbite.

The base camps on both sides of the mountain have dozens of makeshift memorials to dead climbers, some who have been carried off the mountain, some who remain where they took their last breath, and many who, like Hoey, have seemingly vanished into thin air. Naturally, the memorials—and the bodies on the mountain—tend to affect non-climbers more than experienced mountaineers, who often feel that the very meaning of climbing mountains comes from the risk itself.

But it was perhaps the first time Bass truly understood the stakes of what it meant to be a climber. He wrestled with mixed emotions and even wondered aloud to Wells if they should take a break from the Seven Summits. "No chance," was Wells's reaction. Bass didn't fight him. He still wanted the Seven Summits just as badly as Wells, and now wanted Everest most of all. The mountain had him under its spell.

3

The 174TH ASCENT
of MOUNT EVEREST

In the summer of 1982, just a few months after Hoey's tragic death, Wells defiantly announced to Bass that 1983 would be the year they finished the Seven Summits—together. They had become such close friends that they were committed to summiting every mountain in tandem, even the ones Bass had already completed.

The year began on a high note. In January, they went back to Argentina to climb Aconcagua. Wells had befriended Rick Ridgeway, a well-known Southern California–based climber and writer who had made several bold ascents around the world, including of K2. Ridgeway signed on for Aconcagua and even brought along his good friend Yvon Chouinard, the founder of the Patagonia clothing company. Chouinard was forty-five at the time, and Patagonia was a $30 million company. Rich or not, top climbers are notoriously opportunistic when wealthy civilians will pay for their adventure.

Ridgeway and Chouinard had both been vocal about their disapproval of those who had not paid their dues in the mountains. Nevertheless, even a notorious curmudgeon like Chouinard thought it sounded like fun to spend three weeks in South America with this jolly Texan and eccentric Hollywood bigwig, so he put his prejudice aside. "I knew they had no climbing experience, whatsoever," he remembers. "But, still, it just sounded like fun to be with these guys, and with Ridgeway—and to climb Aconcagua and not have to pay for it. But I certainly wasn't a guide on the trip."

Ridgeway, who grew close to Bass and Wells, was later recruited to write the book chronicling their climbing adventures, *Seven Summits*. In it, he openly admitted his initial reservations. "Both of them had so little climbing experience they could hardly be called amateur," he wrote. "What made them think they had a chance? Naivete." Looking back on his early experiences with the pair today, he says, "I had my bullshit detector up and tuned in to why these guys were doing it. I also had to try to judge how much of it was just some sort of ego thing so they could go back to the cocktail parties and brag about what they've done."

To the surprise of the experts, the Aconcagua climb was a success. This time, Bass and Wells stepped onto the summit together. And Bass was as entertaining as Chouinard had hoped. Just as he did on Denali, Bass would stop for no apparent reason and loudly recite lines from Robert Service poems, including one of his favorites, "The Men That Don't Fit In":

> There's a race of men that don't fit in,
>   A race that can't stay still;
> So they break the hearts of kith and kin,
>   And they roam the world at will.
> They range the field and they rove the flood,
>   And they climb the mountain's crest;
> Theirs is the curse of the gypsy blood,
>   And they don't know how to rest.

After Aconcagua, Bass and Wells had hoped to go to Mount Vinson in Antarctica, but ended up missing their window when the weather
was suitable. Instead, their next Seven Summits target would be a second attempt at Everest. Even experienced climbers rarely had the motivation and resources to attempt the mountain two years in a row, but
Bass and Wells were unique. They now had a team behind them of some
of the world's best climbers and guides, who agreed to secure the permit
and organize the expedition so long as Wells and Bass kept finding ways
to pay.

Phil Ershler, one of the talented RMI guides who had been on
the 1982 Whittaker expedition, was the chief organizer and leader
of the spring 1983 Everest trip. Larry Nielson, the man who had
touched the highest point of the group on the north side a year
earlier, also joined the crew. They all wisely agreed to go after the
summit via Nepal's South Col route, which Hillary and Norgay had
first climbed. Once again, the professional climbers were not being
paid to guide, but they did have all their expedition expenses covered. Today, Ershler admits that despite not being responsible for
the two, he certainly took their safety as seriously as he did his own
summit attempt. It wasn't just a matter of owing them a service for
hire. Guiding was part of Ershler's DNA, as well as being his chosen
occupation, and he had grown fond of the two amateurs.

As businessmen who knew how to court investors, Wells and Bass
found ways to avoid paying for the entire trip out of pocket. A documentary about the Whittaker expedition narrated by Robert Redford
had come out. Wells used it to convince Budweiser to put up some cash
for the 1983 attempt in return for high-altitude product placement.
Much of the rest of the cost of the climb was covered by ABC Sports,
which found willing partners and film subjects in Wells and Bass. ABC
even hired Ridgeway to provide on-camera commentary throughout
the expedition; it also brought in a talented young rock climber and

cameraman from Colorado named David Breashears, who had worked for the network before.

Breashears would come to change Bass's life—and Mount Everest—forever.

Breashears had grown up bouncing around the world as an army brat. His father was a military officer with a temper who taught his son to swim by throwing him into the deep end of a pool; he left the family home for good before David was a teenager. As a Boy Scout, Breashears basically taught himself to climb, improvising with an old hemp rope, and found it a welcome distraction throughout his adolescence. Breashears skipped college, making ends meet by laying concrete and repairing remote oil rigs for energy companies, while quietly becoming one of the strongest climbers in the Rockies. Then, in 1976, Bob Godfrey, an English climber, writer, and filmmaker, hired Breashears as a gofer on a film called *Free Climb*, shot on Half Dome in Yosemite (and also narrated by Robert Redford). Breashears shadowed two of the greatest climbing cinematographers, Greg Lowe and Tom Frost, on the project. One day, high on the northwest face of Half Dome, Frost let Breashears look through the viewfinder. Breashears called it a revelation.

In 1978, Lowe hired Breashears as an assistant cameraman for a shoot on the Grand Teton in Wyoming—the resulting film, a fictional short about extreme skiing called *Fall Line*, was nominated for an Academy Award. The next year, Breashears was invited by Frost and Lowe to film on Ama Dablam—a mountain not far from Everest, often referred to as the Matterhorn of the Himalayas for its dramatic shape. He proved so strong at altitude there—even while carrying heavy camera equipment—that ABC hired him to film an expedition on the north side of Everest in 1981 for its popular television program *The American*

Sportsman. As other team members were beaten back by the mountain, Breashears continued on and reached a high point, alone with his camera. The footage he shot won his three-man camera team an Emmy for cinematography. This, of course, made Breashears a shoo-in for the ABC-sponsored 1983 climb with Bass and Wells. When he arrived on Everest that year, at age twenty-seven, he was probably the strongest climber on the entire mountain.

Breashears proved himself once again as both a cameraman and a climber in 1983. "I began thinking, 'I am going to climb Mount Everest,'" he remembers. He was right. He became the 128th person to summit—and even shot live footage from the top. "I had a tangible feeling this would change my life," he says.

In total, eight of the climbers on Bass and Wells's expedition summited, including Nielson and Ang Rita Sherpa, who became the eighth and ninth people to do so without supplemental oxygen. Ang Rita, a popular member of Western expeditions, had already summited four other eight-thousanders.

Bass, however, came face-to-face with a difficult truth at 28,000 feet that he hadn't expected. Though his summit group was only about a thousand feet below the top and he felt quite strong, clouds were building, and the Sherpas he was with were tired out from breaking trail in new snow. They said they were turning around. Bass knew he couldn't make it alone. *If only I had a good rope leader*, he thought, as recounted in *Seven Summits*.

In the following days, Wells, who was on a different summit team than Bass, made it to Camp Four, but ferocious winds then trapped him in his tent for four days, forcing him to ration his remaining oxygen. With his summit ambitions obviously dashed, all he could do was wait for a safe window to descend. Despite coming up short on Everest once again, Bass and Wells were energized by the experience and their greatly improved performances.

A month later, with Ershler serving as their paid guide, they made it to the top of Denali together. Before summer was over, they summited Kilimanjaro and Mount Elbrus. Before the year's end, Wells miraculously pieced together an expedition to Antarctica, convincing the British climbing legend Chris Bonington, whom they had met on Everest's north side in 1982, to join them. Bonington had been part of the first team to summit Nuptse, in 1961, had summited Everest in 1975, and now at nearly fifty was among the most experienced Himalayan climbers in the world. With Bonington's help, Wells and Bass made it up Mount Vinson together, then decided: Why not tag the top of Australia's 7,310-foot Kosciuszko en route back to the United States? Just like that, they had completed six of the Seven Summits. Only Everest remained.

Sadly, Kosciuszko would mark the end of their journey together. Before the Vinson climb, Wells's wife, Luanne, had sat him down and let him know that she was not okay with him returning to Everest for a third time. She had been such a good sport to this point, even purchasing and packing his climbing gear for him before each trip, but she'd finally had enough. He realized it was time to let go of Everest and nurture what he had at home. His career beckoned too, and in 1984 when he was hired to be president of Disney, he truly and completely let go of his Seven Summits dream.

Bass, however, was no longer just under Everest's spell: it was haunting him. He got in touch with Breashears and proposed another Everest expedition for the fall of 1984, all expenses paid. It would be Bass's third attempt in as many years. Fall is a more fickle climbing season, as the temperatures drop and winter looms, but Breashears jumped at the invite. He had been impressed by the Texan twenty-five years his senior on their previous Everest expedition, and the two had since grown close. "Dick could have been a world-class climber if he'd wanted," Breashears says. "He had the gift of utilizing the thin air more efficiently than most" (a reference to Bass's seeming ability to create an unusually high number of red blood cells at altitude).

But Bass wouldn't get the chance to put that gift to the test in 1984. He and Breashears had barely made it past base camp when they got bad news: because of a permitting issue with the Nepalese government, they were forbidden from climbing at all that year.

They wouldn't need to wait long for their next chance. Whereas in 1983 and 1984 it had been Bass inviting Breashears to go to Everest, in 1985 Bass had Breashears to thank for the opportunity. Another wealthy amateur climber, Arne Naess Jr., a Norwegian millionaire, had asked Breashears and Bonington to join a spring 1985 expedition he was putting together. Breashears agreed to come along to climb and film Naess's group on one condition: that Naess invite Dick Bass.

Bass had much in common with Naess. The head of a global shipping firm, Naess had a big personality and lived a big life. (Naess would become famous for marrying the American soul diva Diana Ross in 1986.) Like Bass, he had both the money to support an Everest team and the wisdom to invite climbers who were more experienced than him. (Bass did, however, pay $75,000 to cover his and Breashears's expenses.) Though Naess had spent more time in the mountains than Bass, Bonington would later describe him as "the second least-experienced member of the team" (Bass being the first).

The Norwegian-led expedition was one of only two that spring basing themselves on the Khumbu Glacier. Altogether, including a large team of Sherpas, porters, and cooks, the group comprised about fifty people. Four of the Sherpas would be assigned to Bass and Breashears, one of whom was their friend Ang Rita.

The other team living on the glacier was smaller—about twenty-five people in total—and was primarily made up of American hotshots attempting Everest's perilous west ridge. The group included Jim Bridwell, a Yosemite big-wall pioneer and chain-smoker, and Pete

Athans, a climber who was young but had significant Himalayan experience. In the previous two years Athans had attempted Makalu, Annapurna South, and a winter ascent of Cho Oyu. Both Athans and Bridwell were making their first attempt on Everest, hoping to be added to the list of twenty-four Americans who had done so to date. Bonington had climbed with Bridwell in Yosemite many times and was pleasantly surprised to run into him at Everest base camp; Breashears had met several of the other American climbers over the years. The two teams mingled often during the months they shared the glacier.

Many saw the mid-1980s as the end of an era, a time when Everest came to be more of a logistical challenge than a technical one. At the start of the decade, only around sixty teams had ever attempted to climb the mountain, and 104 people had reached its summit and made it down alive. But between 1980 and 1985 there was a flurry of attempts, with a further fifty expeditions and seventy summits. The roughly seventy-five people who were sharing Nepal's base camp in the spring of 1985 formed the largest contingent that had ever been on the mountain at one time. Climbers were beginning to take advantage of cutting-edge technology in order to increase their odds of summiting. 1985 was the first year that computers were carried to base camp: both Bonington and the Americans had Apple IIcs to type up dispatches and create spreadsheets that helped with the expeditions' logistics. Wires crisscrossed camp in order to strengthen the shortwave radio signal used to receive weather reports and communicate with Nepal's Ministry of Tourism, the government body that regulates and monitors mountaineering. The Americans had a propane heater in their communal kitchen tent, which was becoming increasingly common.

Ed Webster, from the American team, was a climber known for seeking out remote and seldom visited mountains. 1985 marked his first

Himalayan expedition, and he later described base camp as "the most overused, trashed-out campsite in the world." Piles of garbage were starting to fester, as little effort was made to carry it off the mountain. Occasionally, dogs would wander up from the villages below and scavenge for a meal.

It can be fairly assumed that some of the elite climbers wouldn't have taken kindly to the appearance of amateurs like Bass. Bonington was not one of those. "There were plenty of people coming to Everest who didn't have very much experience, in the 1980s," he remembers. "I never really saw that as a problem because you don't really need much climbing experience on Everest. I found Dick Bass to be a lovely guy. Loved his humor, loved his stories—and he was a natural climber, too, physically and in temperament."

Breashears was in agreement with Bonington—most of the time. It was only when Bass did something particularly careless that Breashears was reminded that Bass was not a climber in the same way he and Bonington were. In 1985, as they prepared for their summit push, Breashears was caught off guard when Bass told him he would first need to go back down to the town of Namche Bazaar—a thirty-mile round trip—to collect some gear he had stored there. When the Norwegian expedition picked up pace quicker than expected, Bass needed to retrieve the gear sooner than he'd planned. Most fit climbers break the trek to Namche into two days. Bass being Bass, he decided to do it in one day—even after getting a late start. "Be careful," Breashears told him. "Don't twist an ankle or get any blisters."

Just hours into his descent, Bass already knew he had pushed his feet too far. Nothing reveals inexperience in the mountains like blisters—it's a bit like running out of gas during the rolling start of a NASCAR race. The next morning, his big toenail was black from pushing against the front of his boot. He was convinced that he had blisters on top of his blisters. It was a bruise to the ego as much as the feet. He'd been on the mountain three times before and should have known better.

He had no choice once he reached Namche but to convalesce there for two days until he could walk again. It then took him five days to shuffle his way back up to base camp. Bass knew he'd put himself in a bad position, but he was skilled at hiding the excruciating pain he was in behind his outsize personality. He forced his grimace into a smile as he finally made it to base camp, waved hello, and made small talk with the other climbers.

Bass then collapsed onto the floor of his tent and stared up at the thin nylon walls, which gently fluttered in the ever-present breeze that funnels down the Khumbu Glacier. He later recounted the agonizing moment to Ridgeway: *Oh Lord*, he thought. *I've blown an inner tube.*

"Dick was the most fabulous person, but it could be pretty hard to get him out of his tent," Breashears recalls. "The only way to get him out was to just start walking without him." Out of necessity, that's exactly what Breashears had done. During the time it had taken Bass to get back to base camp, Breashears had needed to forge ahead to Camp Two in order to film the first group of Norwegians who were going to make a summit bid.

So, after getting some rest, Bass got himself up, put a heavy pack on his back, left his tent, and walked out of base camp alone to catch up. He felt a sense of destiny this time. He traveled the treacherous maze of broken ice of the Khumbu Icefall, without help. By the time he reached Camp Two, Bonington, two young Norwegian climbers, and three of the hired Sherpa climbers had already summited and descended. Bonington explained to Bass, Breashears, and Ang Rita that they had climbed the final push to the peak without roping together. Breashears looked at Bass and immediately suggested they do the same. It would give them less protection in the case of a fall, but it would save them time.

A second group of Norwegians, including Naess, was preparing to leave Camp Two to make their climb, but Bass told Breashears and Ang

Rita he wanted one extra day of rest. He suggested they could simply skip Camp Three as a result and climb all the way to Camp Four in one push. Naess looked at Bass as if he were crazy. Breashears was silent. He knew Bass well enough by this point not to underestimate him.

Sure enough, Bass, Breashears, and Ang Rita climbed more than 5,000 vertical feet from Camp Two to Camp Four in a single push, an almost unheard-of effort even from elite climbers. The South Col, where Camp Four is located, is often described as an alien-like moonscape of jagged rock, where the sky is an eerily deep shade of blue. It is the only camp on the south side of Everest that regularly gets pummeled by a ferocious jet stream of cold air and snow—the only camp where, in a bad storm, there is no refuge, not even in your tent. The hostile, 26,250-foot altitude, meanwhile, attacks the body with such force that it's a challenge to sleep, let alone eat or drink. With supplemental oxygen, a fully acclimatized human can survive for up to a week at the South Col; without it, surviving for two days would be a minor miracle.

Yet, Bass, Breashears, and Ang Rita arrived in the afternoon of April 28 feeling good and looking forward to the rest day they had earned by skipping Camp Three. That night, Naess and his group of climbers left Camp Four for the summit. The following day, as Bass and Breashears rested and tended to the arduous chore of melting snow to fill their water bottles, Naess and his team returned to the South Col, victorious. Bass and Breashears went to bed at seven p.m.

At eleven p.m. that night, April 29, Bass, Breashears, and Ang Rita turned on their headlamps and began boiling a few liters of water to drink and cook some simple food, in preparation for their own push to the summit. Bass felt the weight of the moment. He placed pictures of his wife—his second by now—and kids into his pack, as well as a note he had written for Marty Hoey. At two a.m. on April 30, the trio set off, stomping their crampons into the ice. Step by step, with the spotlight from their headlamps illuminating the three feet in front of them, they climbed on. Bass's blisters subsided into the background as a dull ache that kept fading the higher he went.

Near dawn, Bass's headlamp batteries went dead. Thankfully the sun was rising fast on a crystal-clear, windless day. It was light enough for Bass to notice he had reached the same spot where he had turned around two years earlier, at about 28,000 feet. Eventually, Bass, Breashears, and Ang Rita reached an exposed knife-edge. Looking down to his left, Bass saw Camp Two in the Western Cwm, seven thousand feet below. He felt his confidence slipping away, especially without a rope. Breashears had told Bass he would either have to believe in himself and make the traverse unprotected, or turn around.

Bass continued on and, after ascending the forty-foot limestone cliff known as the Hillary Step with the help of a fixed rope, was within a few hundred feet of the top. Clouds began to swirl and there were early signs of inclement weather. But Bass now felt unstoppable.

At noon on April 30, 1985, Bass, Breashears, and Ang Rita stepped onto the summit of Mount Everest. Bass was the 174th person to stand on top of the world, and at fifty-five, the oldest person to have done so. He and Breashears hugged. Bass held a flag emblazoned with a Seven Summits logo and had his picture taken. He was moved to tears. Bass had lost his dear friend to the mountain just three years earlier. On the summit, he removed the piece of paper on which he had written his note to her, placed it in a plastic bag with a rock in it, and threw it over the north side into Tibet, where she had fallen.

Breashears, having been on the summit once before, knew well enough their climb was far from over. The descent from a peak of high consequence is often a cruel twist in what should be a happy ending. Some of the most legendary climbers and mountaineers in history have accomplished seemingly impossible ascents—achieved lifelong dreams, culminations of decades of preparation—only to perish on the return trip. As adrenaline wanes it is not uncommon for the body to simply give up. The assist from gravity on the way down is effectively erased by debilitating exhaustion.

Ang Rita had already left because he had started to suffer from snow blindness. As the cloud around them thickened, Breashears checked Bass's oxygen bottle one last time and found that it was empty. Bass had turned up the flow during the summit push to keep himself going.

Breashears gave Bass what was left of his own bottle and steeled himself for a long battle. Having no oxygen for the descent from Everest is often a death sentence. As Breashears remembers: "He was tired. I was tired—there was no point in asking him why he had turned the flow rate up. So it was just me and Dick. I'm with a fifty-five-year-old guy who's not as acclimatized as he should be because of that big climb from Camp Two to Four.

"And then the remainder of my bottle runs out, and this just flattens Dick. He can no longer even stand and so I have to get him to scoot on his butt, ten, fifteen feet at a time. I'm horrified because it's still a long way down to the bottle of oxygen we had stashed lower.

"At one point Dick just stops and says, 'I'm not sure I can descend.' It was an awful moment—I was completely unprepared to hear those words."

Breashears had one last hope. "The last cards I was holding were to encourage him to keep moving for his family," he says.

"I kept thinking, 'If this guy doesn't get down to that bottle, he's going to die up here.' Because he never would have made it through the night as we waited for rescue. And I don't know what would have happened to me, because I never would have left him."

They inched downward together, stopping often so Breashears could wrap his arms around Bass and tell him everything was going to be okay. Eventually, they made it below the cloud into what was a clear day below. They could now see Camp Four and were only a few hundred feet from their oxygen stash. Breashears rushed ahead to get the tank. Bass began to recite poetry. He thought about his kids. He saw Breashears ahead, but there was someone else, too: Hoey. He heard her speaking to him: "Step . . . breath . . . step . . . breath." Bass finally made it to the oxygen bottle. Breathing in big lungfuls of air, he began coming back to life.

After fifteen hours on the move, Bass and Breashears stumbled into Camp Four and collapsed into their tent. They were the only people from any expedition left at the South Col. After spending one more night at the Col, Bass and Breashears descended to Camp Two.

The legend of Dick Bass was born not in the moment when he staggered into Everest base camp safely the following day, after having spent three and half full days in the death zone above 26,000 feet. It was when the man they called Large Mouth Bass began telling stories again. That's when Breashears truly knew the worst was over. And that's also when the whole idea of climbing Everest began to change in the public eye.

Bass knew full well his accomplishment had little to do with climbing. He was never a "real" climber, nor did he want to become one. His dream—to reach the top of Everest and complete the Seven Summits—was not a mountaineering objective, but a test of character and determination. If you asked him, Bass would say the century that preceded his 1985 climb was just a long, drawn-out prologue to the discovery of Everest's most revolutionary new route: the easy way.

"I'm not a mountaineer," he said while still in base camp in 1985. "I never jogged, never pumped iron. All I do is talk a lot and run through airports, trying to catch an airplane at the last second."

Two weeks later, millions of average Americans sitting at home watching Johnny Carson were thinking, *Huh, so that guy climbed Mount Everest* . . .

After returning from the commercial break, Carson asked Bass what was next.

"Well, I'm sure I'm going to have some figurative mountains to climb in this life," Bass said. "But that's going to wind up my big mountain expeditions. Oh, and I'd like to say, the only reason I really made this, I had a fellow, Dave Breashears—he was my partner in all this and I want to give him credit for that."

While it was pretty much the last serious climbing Dick Bass would do, he became a folk hero for dreamers like him. And he set something in motion that irrevocably changed the way people thought about Everest, and mountaineering in general.

Meanwhile, a few entrepreneurial-minded mountain guides sensed an opportunity. Guiding on Everest still seemed far-fetched—Breashears was Bass's climbing partner, after all, not a guide—but taking people up the other Seven Summits was a different story. If they could market the endeavor, there were careers to be made.

4

SEVEN SUMMITS FEVER

Within a year of Dick Bass becoming the first person in history to climb to the highest point on each of the seven continents, the book that he and Wells commissioned Rick Ridgeway to help them write was published. *Seven Summits*, "by Dick Bass and Frank Wells, with Rick Ridgeway," recounted the duo's improbable four-year adventure. Among those who contributed effusive endorsements were former president Gerald Ford, future presidential candidate Ross Perot, NBC anchorman Tom Brokaw, the actors Robert Redford and Clint Eastwood, and Chris Bonington.

"It's going to cause a revolution in the boardrooms of the U.S.," Bonington wrote, "as countless executives relate to Frank and Dick and take off on far-flung adventures."

He was right: the Seven Summits were suddenly being discussed at watercoolers in much the same way that people talked about running a charity marathon or backpacking through India. It captured the imagination of restless, adventure-hungry people who knew little enough about mountaineering to be ignorant of the dangers. Swept up in the romanticism of it all, people simply thought, *If Dick Bass can do it, so can I.*

Meanwhile, serious climbers ranged from unimpressed to derisive of the very concept of the Seven Summits. Bonington's feelings were in line with those of his climbing-community peers, despite his having come to like Bass and having written a blurb for his book. He had once thought of trying to become the first to scale the Seven Summits himself, but on reflection decided, "It was so boring. I think I'd done three of them when I was asked to go on a more exciting expedition and I just abandoned the idea." Eric Simonson, who had been with Bass and Wells on the 1982 Whittaker expedition, didn't make much of the endeavor either. "I remember when Marty first described the Seven Summits thing to me," he says. "I thought 'Well, that sounds stupid, who cares about that?' It sounded like a gimmick." To put it simply, most of the mountains were just too easy. (That same criticism remains—these days, people can ride a snowmobile to the top of Mount Elbrus.)

Simonson, meanwhile, had spent the late 1970s and early 1980s building a résumé as one of the most prolific climbers in the Himalayas. After racking up ascents on Denali and Rainier as a guide for Whittaker's company, RMI, he'd fly across the world, most often to Nepal, and spend his paycheck. "Kathmandu in the seventies and eighties was magical," Simonson remembers. "There was no pollution and you could ride your bike around the ring road, be out among the rice paddies. For a kid from Tacoma [Washington], it was amazing." Of the climbing, he says, "People forget how remote it was. There was so much more to it than just the mountaineering—it was a psychological challenge, it was real adventure."

Unique among American guides, he began to make these adventures possible for client climbers on a regular basis. Standing atop Denali or Rainier with a strong client as the sun was rising, he made a habit of asking, "Ever thought about climbing in the Himalaya?" In 1981, he brought some former Rainier clients to a 21,100-foot peak near Annapurna called Hiunchuli. In 1982, he attempted another 21,000-foot peak called Singu Chuli with some former clients, and the following year he was back on Hiunchuli, again with former clients.

Simonson was not guiding on these trips. He did not venture above 7,000 meters bearing explicit—or even implied—responsibility for anyone. Clients would get his expertise and informal oversight, and he would get an all-expenses-paid expedition. Simonson did, however, harbor the ambition of guiding in the Himalayas, especially on Everest.

In 1986, Simonson and his friends Phil Ershler and George Dunn cofounded International Mountain Guides (IMG). Lou Whittaker allowed the three to continue working for RMI as long as IMG exclusively operated outside the United States. At first, IMG was essentially a collective, in which each of the owners would focus on a particular region of the world. Simonson, naturally, handled climbs in Nepal, where he had built up important connections, while Dunn oversaw Africa, and Ershler focused on South America. "One of Eric's big strengths back then was developing relationships with Sherpas," remembers Dunn. "And he became super loyal to them."

IMG created newsletters that they would send out to their vast network of former RMI clients to advertise their upcoming expeditions. In 1987, IMG announced that Simonson and Dunn would be headed to the north side of Everest and were willing to "take some additional climbers in a support role at a premium price." By then, Ershler was the only one of the three who had summited.

"Personally, I wasn't really into the idea of guiding Everest," says Dunn, whom Simonson describes as a Boy Scout. "I didn't think it sounded sensible—it was hard enough for me."

If things had played out differently, it's possible that this trip could have turned into the first true attempt at a guided climb of Everest. However, the 1987 trip had an awkward dynamic. The permit holder and expedition leader was Jack Allsup, an engineer in his late fifties from Arkansas, whom Simonson had met through a former client. Simonson and Dunn were the ones joining Allsup's expedition instead of running it themselves, and in the end they didn't even go in an official capacity for IMG. If he had in fact been guiding, Simonson says, he never would have signed off on some of the scary decision-making he witnessed. No one summited. "The mountain was just too big for them," Simonson says of the Allsup group, with a chuckle.

While it was far from a rousing success, the Allsup expedition was part of a seismic shift that was underway. Allsup had hoped to become the first to climb the Seven Summits before Bass beat him to it. And Simonson was starting to shed his Seven Summits skepticism and take seriously the potential it had to set his upstart guiding company apart. The six peaks besides Everest, all easier to climb and guide, relatively speaking, could potentially generate large and predictable revenue streams and create repeat customers for IMG. "I realized it was basically like farming," he says. "It might be three, four, five years before a farmer gets a good crop. I started nurturing clients the same way—fertilize, water, and eventually you can harvest your corn. Rainier clients became Denali clients, Denali clients became Aconcagua clients, Aconcagua clients became Seven Summits clients."

By the end of 1987, IMG became one of the first guide services in the world to explicitly offer guided climbs on the Seven Summits. Many others soon followed. This despite the fact that no one, including Simonson, had figured out how to tackle Everest.

To this day, Ershler looks back on the 1982 Whittaker expedition as the inciting event of this watershed moment. "Our trips to Everest with Dick and Frank were the beginning, in my opinion" he says. "I find

it hard to separate what happened with guiding on the Seven Summits, and then later with guiding on Everest, from what they did. Every
international guide in America should worship at the feet of Dick and
Frank."

Among the other entrepreneurs who spotted the Seven Summits
market early on was an Alaskan named Harry Johnson. Johnson had
bought a company called Genet Expeditions from the widow of Ray
Genet, a climber who, as it happened, had died on Everest in 1979.
The company was based in the tiny town of Talkeetna, on the doorstep
of Denali National Park. After news of Bass's accomplishment spread
in 1985, Johnson took note of the influx of Seven Summits pilgrims
coming to Denali. Most, like Bass, were what guides called "Sunday
mountaineers"—those more interested in bagging summits than learning climbing skills. Johnson began marketing Genet Expeditions as a
Seven Summits guiding service and cultivated a small team of talented
guides, including a fellow Alaskan named Vern Tejas.

Tejas says, "I asked Harry, 'What are we going to do about Everest?
He just said, 'We'll worry about that later.'" Johnson assumed that if any
of his clients got to that point, he'd just subcontract the work to another
company, assuming there was one that had figured out how to guide the
mountain by then. "Everest was beyond our scope," he says.

Some of the first client climbers to attempt the Seven Summits were
a couple of expats living and working in Hong Kong: Keith Kerr and
Frank Fischbeck. Kerr, originally from England, and Fischbeck, from
South Africa, had climbed Denali with Tejas in 1986, before he was
working for Johnson. They were relative amateurs with big jobs and disposable incomes but little time to plan expeditions, so they used guides
as much as possible. They had taken a liking to the perennially popular
Tejas, who was known as a "type A athlete with a type B personality,"

as one Denali ranger likes to say. Seemingly immune to fatigue, Tejas would entertain clients by playing his harmonica, guitar, fiddle, or whatever other instrument he had dragged up to the glacier. After climbing Denali, the trio floated the idea of bringing Tejas along on their other Seven Summits expeditions, all expenses paid, in return for some expert planning and supervision. Tejas was thrilled. In 1988, he guided the duo up Elbrus and Vinson.

"At first, I just wanted to be the first Alaskan to do the Seven Summits," Tejas says. But soon that ambition grew to being the first person, from anywhere, to guide the Seven Summits. "We were just taking each mountain one at a time," says Fischbeck. "We hadn't even thought about guides on Everest."

There were two other early Seven Summits disciples who were on a similar track as Kerr and Fischbeck: the Americans Bob John and Mike Gordon. John was a glutton for punishment. An IBM executive from Trenton, New Jersey, he would wake up before sunrise for two hours of endurance training. He finished an Ironman triathlon—a twenty-five-mile run, one-hundred-mile bike ride, and two-mile swim. But in 1986, at the age of thirty-six, his life wasn't going the way he wanted. He was living apart from his wife and divorce was all but certain. After reading *Seven Summits*, he knew exactly where he wanted to turn his attention to clear his head. He signed up for a climb on Rainier and almost immediately afterward phoned up Genet Expeditions to find out how he could climb Denali. Johnson suggested he test himself at altitude on easier terrain first and pointed him toward their Kilimanjaro climb. That August, John headed off to Tanzania and excelled on the mountain. That's when he really got the bug. "I read all the books—I just couldn't get enough of it," he says.

Having earned his spot on the Denali expedition, where Tejas would be his guide, he successfully begged for three weeks off work and headed to Alaska in May 1989. There he met fellow client Mike Gordon, who, at the time, owned the biggest bar in Alaska, Chilkoot Charlie's, in Anchorage. Gordon was forty-seven years old and says reading *Seven Summits* changed his life, too. "At the time, I had my priorities turned upside down," Gordon remembers. "My wife and I were separated, and I had a problem with cocaine, and it seemed like a good way to square my life away."

Gordon and John shared a tent for three weeks while attempting to climb North America's highest peak and bonded over their midlife crises and Seven Summits dreams. On summit day, John waited for Gordon so the two could walk to the top together. Gordon's new sense of purpose helped him turn his life around.

As the phones continued ringing at the companies that offered guided ascents on the Seven Summits in the late 1980s, the guides themselves kept kicking the Everest can down the road and cashing in on the other six, much-safer peaks. But Simonson and Tejas were among a small group of guides who were intrigued by the idea of bringing clients to Everest. However, they toggled between the dream and the dread of having to look after someone in the death zone. As experienced mountain guides, they understood how unprecedented doing anything like that was within the storied tradition of mountain guiding.

Bringing clients to Everest would require guides to harness decades' worth of experience. Simultaneously, it would require them to turn their back on a two-hundred-year-old ethos.

Mountain guiding as an occupation was born in earnest in eighteenth-century Europe, when a critical mass of people started finding the mountains more majestic than menacing. Wealthy Europeans— especially the British—would travel to Alpine villages such as Chamonix in France to gape at 15,000-foot-high snowcapped granite spires, including Western Europe's highest peak, Mont Blanc. Inevitably, looking up at the high peaks wasn't enough. People started to pile on the wool and put on a pair of hobnail boots and venture upward, in search of solitude, freedom, and a sense of awe.

As is found in other mountain-dwelling cultures and societies across the world, local farmers and sheepherders in Scotland, Switzerland, France, and Italy were already fairly adept at navigating steep and icy slopes. Unsurprisingly, therefore, it was two local Frenchmen who first climbed Mont Blanc's 15,774-foot summit, in 1786. Just a year later, one of those same French climbers was hired by a Swiss man to guide him on the peak. Soon the popularity of being guided up Mont Blanc exploded. (Today, more than ten thousand people attempt to climb it each year.)

After the death of three guides on the mountain in 1820, however, it became clear that guiding would need to be regulated, restricted to the most capable mountaineers. Local French climbers formed the Compagnie des guides de Chamonix, the oldest, most respected, and most emulated guides collective in the world. Its endless rules, codes, and technical handbooks have been argued over, refined, and redesigned for two centuries, and you can still walk into Maison de la Montagne—its original headquarters in Chamonix—to hire a mountain guide today.

Britain, Australia, New Zealand, and Canada didn't take long to set up regulated guiding organizations of their own in the model of France's. The Americans, however, lagged behind. In 1902 the American Alpine Club was finally set up, but it was more of a fraternity than a regulating body. Its members actually decided *against* creating an official guiding certification.

The unique American mountain guiding ethic would instead be shaped more quietly by a young climber named Paul Petzoldt. In 1924, at just sixteen years old, Petzoldt climbed the Grand Teton in Wyoming and soon began leading others to the top, including some visiting British royalty. European guides were well known by that time for their overbearing "rope 'em up, keep 'em close" style—"always assume your client is trying to kill you" was their early-adopted rule—but Petzoldt thought differently. He created a hybrid system of guiding clients while also teaching them self-sufficiency, and he went on to found some of the best climbing and outdoor schools in the country. These included the US branch of the British-founded Outward Bound, and the more technically oriented National Outdoor Leadership School (NOLS), which is still based in Wyoming, and is where many renowned climbers—including David Breashears—got their early training.

Meanwhile, the European model of guiding certification was so influential by the mid-twentieth century that a global organization called the International Federation of Mountain Guides Associations (IFMGA) was formed in 1965 as a way of creating global standards. While a climber could become a certified guide via their own national organization in, say, Switzerland, Australia, or Argentina, many countries would allow foreigners to guide in their country only if they had IFMGA certification.

For the most part, the proudly independent Americans turned up their noses at the whole idea. They continued to climb and guide informally, and often illegally, throughout the twentieth century. When Europeans came to the Yosemite Valley in California, where a true climbing revolution was happening in the 1960s and 1970s, they often encountered an anarchic Wild West environment of unshowered men who climbed with their shirts off while smoking cigarettes. Fall, the main rock climbing season, was like Woodstock for people with six-pack abs. Yvon Chouinard, Jim Bridwell, and others lived in their cars or in campgrounds, fiercely championing clean and minimum-impact styles of rock climbing by day, getting high and singing by the fire at night.

In addition to becoming famous for founding Patagonia, Chouinard is known for his cynicism toward guided climbing, especially on

Everest. He once called guides "enablers and manservants" because of how they can allow climbers to avoid developing their own skills. But few people realize that it was actually Chouinard—along with other climbers of note like Jim Donini and Peter Lev—who proposed the formation of an "American Professional Mountain Guides Association" in 1979. The stated goal was to enforce more competence, not hand out meaningless rubber stamps.

"Back then, I saw it as a really great profession," says Chouinard of guiding. "I spent a lot of time climbing in Europe and those guys were real professionals. When a guide walked into a bar, everybody would spin around and whisper. They had a very high level of guiding and I thought we should emulate what they're doing. In this country, like at Exum [an influential guiding company based in the Tetons, cofounded by Petzoldt and Glenn Exum in 1929, where Chouinard taught guides for a short time], the guides didn't know how to ice climb, Rainier guides didn't know how to rock climb, and none of them knew how to ski!"

It was pretty hard to convince a rock climbing guide who rarely touched snow, however, that they needed to learn to ski, and the guiding certification system Chouinard proposed never materialized. "A lot of guides were really opposed to a certification—they saw it as a threat," he says. "They didn't want to have to learn these other skills that they wouldn't be using regularly."

The only thing that did impose some structure around American guiding was the national park system. As the country's most iconic mountains and rock walls sat mainly within federal land, guides like Lou Whittaker sought exclusive permission from the government to operate businesses within them. (The Whittakers' friendship with the Kennedy family didn't hurt—Jim had guided then senator Robert F. Kennedy to the top of Mount Kennedy, in Canada, in 1965.) Most of America's early guide services established themselves in this way, building their businesses around a specific mountain or area that they alone or with a select few others had access to, such as Rainier or the Tetons. This privatized approach was another reason that through the mid-1980s, the closest things to standardized training programs for guides in America were the handbooks and personal philosophies taught by Whittaker at RMI, or by Glenn Exum and Exum's longtime president and eventual co-owner, Al Read, in the Tetons.

When guides and guiding companies came under pressure from insurance companies, a handful of guides finally formed the American Mountain Guides Association (AMGA), in 1986. Nonetheless, most American mountain guides hardly took notice—especially since their jobs on mountains like Rainier and Denali didn't require AMGA certification. The AMGA was eventually accepted into the IFMGA in 1997. Few cared about the milestone.

No matter what country they were from or which certification they did or did not have, most climbers and guides around the world believed the idea of guiding on Everest was asking for trouble. The prevailing wisdom was that no mountain guide in their right mind would try. They were certain of this because they were struggling, and sometimes dying, trying to climb 8,000-meter peaks themselves—especially when they joined expeditions with less experienced climbers, and the line between their responsibilities to themselves and to others blurred.

No one understood this better than the second New Zealander to summit Everest, Nick Banks.

Nick Banks's first time on Everest was in 1977. An ambitious twenty-five-year-old, he and his tiny team of eight were attempting the mountain without Sherpa support beyond base camp. This unsupported style of climbing on eight-thousanders was almost unheard of at the time.

Banks had grown up in New Zealand as part of a tight-knit crew of Kiwi climbers that included Gary Ball, Russell Brice, and Bill King.

The group earned steady paychecks guiding in their country's Southern Alps. By their early twenties, Banks and his friends were rock stars of the climbing and guiding world in New Zealand, and looked the part, with their corduroy flares and shaggy hair (Ball's nickname was "the Blond Bombshell"). Banks wasn't satisfied by drafting off the pride of a fellow New Zealander having made the first ascent of Everest, though, and set off to ascend it himself.

On the Khumbu Glacier, Banks shared base camp with a wealthy German couple named Gerhard and Hannelore Schmatz, who were using the camp to attempt the neighboring peak of Lhotse. Though Gerhard was a lawyer back home, climbing was not a lark for him—he took it seriously and worked to develop his own skills. The same could be said for Hannelore, who had attempted Manaslu with Gerhard in 1973 and more recently had summited Denali. While Hannelore didn't make it to the top of Lhotse in 1977, Gerhard did, with other members of his team and some Sherpa climbers in support.

Banks and his crew did not summit Everest that year. However, Gerhard was impressed by Banks and the two kept in touch and became friends. Banks and his wife soon visited the Schmatzes in Germany. It turned out that the Schmatzes had their sights set on taking a shot at Everest in 1979. When it came time to put a team together, Banks was among the first to get the call. Gerhard offered him an all-expenses-paid spot. Despite being a deeply respected and experienced guide, Banks was living on cans of beans, and the opportunity was just too good to be true. "My wife and I literally had about three hundred American dollars between us," he remembers.

The Schmatzes also invited the guide who had helped Hannelore get to the top of Denali a few years earlier, Ray Genet (the founder of Harry Johnson's guiding company). Though Banks and Genet were not there as guides, it would be fair to say that, much as with Bass and Breashears, the Schmatzes saw them as a safety net. "I wasn't guiding but I was certainly there because I was a guide," is how Banks explains it. "Gerhard was fifty years old and wanted to surround himself with some young, strong climbers."

Genet was certainly that. A legendary Swiss-born climber who had long been living in Alaska, he was said to have been Denali's very first guide, and by the time of the Schmatz expedition, he was certainly its best-known. His womanizing ways, burly beard, and burlier reputation led to his being nicknamed "Pirate."

The Schmatz expedition arrived at Everest in the fall of 1979. On October 16, Banks and Genet were climbing, roped together, ahead of Hannelore and her hired partner, Sungdare Sherpa. As they reached higher elevations, Genet decided to unrope from Banks and slow down while Banks carried on alone. Hannelore eventually caught up with Genet. Banks summited, becoming the first New Zealander to touch the top since Hillary twenty-five years earlier. As he descended, he passed Genet, Hannelore, and Sungdare, who were still moving steadily. All three also made it to the top.

On their descent, however, Hannelore's faculties deteriorated, and she collapsed. It was late, and there was a discussion about whether they should bivouac—stay put and try to survive the night huddled together at 28,000 feet—then continue the descent in the light of morning. Sungdare knew that an unplanned bivouac that high on Everest is rarely survived, and he tried to convince Hannelore to carry on, but she refused. To make matters worse, Genet himself was low on oxygen and was beginning to fade. Nevertheless, Sungdare and Genet stayed with Hannelore through the cold, dark hours.

By the time the faint glow of sunrise appeared, Genet was dead. Hannelore and Sungdare managed to start descending. But then Hannelore collapsed again and, this time, she never got up. Sungdare survived and had to continue down without her. Instead of becoming the fourth woman in history to summit and get down safely, Hannelore became the first woman to die on Everest. She was thirty-nine years old. Her frozen body sat in its final resting place for nearly twenty years, her eyes wide open, her dark hair eerily blowing in the wind for passing climbers to see on their way to the summit, before she was finally extricated from the ice, either by unknown climbers or the elements, and was either dropped or fell down the Kangshung Face.

Banks looks back on that day as a stark example of why the notion of guiding on Everest was considered beyond the pale at the time. "Ray might have been suffering from the onset of cerebral edema," Banks says. "Earlier in the day, he and I were roped together and he became very irritable and bad tempered, asking me to slow down. It was very out of character—not the guy I'd known on the lower mountain. So then he just unroped completely and soloed behind us. I was very much against it, but he wouldn't have it. That's when he joined up with Hannelore."

Just as Breashears believes he would have perished had Bass given up during their descent from Everest, simply because he would not have abandoned Bass, Genet's and Hannelore's destinies that day were one. Banks is certain that a guide of Genet's pedigree and experience would never have abandoned her and continued descending, no matter the fact that there was no agreement in place or fee paid for him to protect her. As a result, he never stood a chance. Few survive a night spent in the death zone without shelter, warm layers, and a healthy reserve of oxygen. Yet climbing in the death zone while carrying enough oxygen to survive a potential overnight is equally dangerous. It's one of the many reasons so few believed that guiding on Everest would ever be possible.

"It's just so utterly unpredictable," Banks says of guiding at extreme altitude. "I think you can certainly provide inspiration and supervision above eight thousand meters, but you can't guide in the traditional sense. You can go to the Himalaya safely twenty times and die on the twenty-first time, or you can go once and die from altitude on your first climb."

5

The NEW RACE
to the TOP

Hannelore's frozen corpse is only one of dozens that have been visible between Camp Four and the summit over the years. A frozen dead body can weigh up to two times more than one that is not frozen, as it absorbs moisture and becomes encrusted with ice. It typically takes a team of climbers to move such a body. They must spend several hours chipping it free from the mountain, and then hours or days carrying it down to Camp Two. This is why there are supposedly up to two hundred bodies on Everest, though most are deep under snow and ice or have been moved out of view. Some are buried only partially by the constantly drifting snow, whereas others will dangle in plain view from old rope until someone cuts them free. All are basically suspended in time as the average temperature on the upper part of Everest is about the same as a morgue's cold chamber.

For Everest climbers who are still breathing, the cold is the least of their worries. It's intense, but with proper gear and constant movement, manageable. Above 26,000 feet, there are in fact fewer avalanches, rockfalls, and crevasses than below. On the upper reaches, where there are deceptively steep and technical stretches of climbing, mountaineers can fall to their deaths if they are lost or snow blind. However, what kills most people above that altitude is, to put it simply, time.

In 1953, the same year of Everest's first ascent, a Swiss doctor who was on the mountain referred to its upper reaches as the "lethal zone." Today, anywhere above 26,000 feet is referred to as the death zone. At that altitude, "the deterioration of the body is pretty rapid," says Peter Hackett, the foremost expert in high-altitude physiology. He summited Everest in 1981 and has spent a lot of time in the Khumbu Valley studying trekkers, Sherpas, and climbers. "'Wasting away' is another good term," he says. "Or 'dying.'"

A fit person who has been properly acclimatized to the altitude of the death zone—but with little or no supplemental oxygen—could last up to a day on the summit in a best-case scenario. But according to Hackett, a person just plucked from a sofa at sea level and dropped onto the summit would have about one minute of normal brain function. This is due to sudden hypoxia, or lack of oxygen. Their body would be furiously trying to increase oxygen intake through rapid breathing and a racing heartbeat. A lethal sense of well-being, even a morphine-like euphoria, would wash over the person. Approximately ten minutes after that, their brain would no longer be sending signals out to the rest of their body, and their heart and lungs would go into a sort of standby mode. Then the person would die.

While hypoxia is an incredibly real danger, the most common ailments on Everest are high-altitude pulmonary edema (HAPE) and high-altitude cerebral edema (HACE). Both fall under the umbrella of altitude sickness, and can strike as low as 10,000 feet (mild symptoms can occur even lower). They are essentially the buildup of fluid and swelling in the lungs (for HAPE) or brain (for HACE). HAPE is easier to spot, with its trademark cough and pink blood-tinged spit, and it goes from bad to worse more quickly, at which point it is extremely hard to reverse. HACE is trickier to identify—the symptoms that precede it, such as dizziness, headache, and a lack of coordination, are common and unclear—but a person's inability to perform easy cognitive tasks such as telling time on a clock or saying where they are from often proves to be a helpful red flag.

In severe cases of altitude sickness higher up, climbers often become belligerently combative. People in those situations are usually savable, but if they refuse help and keep ascending instead of turning around, things get exponentially more serious. Hypothermic climbers begin shedding clothing for no apparent reason. "It's a downward spiral," says Hackett. "Eventually, they just give up and think that they are going to die, when just a little help from another climber can easily save them."

HAPE and HACE can strike anyone, anytime, on Everest, and are hard to prevent, but even the earliest Everest climbers were looking for a viable workaround to the solvable problem of lack of oxygen at altitude. George Mallory used a rudimentary oxygen apparatus on his ill-fated 1924 expedition. Early oxygen systems malfunctioned frequently and the masks were leaky. They have improved greatly but still require tinkering. Today, climbers suck on anywhere from three to six liters per minute during their summit pushes, tricking their bodies and brains into thinking they are at only about 24,000 feet all the way to the top. Even then, it's difficult to breathe, especially at the level of exertion required, and it's a race against time.

Delirious climbers are notoriously bad at deciding what flow rate of oxygen they need as they get closer to the summit. Client climbers have been known to instruct Sherpa climbers to crank the dial up much higher than they are supposed to; others forget to turn their oxygen on altogether—or they turn it off by accident—and don't notice their mistake until they are too far gone. Summiting can be a bittersweet moment, as it is then that many climbers are able to finally process the oxygen predicament they are in.

．　　．　　．

When Eric Simonson was dreaming of guiding Everest in the late 1980s, the challenges posed by the lack of oxygen at the mountain's extreme altitude weighed heavily on his mind. "The less oxygen, the less bandwidth to go around," he explains. "If you're a really proficient climber, maybe you're only spending twenty percent of your bandwidth on yourself and you've got eighty percent left for your client. On Everest, you might have fifty or sixty percent left for a client. Without oxygen, maybe ten percent."

Nevertheless, he knew once IMG announced it would be a Seven Summits company in 1987 that offering six of the mountains would never be enough. It was the seventh that would truly set a guide company apart. The other companies offering the Seven Summits knew the same. The question was: Which would be the first to stick its neck out and try to guide Everest?

In July 1989, two months after climbing Denali with his guide, Vern Tejas, and his new friend Mike Gordon, Bob John was home in New Jersey, kicking back with a bottle of light lager and the latest issue of *Outside* magazine. On the cover was a woman model with big hair, decked out in L.L. Bean, looking far too squeaky clean to actually be doing anything the magazine's readers enjoyed. In the back was a section called The Active Traveler—essentially classified ads for high-end adventures. There was a hot springs tour on horseback in Colorado, sea kayaking and whale watching in Baja, and an inn-to-inn canoe trip from Maine to Florida.

Then John noticed a listing that he had to read twice before it sank in. Sandwiched between an ad for a network of hostels and one for an Indiana-based sailing school, opposite splashy campaigns for fanny packs and Subaru Outbacks, was the following copy:

Join a group led by Todd Burleson, Peter Habeler, Martyn [sic]
Zabaleta, and Larry Nielson on the North Face of Everest in

spring 1990. Guided ascent and 1st American ascent of the Super Couloir.

Though John didn't know it at the time, he was looking at history—the first guided trip to Everest offered on the open market. This would not be like the "client funded" trips of the past, but an explicitly guided expedition available to a huge reading public for purchase, and a potentially lucrative payday for its organizers.

A *Washington Post* journalist spotted the ad and wrote an op-ed with the headline "The Sky Is the Limit for a Mere $35,000." It noted that "until about two years ago, no one was prepared to offer a public opportunity to climb any of the eight-thousand-meter peaks." A local paper out of Tulsa, Oklahoma, characterized the trip as part of a trend toward seemingly unattainable "dream vacations" like baseball fantasy camp, a weeklong cattle drive, or Skip Barber's race car driving school.

As soon as John saw the ad, he got in touch with Gordon. Both men agreed: it was a sign. "I just called the number," says Gordon. John was in charge of three hundred employees at IBM in a department that did $100 million in annual revenue, and his employer was getting a little tired of his frequent vacation requests, but John says he would have quit his job if he had to. This was Everest.

It helped that the guide team had serious star power. Peter Habeler was the first person in history to climb Everest without supplemental oxygen, which he did in 1980 with Reinhold Messner, a fellow Austrian and a mountaineering superstar. The Spanish climber Martín Zabaleta was South America's most famous guide. Larry Nielson had become the first American to climb Everest without supplemental oxygen during Bass and Wells's 1983 expedition. And the Super Couloir route—also known as the Hornbein Couloir after the first ascender—was nearly as famous among mountaineers as the guides themselves.

But who the hell was Todd Burleson?

The first time many veteran Himalayan climbers heard Burleson's name was when it appeared in that summer 1989 issue of *Outside*, next to the names of three of the greatest high-altitude mountaineers of their generation.

"I'd never heard of him," says Simonson, who knew the others well (Nielson, in particular, who had become a mentor of his). "And I certainly didn't have the money to buy ads in *Outside* magazine—or even print fancy brochures, for that matter. We just had these xeroxed newsletters."

As it turned out, Burleson, like Simonson, was a climber living in the Pacific Northwest who had also spent time in Nepal. But, more important, he had a knack for thinking five steps ahead and he'd long ago decided his destination was Everest.

Burleson grew up on a remote island off Kodiak, Alaska, called Sitka-lidak. By 1977, at the age of seventeen, he had become adept in the art of subsistence living and was out on his own, scrambling up the peaks and glaciers of his state. He then cut his teeth as a climber in Joshua Tree and on the big walls of Yosemite. In his early twenties, blond, fit, and with a boyish face, he brought his climbing gear to the Himalayas, explored some lower peaks, then got sidetracked by a two-and-a-half-year spiritual detour in India. Upon his return to the States, he rededicated himself to mountaineering, signed up for some climbing courses, and traveled all over North America honing his skills. In 1987, along with his best friend and trusted climbing partner, Willi Prittie, he went to work for the esteemed American Alpine Institute in Washington State for several months to, as he puts it, "learn the business a bit." Even this early in his career, he had ambitions to own his own guide service and was developing his own climbing and guiding skills in tandem with a business plan.

But Burleson and the American Alpine Institute's founder, Dunham Gooding, butted heads. Gooding was well respected and old school—his approach was one of long apprenticeship, which had worked well for many great American climbers—and Burleson's ambition and impatience rubbed Gooding the wrong way. Burleson had even established his own guiding entity before coming to work for Gooding, enlisting Willi Prittie as his right-hand man, a fact that he kept to himself.

In 1988, Burleson secured space on a permit for the north side of Everest for a spring 1989 expedition. He suggested to Gooding that he and Prittie could use it to lead a small American Alpine Institute trip. Gooding didn't feel Burleson had the experience to pull off such a thing so early in his guiding career and flatly dismissed the idea. Though Burleson had befriended the Everest vet Pete Athans and had been to the Nepal side of Everest twice by that time—a claim corroborated by several others who remember seeing him there in the late 1980s—his climbs weren't recorded by the Himalayan Database (the undisputed record-keeping authority on all Himalayan climbs). That wasn't uncommon back then, as people sometimes managed to fly under the radar to avoid the difficulty of the permitting process. In any case, he was green. He had certainly not summited Everest, or any other 8,000-meter peak.

"Todd's pretty bold," Gooding says. "I told him we felt it would be unsafe and unethical for him to take clients to Everest. He decided he wanted to do that more than work for us."

As the relationship between the two men frayed, Gooding learned that Burleson was calling his own guiding business Alpine Ascents International, or AAI. It was the same three initials as Gooding's company, and it felt like a cheap shot.

"The name thing was no coincidence," says Gooding. "And it still feels like a rip-off." (Burleson insists he had incorporated as "Alpine Ascents" in 1986 while living in Nevada, before going to work for

Gooding, and added "International" later, with no intention of usurping Gooding's business.)

The truth is, the initials were about the only thing Burleson could take from Gooding, because Gooding's AAI was mostly focused on skills training and was not much in the international guiding business anyway. In fact, many of Gooding's guided trips were outsourced to other companies. Burleson, on the other hand, was attempting to build a full-service Seven Summits guiding company. He began by putting together trips to mountains like Aconcagua. But Burleson had balls—in business and in the mountains—and his focus was squarely set on the one peak that would set him apart.

Within just a few weeks of placing the ad in *Outside*, Burleson embarked for the Tibet side of Everest on a sort of dress rehearsal. This expedition, half a year before he was scheduled to bring clients to the mountain in the spring of 1990, was a dual climbing and scouting trip. He wanted to summit but spent his downtime exploring and tinkering with oxygen systems. "We had three huge tanks of liquid oxygen shipped in from Beijing just so we could experiment," he recalls.

The expedition he had joined was led by an Antarctic outfitter and entrepreneur from Australia, Mike McDowell, and an American adventurer of esteem, Mike Dunn. McDowell and Dunn were savvy logisticians but didn't have much experience on mountains of this caliber, so they had the good sense to bring a couple more seasoned climbers with them: Vern Tejas and a well-known Idaho-based guide named Skip Horner.

Horner and Tejas knew of each other but had not met before. Unbeknownst to Tejas, Horner was gunning for the same prize of becoming the first person to guide all the Seven Summits and had several under his belt already. "I had guided three or four of them by then, so it was in the back of my mind to become the first," says Horner. "I didn't talk about it much, because I didn't want someone else to pick up on the idea and beat me to it." Tejas was not only in the same race, but ahead. After guiding the Hong Kong–based duo of Keith Kerr and Frank Fischbeck to the summit of Aconcagua in early 1989, Tejas had tallied five of the seven peaks. The Everest expedition where they met Burleson, however, was not set up as a guided climb, so Tejas and Horner would have to settle for simply trying to summit the tallest mountain in the world, and perhaps gather a little intel for any future opportunities to guide it.

In the end, no one ended up summiting during the fall 1989 trip, but one very important partnership was formed. During the climb, Tejas and Burleson ended up high on the mountain together. Tejas didn't like the look of a slope of heavy snow. He stopped and began trying to trigger an intentional avalanche to stabilize the ground around them by stomping on the snow above the slide zone. Burleson began jumping up and down, too. It worked. They braced themselves and watched the loose snow, which otherwise could easily have swept them down the mountain, fall away. Burleson was impressed with Tejas's instincts as well as his guiding ambitions. He asked Tejas to come work for him. Tejas agreed. (Tejas also continued working for Harry Johnson at Genet Expeditions on Denali, since Burleson did not have a permit for that mountain.)

By 1990, most experienced Himalayan climbers would agree that the list of veteran mountain guides with the experience, nerves, and logistical prowess to pull off a guided Everest climb could probably fit in a fortune cookie. Burleson was not on that list. Neither were two relative unknowns in the Himalayan climbing world who were in pursuit of the same dream.

The New Zealanders Rob Hall and Gary Ball were unlikely partners, according to friends. "Gary was a wild man—like a live hand grenade," says his friend Nick Banks. Hall, meanwhile, was eight years younger but more serious and business minded. Hall had been climbing in the Himalayas since he was nineteen, when he tagged along with the older Russell Brice—a member of Ball's and Banks's fraternity of New Zealand guides—to attempt Ama Dablam in 1980. Ball had also made his first Himalayan trip with Brice—as well as Banks, and Bill King— but not until 1984, when he was thirty-one, on Kangchenjunga.

By 1988, Hall was twenty-seven and had been on three Himalayan expeditions. He felt ready to take on Everest. Ball had still been on only the one Himalayan expedition in 1984, but the two joined forces and attempted Everest together. They decided not to use supplemental oxygen, hoping to join the tiny cohort of people who had summited without. While they came up short, another Kiwi they were climbing with named Lydia Bradey, who was one of the very few woman guides at the time, became the first woman in history to summit without supplemental oxygen (a feat only eight other women have repeated since).

Hall and Ball returned to Everest the very next year, but once again failed to summit. Nevertheless, they started talking about partnering up in business, sharing the vision of Everest as their flagship product— even though they had neither been to the top of that mountain themselves nor guided on a single Himalayan peak.

Like Burleson, what the two lacked in Himalayan guiding experience, they made up for in bravado and foresight. They shared a compulsion to always be out front, pushing the edge—"on the sharp end of the rope," as climbers refer to it, and imagined an industry eventually forming around Everest, much like the one around Denali.

"I guess I was a bit of an entrepreneur, but a lot of it was naivete," says Burleson. "Everest was a big bite to take on, there's no doubt about it. That first trip, my attitude was, 'Let's just try it.'"

When Bob John and Mike Gordon reached out to Burleson with the hope of joining AAI's spring 1990 guided Everest climb, Burleson told

them that he wouldn't be bringing anyone whom he had not personally climbed with. But if they signed up for his upcoming Aconcagua
expedition, he suggested, they could all get to know each other. John
and Gordon were happy to oblige. They could tick off another one of
the Seven Summits and set new altitude records for themselves. The
two others who answered Burleson's Everest ad and similarly agreed to
climb Aconcagua in preparation were Brad Nieman, a Denver real estate
agent, and Normand Bergeron, an environmental science researcher living in Boston. Vern Tejas would coguide the Aconcagua trip with Burleson.

The four clients arrived in Argentina in the winter of 1989. "I loved
Todd right away," says John. "I totally respected him. And Vern is just
such a character. After that trip, knowing that these were going to be
our guides on Everest gave me a lot of confidence." It certainly helped
that Burleson and Tejas got Gordon and John to the summit of Aconcagua. Neither Bergeron nor Nieman summited, but nonetheless, Burleson said that all had proved themselves enough to earn a spot on the
Everest climb.

In February 1990, John turned forty. The next month he was on his
way to Tibet. Though the *Outside* ad had gotten some media attention,
Burleson's thirteen-person expedition, which included five guides, four
clients, and four Sherpa climbers, still arrived on the mountain without
much fanfare. The private expeditions they were sharing the north side's
base camp with weren't even aware that theirs was a guided trip.

On the south side of the mountain, and also unaware of the details
of the AAI expedition, were Rob Hall and Gary Ball. This time their
mission was twofold, and audacious: summit Everest, and then drum up
publicity for their new company, Adventure Consultants, by climbing
all Seven Summits in the span of seven months.

Their third attempt at Everest was a success. They summited together
on May 10, this time using oxygen. They whipped up extra excitement

by helping Edmund Hillary's son, Peter, get to the top, where he used a satellite phone to speak with his father and the prime minister of New Zealand.

Simonson was in the Himalayas that season, too, though seventy-five miles away from Everest. He'd been unable to get a spring 1990 permit for Everest, so he'd settled for Shishapangma in Tibet, the world's fourteenth-tallest mountain and last in the list of eight-thousanders. His IMG team—of mostly guides—was turned back at 23,000 feet and nobody summited.

Things didn't go much better for Burleson and AAI. In the end, while Burleson could forever—and justly—claim that his company was the first in the world to undertake a guided climb of Everest, three of his four clients barely made it past base camp. Gordon, Nieman, and Bergeron succumbed to violent coughs, boredom, fear, and utter fatigue, as those who are inexperienced at altitude often do. John, however, lived up to his reputation as an Energizer bunny and performed surprisingly well during several rotations to set up higher camps. And he was having the time of his life.

"I think the others were just overwhelmed by it," he says. "I knew I was probably also one of the least-experienced guys on that mountain but I was moving pretty well—like Dick Bass. It wasn't until we were headed from Camp Three to Camp Four, at about 27,400 feet, that I started slowing down. We weren't using oxygen yet. Next thing we know, we see Zabaleta and Habeler walking down from Camp Four toward us. They just pointed up at a huge lenticular cloud forming high on the mountain. Zabaleta tied me to his rope and we just descended quickly all the way to Camp One. And that was fine with me. It's what I paid these guys to do. My climb was over."

Thirty years after the first ascent of Everest, the race to the top was back on. This time, it was the race among mountain guides to put a paying client on the summit and bring them down safely. And just like in

1953, mountaineers from a half dozen different countries around the world felt they had a good shot. In addition to Simonson, who got an Everest permit for the spring of 1991, Hall and Ball, who successfully completed their Seven-Summits-in-seven-months mission, and Burleson, there were European guides with the bona fides to try. Bernard Muller of France, Ralf Dujmovitz of Germany, and Ronald Naar of the Netherlands had all been pushing the envelope by guiding other 8,000-meter peaks in the mid- and late 1980s.

Unfortunately for Simonson, the type of clients he was looking for never materialized in 1991, and he didn't get a shot to win the race that year. It was a shame, as neither AAI nor Adventure Consultants was on Everest in 1991—their next permits were for 1992. Simonson had to settle for leading another "client funded" trip made up of mostly independent climbers—in this case, wealthy businessmen who put down the cash for the trip and allowed a bunch of hotshot guides, mostly from RMI, to come along on a free ride. "I really wanted to go to Everest, and so I told Eric I could probably raise $400 or $500K," remembers Charlie Peck, an investment banker from Pasadena, who was forty-four years old. "He was blown away. So, there were us four corporate guys and the rest of the group was like this dream team of guides. But, still, we never thought of ourselves as clients as much as we were expedition organizers."

Unsurprisingly, the amateur climbers ended up being in over their heads, but the expedition was a huge success, nonetheless. Ten of the more experienced climbers summited, including Simonson and George Dunn. After having come up short in his attempts in 1982 and 1987, Simonson felt palpable relief. *Thank God, I can finally get on with my life*, he remembers thinking. His focus, as he explains it, could now fully turn to getting other people to the top.

6

ONE HUNDRED
PERCENT SUCCESS

In the autumn of 1991, Steve Bell reached across his desk in Bristol, England, and picked up the telephone. The veteran British climber with the deep voice, proper English accent, and good looks of a television adventure show host knew that the call he was about make couldn't be undone. He wondered if it was the right thing for his fledgling company, Himalayan Kingdoms. As a mountaineer who had spent significant time in the Himalayas above 8,000 meters and was well aware of the risks, he wondered if it was the right thing to do at all.

Bell dialed Geoff Birtles, the editor of a well-respected UK climbing magazine called *High*, one of the few periodicals that chronicled the oddball exploits of mountaineers.

"Geoff, we've got some news," Bell said. "We'd like to place an ad—it's for Everest."

Like a lot of climbers, Bell was unaware of Burleson's 1990 guided expedition. He certainly would have learned about it if some of Burleson's AAI clients had summited, but they hadn't, so news didn't spread.

Bell had founded Himalayan Kingdoms with two friends, Steve Berry and John Knowles, in 1987. Their office in Bristol was an attic above a real estate agency, with a small brass plaque beside the doorbell being the sole indication it was a company headquarters. They initially offered an assortment of exotic but only modestly strenuous treks in Nepal, Europe, and Africa, including through the Khumbu Valley to base camp, which nearly ten thousand tourists a year were doing at the time. Yet while Knowles and Berry were happy to continue focusing on these relatively mild trekking adventures, Bell was a climber long drawn to high-altitude challenges, and he wanted the company to be known for more.

"The day I left secondary school—at eighteen—I hitchhiked to Chamonix and spent six weeks climbing," he recalls. "I nearly killed myself a few times. At twenty I did the north face of the Eiger. Then me and two friends went to the Himalayas and we attempted the northeast ridge of Annapurna III." He then served in the Royal Marines between 1983 and 1987, which allowed him to participate in several British military expeditions to the Himalayas.

In 1987, he left the marines, but he was still a reservist and in 1988 was given the opportunity to go with the military to Everest and attempt the west ridge. There, he ran into a New Zealander named Mike Perry, who was guiding clients for High Country Expeditions, the company Perry co-owned, on nearby Changtse, a 24,747-foot point that some call the north peak of Everest. High Country was another outfitter testing the waters of bringing clients to the Himalayas. It was the first time Bell had heard of anyone bringing clients above 7,000 meters, in the Himalayas or anywhere else, for that matter.

Bell approached Perry and asked him if he'd consider setting up another big climb that could be marketed separately—by Bell as Himalayan Kingdoms and by Perry as High Country Expeditions—but run in conjunction. Sharing the risk and reward was a smart move at a time when mountain guides were making it up as they went along, and Himalayan Kingdoms didn't yet have the resources or the client list to organize expeditions on its own. Bell and Perry shook hands. The following year, in 1989, Bell and Russell Brice—who was working for High Country—successfully guided clients to the top of Himalchuli West. It was High Country's first successful guided ascent of a 7,000-meter peak. During the climb, Brice told Bell that he too harbored ambitions of establishing his own Himalayan guiding company. But, true to his type, Brice was playing the long game, fixated on becoming the best outfitter on Everest over time, while Bell was intoxicated by the same thing Rob Hall, Gary Ball, and Todd Burleson were: he wanted to be the first to bring clients to the top. As a patriotic Brit, he would have loved nothing more than to live up to his nation's pioneering legacy on the mountain.

In 1989, Bell ran two expeditions under the shared Himalayan Kingdoms–High Country Expeditions banner, then two more in 1990 without High Country. On one of those trips, he got one Himalayan Kingdoms client to the summit of Broad Peak—the twelfth-highest mountain in the world, at 26,414 feet. This was a game-changer: the first-ever British-guided ascent of an eight-thousander. Any first means something in the world of climbing mountains. Then he placed his Everest ad. When he opened *High* magazine in the fall of 1991, he eagerly flipped through until he spotted the small but unforgettable lines announcing that Himalayan Kingdoms "has Everest booked for 1993."

Bell soon got a phone call he was half expecting. It was from Peter Gillman, a *Sunday Times* journalist and an amateur climber he had gotten to know over the years. It seemed Himalayan Kingdoms' Everest climb was newsworthy enough for a few inches in Britain's most popular Sunday broadsheet.

Then Bell got a call from another journalist with an interest in climbing, Jules Stewart from Reuters. Stewart was fascinated by the concept of a guided Everest climb offered on the open market, and he asked Bell to share details for a story.

"It basically went the 1991 equivalent of viral, and not necessarily in a good way," Bell recalls of the piece Stewart wrote. Unlike the *Sunday Times*, Reuters was a wire service available to any media outlet across the globe. "Newspapers all over the world picked it up. It was in the *New York Times*, *Los Angeles Times*, Johannesburg *Times*, the *South China Morning Post* . . . I mean, it literally went everywhere. These articles were mostly saying how outrageous it was. In the UK it was portrayed as extreme tourism or a package holiday to the summit of Everest."

Famous for their mix of sensationalism and condescension, the British tabloids had a field day. The *Weekly News* led with, "If you're looking for a holiday that's a little more challenging than the usual jaunt to the sun . . ." The *Sunday Sport* reported, "Dangers include: freezing your balls off and being squashed by an avalanche."

"I put a lot of them into a scrapbook, which I still have," says Bell of the clippings. "I had this sense that what we were doing was important. We were inundated with applicants—more than fifty people sent us hundred-pound-deposit checks. What surprised us was the inexperience of people that were applying. The climb was set up for 'experienced mountaineers,' who wouldn't normally have the opportunity to go to Everest unless they organized an expedition themselves. But we heard from all these people who'd done bugger all climbing—just, you know, 'Hey, I saw your ad, can I come?!'"

Bell discarded the applications that made no mention of climbing or mountaineering experience, and singled out the people who said they had experience at altitude, or at least seemed eager to sign on to a program that would prepare them over the next two years.

. . .

One hundred and eighty miles north of Bristol was the headquarters of another British trekking company that, unbeknownst to Bell, also had its eye on the Everest prize. Out There Trekking, known locally as OTT, was co-owned by a hulking and rebellious mountaineer named Mark Miller who had a disdain for the climbing establishment. OTT's other owner was Andy Broom, a nonclimber with skills in logistics and problem-solving on far-flung expeditions.

The company's "office" was really just a landline telephone sitting in a disheveled flat on Nettleham Road on the south side of Sheffield, a medium-size blue-collar city. At the time, however, Sheffield was the epicenter of the United Kingdom's climbing scene, with the famous gritstone cliffs of the Peak District just a few miles away.

The OTT flat was strewn with half-full pints of lager, full ashtrays, and at least one couch-surfing climber at any given time. It was an era when all-night raves and electronic music were picking up steam across the British Midlands, but OTT was founded on more of a counter-culture punk rock ethos, and thanks largely to Miller, garnered respect within the climbing community for its authenticity. With the build of a rugby player and the athleticism of a gymnast, no one epitomized the Sheffield climbing scene quite like Miller. And he couldn't have been more different than Bell—it was Johnny Rotten going up against the military man.

"Mark was a bit younger than me," says Bell. "He turned up around the mideighties and he just exploded on the scene as this really ballsy climber. If he wasn't doing something really hard in the mountains, he was in the bar getting smashed or beating someone up. He was sort of a rough diamond."

"I'm not sure about the diamond part," says Richard Jones, Miller's childhood friend and longtime climbing partner, only half joking. "We went to boarding school together. He was quite a big lad, even at thirteen."

Miller was part of a famed crew of British climbers referred to as the Alpine Binmen. These young men were so dedicated to pushing themselves up impossible spires of rock and ice above Chamonix that they would spend the spring and summer there, living ten to an apartment, subsisting on pub snacks and stolen beer, working the least amount of shifts they could as trash collectors. The revered *Alpine Journal* described them as "notorious for their poverty and simple love of the mountains."

"I think Mark went to college for about a month," says Jones. "Thatcher had just arrived, there were three million unemployed, no jobs . . . and Mark just decided to lose himself in climbing."

Miller used his unemployment checks to begin flying to Pakistan to climb as often as he could, and he loved the country so much that he began leading treks for a company called Karakoram Expeditions in the late 1980s, which is how he met Broom, who handled its logistics and travel planning. Miller and Broom hit it off, and in 1990, the two founded OTT. When Miller saw Himalayan Kingdoms' ad for the guided Everest climb in *High* magazine, he realized how easy it would be to attract the clients whom Bell would inevitably turn away. A few months later, Bell got hold of some of OTT's promotional material. Thumbing through it, he spotted one of his own photographs and some very familiar wording. OTT had set an Everest expedition of its own for the exact same time, the autumn of 1993.

Broom was proud of the quick work he and Miller were doing to establish OTT. "We had this one expedition to a seven-thousand-meter peak and then we were offering clients the opportunity to go to Everest," he says. "We were pretty ambitious and we moved very fast."

"Mark definitely saw the market was there," says Jones.

"They say competition is good for business," Bell says. "But OTT were cutting corners and taking business from us. We had put a lot of effort into getting our travel agency license, for instance—which is needed to legally book travel for clients—whereas OTT just went ahead and booked travel without a license. It bothered us so much that we even notified the local trading standards office in Sheffield. That basically started World War III and we became archrivals."

"It's true," Broom admits. "We just didn't have the resources Himalayan Kingdoms did."

As much as Bell and Miller were ready to go head-to-head to become the first company to guide paying clients to the top of Everest, they were also aware that there were two full Everest climbing seasons before they would have their chance, during which time someone else could grab the prize. Hall and Ball's recently founded Adventure Consultants was quickly overtaking Perry's High Country as New Zealand's most famous guide firm, in the wake of its seven-month Seven Summits success. Bell had heard of IMG's Shishapangma climb in 1990, and of the eight-thousander expeditions that Europeans were guiding. He knew the record could fall any season.

In the spring of 1992, Bell headed to Everest to attempt the mountain again himself and to prepare for taking his clients there the next year. He hadn't yet touched the top in his previous two attempts and was still living with the same monkey on his back Simonson had worn until he summited in 1991. As he set up at base camp on the south side, he kept an eye on two of his stiffest competitors: Todd Burleson's AAI, which Bell was now aware of, and Adventure Consultants. Both had permits and were there with clients. All Bell could do was wait to see if he would have a front-row seat to guiding history being made by someone other than him.

The Adventure Consultants clients were an intentionally eclectic bunch. Ned Gillette, an American, was part climber, part showman—an able mountaineer and savvy self-promoter, with an expertise in financing his exploits with other people's money. Among those mingling with him in the mess tent at base camp were Doug Mantle, a forty-two-year-old attorney from Los Angeles; Ingrid Baeyens, a thirty-six-year-old physical therapist and climber from Belgium; and Yick-Kai Chan, a thirty-three-year-old sheet metal worker from Hong Kong. The guides were Rob Hall, Gary Ball, and their Kiwi friend Guy Cotter, the son of Ed Cotter, a renowned mountaineer and climbing partner of Edmund Hillary. The twenty-seven-year-old Ang Dorjee Sherpa was also on staff, and making his first attempt on an 8,000-meter peak.

"A few years earlier, I had gone to New Zealand to try and climb Mount Cook, and my guide on that trip was Guy Cotter," remembers Mantle. "I didn't make it to the top so I returned the following year and it was during that trip that Gary Ball horns his way into our table at dinner and hands me a business card. A few months later I get this letter from Adventure Consultants saying, 'This could be your chance to stand on top of the world' . . . I wasn't aware of anyone offering anything like this."

Cotter shared Hall's and Ball's optimism about Adventure Consultants' ability to put inexperienced but gutsy climbers on the Everest summit, through teamwork and exceptional client management. As Cotter puts it: "Everest expeditions had always had a management problem. I saw quite a few private expeditions fall apart because the team members were drawn together from all over one country. I saw an American expedition leader—a marketing and finance guy—pull the money together and then get the best climbers from all across the US to try and work together. They didn't want to work together—they wanted to summit. I watched a French national team fail, while everyday Joe Blogs managed to summit. That's exactly what Rob and Gary were excited about, that there were people, unknown to the world, who wanted to climb Mount Everest for their holiday—they'd just never been given an opportunity."

Burleson's AAI guiding team was made up of himself, Vern Tejas,

Skip Horner, and Pete Athans, with the twenty-six-year-old Lakpa Rita Sherpa in support. By 1992, Athans was already the most experienced Everest climber in the world, with six attempts and two summits. Tejas had signed up his duo of Frank Fischbeck and Keith Kerr as AAI clients, and they had invited another Hong Kong transplant and a good friend of theirs, Louis Bowen, an American.

Mike Gordon, the Alaskan bar owner, was back as a client as well, making his second attempt with Burleson and receiving a small discount as a returning customer. Notably absent was Gordon's friend Bob John, who had retired from his Seven Summits quest after climbing Elbrus in 1990. "I had four of the Seven Summits, I had gotten remarried, had gotten a promotion—when I got back from Elbrus, I just stopped climbing. I moved on to other stuff," John says.

As the weeks went by on the Khumbu Glacier, the AAI and Adventure Consultants teams intermingled and essentially merged into one entity. AAI's client Bowen, for example, grew close to Rob Hall, and when Bowen, Tejas, and a few of the others from the AAI team ended up with pneumonia and had to descend to the village of Pheriche for several days, Hall sent his wife, Jan Arnold, a doctor who was at base camp, down to look after their recovery.

"In 1992 it wasn't really an industry yet and there weren't that many groups on the mountain," remembers Bowen. "We were all really very close. We got to know each other and we helped each other. It was like a close-knit community."

Even once the teams got higher on the mountain there was more camaraderie than competition. Adventure Consultants had an impressive six clients who were still fit enough to make a summit attempt: Mantle, Gillette, Baeyens, Chan, and two others. AAI had two clients left with a realistic shot at the top: Bowen and Kerr. Fischbeck had dropped out of the climb. The plan was for Bowen to head up with Tejas and Horner first; Kerr was to go up with Burleson, Athans, and Lakpa

Rita a few days later. But Bowen, Tejas, and Horner wouldn't be alone. They climbed right alongside Hall, Ball, Cotter, Ang Dorjee, and their Adventure Consultants clients nearly the whole way.

On May 12, 1992, the two companies made history. Adventure Consultants got all six of its remaining clients to the top. That it had succeeded on its very first attempt at guiding Everest made it all the more impressive. Minutes later, Horner, Bowen, and Tejas stepped onto the summit. "I was right between Skip and Vern on a rope," Bowen says.

The first two successful guided Everest climbs had happened all at once.

That day, Horner and Tejas simultaneously became the first people to guide each of the Seven Summits (and the fifteenth and sixteenth people to complete them). Tejas had also succeeded in being the first Alaskan to complete them. Three days later, Kerr summited with Burleson, Athans, and Lakpa Rita (and became the seventeenth person to complete the Seven Summits.) Bowen hadn't yet climbed Kilimanjaro, but he rectified that in 1998. (Burleson completed the Seven Summits in 1997, as did Steve Bell.)

It had been seven years since Dick Bass stood on top of Everest, but his influence on the birth of the Everest guiding industry was palpable. In kicking off the Seven Summits concept, he'd created a new type of client climber—and guide to serve them—that led to this momentous day.

"I actually had dinner with Dick Bass in Hong Kong, about six months before the climb," says Bowen. "He was a real inspiration to a lot of people who never thought that climbing mountains was something that would be in their life plan."

Between Adventure Consultants and AAI, eight average Joes had planted their feet on top of the world. All had made it down with their lives and limbs intact. The race to be first was over.

.   .   .

Steve Bell celebrated with the two teams in base camp afterward, but he had a bittersweet feeling. Not only was the record he was after already in the history books, but he was a bit uncomfortable with how, as he saw it, some were rushing into the Everest guiding business a little hastily. "I wasn't taking the idea of guiding at eight thousand meters lightly, which is why I built up to it slowly," explains Bell. "It seemed to me, Rob and Gary were just jumping straight into the deep end. They had done their own Himalayan expeditions, but none as guides, looking after clients. It felt like they climbed the Seven Summits in seven months, got massive publicity, and then just said, 'Hey, let's take people up Everest.' At the same time, I was also very inspired by Rob."

Another source of frustration was the fact that Bell—and the rest of the British military climbing team that was with him—had come up short once again in their own attempt to summit Everest. To be fair, they had not taken the South Col route like AAI and Adventure Consultants but had attempted the dreaded, much more technical west ridge and Hornbein Couloir.

While Himalayan Kingdoms had missed the chance to put the first client on top of Everest, Bell still wanted it to be the first British company to do so. This was the prize left to play for, and it kept Bell's rivalry with Mark Miller and OTT burning hot. While Miller found ways to keep his prices lower and margins higher in advance of his fall 1993 expedition, Bell spent his free time vetting clients and thinking of ways to distinguish the Himalayan Kingdoms experience from OTT's. Bell secretly hoped something would disrupt OTT's momentum. It's a wish he now regrets.

In September 1992, Miller went to Pakistan on a personal climbing trip. Afterward, he boarded a plane to Kathmandu to meet a group of OTT clients hoping to climb Manaslu. On approach to landing, Pakistan Air flight 268 flew into the side of a mountain and disintegrated on impact. All 167 passengers aboard were killed. Miller was just twenty-eight at the time. His obituary in Britain's *Alpine Journal* said his death "deprived British mountaineering of one of its most talented and prolific sons."

Jon Tinker—a talented climber who had done some guiding for OTT, and cowritten Miller's obituary—had struck up a deal with Andy Broom to become part owner of OTT and started leading all the company's big Himalayan climbs. Bell, who knew Tinker as well, hadn't seen that coming.

"I considered Jon a friend at the time," recalls Bell. "He and I climbed together, we'd had a lot of deep, meaningful conversations. We'd slept on the sides of mountains together. So, when he took over for Mark, we still had a mutual respect, but it's not like we could go down to the pub and have a pint anymore. Let's just say the friendship was put on hold. We were now competitors."

Bell kept his focus on his own upcoming trip. However, the timing of his fall 1993 permit meant AAI and Adventure Consultants would have a second chance to climb the mountain with clients—in the spring of 1993—before he even had his first.

Burleson, Hall, and Ball arrived at base camp that spring understandably cocky. Their guide teams were now Everest veterans—it was Athans's seventh climb, Burleson and Cotter's second each, and both Ball's and Hall's fifth attempts. Adventure Consultants had seven clients. AAI brought fourteen clients this time, including four repeat customers who had been unsuccessful the previous year. Once again Mike Gordon was there, making his third and final attempt. "Every time I went to Everest I had to buy my wife a car," he says. "So it got a little harder."

The conditions were more challenging than they had been in 1992. Nonetheless, AAI and Adventure Consultants managed to get two clients to the top, each. They'd repeated their feat and cemented their status on the mountain.

At last, the autumn of 1993 rolled around. Himalayan Kingdoms' permit was for the south side; OTT's was for the north. As Bell was packing duffel bags and calming his clients' last-minute jitters, the Nepalese Ministry of Tourism announced out of the blue that effective September 1, just days before Bell was due to arrive in the country, each Everest permit would cost $10,000 per person, instead of the previous $10,000 total. The minimum permit fee was $50,000 for a five-person permit (with an option to pay an additional $10,000 each for up to two more climbers, for a maximum total of seven climbers on each permit). With fourteen climbers—eleven clients and three guides—Bell would now need two seven-person permits and be required to hand over $140,000 to the Nepalese government. It was $130,000 more than he'd expected.

Unable to process the thought of canceling, in haste Bell resorted to looking for a loophole. He purchased one $70,000 permit to cover half of his team and said the other half would instead climb Lhotse. The permit for Lhotse cost only $9,600, total. Bell told officials he would happily pay an additional $10,000 for each Lhotse climber who happened to summit Everest (something, to this day, he says he believed was allowed at the time).

Bell and his team proceeded with their trip. And at last, after years of planning and all his hard work, he achieved two milestones. On the personal front, he made good on his third attempt and finally summited Everest himself. But for Bell, helping others summit mountains was even more satisfying, so he was prouder yet of his historic achievement as a guide. He got seven of his clients to the top at once—the most any single guide or company had done—and became the first Brit to guide paying clients to the Everest summit. He had thoroughly beaten his rival OTT, which, it turned out, wasn't able to put any clients on top that year.

Himalayan Kingdoms' fall 1993 Everest expedition had been an undeniable success. However, the company was dealt a nearly fatal blow when the Nepalese government hit it with a huge permitting fine. The officials decided it was not in fact okay for Bell's climbers to attempt Everest while on a Lhotse permit, and fined the company $100,000. It took years for Bell to negotiate and pay his way through the mess.

More climbers had summited Everest in 1993 alone than in the twenty-six-year period after its first ascent. However, the year ended on a somber note that underscored the seriousness of climbing in the death zone, clients in tow or not. In October, Hall and Ball were attempting the world's seventh-highest mountain, Dhaulagiri, together on a personal climb. Even though they were using oxygen, Ball was moving slower than usual. At one point he said he was getting cold. At 24,000 feet, he stopped moving altogether. Ball was succumbing to the effects of HAPE. Hall and his other climbing partners began the arduous process of getting him down to a lower camp, but Ball's condition deteriorated too rapidly. Neither medication nor oxygen was helping. Ball died suddenly at 21,300 feet. His body was lowered into a crevasse. He was forty years old.

"He was a great guy, one of the most charismatic people you'll ever meet," Nick Banks remembers. But "Gary did have a self-destructive side," he notes. "We all told him to stay off the high peaks after K2 [where he'd had a close call with HAPE in 1992]. He drove himself to the limit in all aspects of his life."

Tragic as it was, death in the Himalayas was nothing new to climbers, and the following season, the spring of 1994, was seen as a pivotal moment for the burgeoning guiding industry on Everest. With the race to the top well and truly over, now the mission was to build a business that could grow reliably each year. On the Tibet side, three major guide firms arrived with clients: Simonson's IMG, Bell's Himalayan Kingdoms, and Russell Brice's newly launched Himalayan Experience (Himex). Four

IMG guides summited. However, due to atrocious weather—coupled with the fact that summiting from the north remained considerably more difficult than from the south—none of the companies got any of their clients to the top.

On the Nepal side, AAI and Adventure Consultants had also returned with clients and had experience in their favor. Hall, now without the late Ball, and also without Guy Cotter that year, hired Ed Viesturs, an American guide who had climbed three 8,000-meter peaks without supplemental oxygen (and went on to become the first American in history to climb the fourteen eight-thousanders). Adventure Consultants put all six of its paying clients on the summit of Everest at once that season, giving Hall license to place ads in several magazines and create posters boasting of his company's "100 percent success!" AAI put clients on the top as well, and in total, the two pioneering outfitters put twenty-five people on the top of Everest in 1994—equating to nearly 70 percent of all climbers who summited from the Nepal side that year—including clients, guides, and hired Sherpa climbers. The spring 1994 Everest season was clear proof of concept for AAI and Adventure Consultants, but all five guide company owners believed in that moment that the number of people summiting Everest each year—safely, under the supervision of an experienced guide—could continue growing exponentially.

Ironically, the new permit rules in Nepal worked in their favor and became a major factor in the blossoming of the industry. The permits were more expensive but there were suddenly far fewer limitations on them: many more expeditions were allowed to be on the mountain at any given time, and companies could reliably buy permits for future dates, setting themselves up to come back season after season. It was an obvious boon for Nepal's tourism revenue, but also the beginning of hard questions being asked about the mountain's capacity.

The following year, 1995, all but two of the major guide firms returned to Everest with clients. Bell, excited by what he saw ahead, took the year off and decided it was time to split with his Himalayan Kingdoms partners to form the global climbing-focused guide company he'd always envisioned. He phoned up his old climbing buddy and fellow former soldier, Simon Lowe, who had led the successful Everest expedition for Bell in 1993. He thought Lowe would make the perfect partner. They set up shop in Sheffield and called their new company Jagged Globe.

Meanwhile, AAI, Adventure Consultants, OTT, and Himex were back on the mountain in 1995 with paying clients. (IMG brought clients to Cho Oyu that year, but not Everest.) There were two others as well—smaller startups trying to emulate what the pioneers had done—and across the six total guided expeditions on Everest in 1995, twenty-eight guides, clients, and Sherpas reached the summit.

The industry was essentially doubling in size each year, in terms of the number of outfitters offering guided Everest climbs. Guided expeditions were quickly taking over base camps on both sides of the mountain. For the expedition companies, this was unreservedly a good thing, but it did leave them a bit short staffed. A ratio of one guide for every two clients was generally considered to be ideal. An elite high-altitude guide is a very different thing from an elite high-altitude climber, and at the time, there were a few dozen people at best both qualified to guide on Everest, and willing to take the risks of doing so.

7

The ART *of* GUIDING

Conrad Anker is America's most famous alpinist and, arguably, its greatest living one. There is an international alpinism award called the Piolet d'Or (the "Golden Ice Ax") given annually to the climber who took on such a cutting-edge and dangerous route they deserve what is essentially the Oscar of mountaineering. As with the Oscar, winning is as much a political affair as an artistic one, and just getting nominated is a huge achievement, especially since Americans rarely get the honor. In 2012, however, Anker was nominated for successfully ascending a route called the Shark's Fin on Mount Meru in India. It's still considered one of the hardest alpine climbs in the world, and it cemented his status as the elder statesman of American alpinism. The achievement was documented on film by Jimmy Chin, a mentee of Anker's, and made into an award-winning documentary called *Meru*. Anker is also a mentor of the climber Alex Honnold, the subject of Chin's Oscar-winning documentary *Free Solo*.

Having devoted his life to scaling seemingly impossible lines on the remotest mountains in the world, Anker wouldn't seem to be frightened by any type of climbing. But that isn't the case. Guiding scares the shit out of him.

His aversion to guiding has a lot to do with the story of his own mentor, a beloved alpinist named Terry Stump, known to the climbing world as Mugs. Mugs was thirteen years older than Anker, and they met in 1988 while Anker was in college in Utah. Anker traded a bicycle for some of Mugs's old climbing gear. Mugs had already climbed extensively in the Himalayas and was turning his attention to Alaska, where he notched up several goundbreaking first ascents, most notably on the east face of the Moose's Tooth and on the north buttress of Mount Hunter. Anker was soon following Mugs up these routes, and the two formed a brotherhood. "Mugs was tough love," Anker says. "He played football for Joe Paterno at Penn State in the seventies. I remember seeing him get into arguments about climbing style—Mugs didn't suffer fools lightly."

Anker says the only time Mugs ever mentioned Everest was when he talked about maybe wanting to climb the north face without oxygen someday. Everest was barely on Anker's own radar as a young climber, and it was certainly never a fixation, as it was for so many of his peers. "My dad was a climber, and after Everest was climbed by Jim Whittaker in 1963, he had a big poster of the north ridge on our wall," he remembers. "It hadn't been climbed yet, so it sort of felt like that could be the apex of a climbing career. But, by the nineties, I just felt like it could wait. Once I'd seen that Dick Bass had done it, I thought it was an old guy's peak."

Anker says Mugs talked a lot about getting a license to guide on Denali, a peak he knew intimately. Only about a half dozen companies were legally allowed to guide on Denali—including Genet Expeditions and Mugs's employer, Mountain Trip, owned by Gary Bocarde—and it would be a lucrative contract. In the meantime, Mugs worked as a guide for the companies that had licenses.

Meanwhile, Anker reluctantly picked up domestic guiding jobs here and there, just to feed his habit, though he preferred carpentry work. He says he did love taking people into the mountains for their first time and getting them excited about climbing, but it was clear his Alpine dreams were more personal, almost in another realm of what was possible. "I just wanted to do cutting-edge climbing at the time," he remembers. "But, back then, you couldn't make a living off equipment sponsorships, so you had to guide." As one example, he points out, "It was the only way to get to Antarctica in the nineties."

Mugs, however, kept leaning into the guide life on Denali every spring. And it wasn't just a side hustle; he formed a real bond with many of his clients. In 1991, he was at the bedside of Gavin Borden, a wealthy former client turned friend, when he died of cancer. Another former client, Bob Hoffman, called Mugs the most considerate, capable, and likable guide he knew. "I climbed on and off with him for thirty years," said Hoffman. "He had a gift for bringing out the best in people, for showing them how to overcome fear."

Unfortunately, Hoffman said this while eulogizing his dear friend.

In May 1992, the same month AAI and Adventure Consultants were putting the first paying clients atop Everest, Mugs was guiding Hoffman and a friend down the south buttress of Denali after they'd summited. The three were roped together on a gentle slope, which is customary. As guide, Mugs was in the rear, ready to arrest a slip, if there was one.

Then Hoffman stopped at what appeared to be a crevasse. He didn't feel comfortable going any farther without Mugs's assessment of the best way around or over it. He waved Mugs forward. There were roughly forty feet of rope between the three men, so Mugs walked toward the edge, creating a big loop. As he stood at the precipice, assessing the situation, the snow beneath his feet disappeared from under him. He was free-falling. The other two climbers dropped to the ground to catch the fall by plunging their ice axes into the snow. But so much snow and ice had broken away and come tumbling down on top of Mugs, he was crushed. Mugs's clients rappelled into the crevasse to look for him, but it was clear he was under too much ice and snow to be saved. The rangers never bothered with a body recovery. Mugs Stump was forever part of the mountain he loved.

Anker was devastated. "It was like night and day," he says. "That was the year I quit guiding completely. My parents knew Mugs—they even went to his service—and they said, 'You can still climb mountains, but don't guide in the mountains.'"

Those who choose to dedicate their lives to guiding do so for reasons that are hard to explain. The standard opinion that greed must be the motivating factor has always been untrue: to this day, guides are not getting rich. At most, an Everest guide can make $15,000 to $20,000 in a two-month season, and many barely make ends meet. The company owners weren't raking in the dough on Everest either. Every major outfitter still refers to its Everest expeditions as loss leaders, returning each year to the mountain primarily to maintain its status as a top-tier guiding company in the hope of attracting clients to sign up to more lucrative expeditions on Rainier, Denali, or Mont Blanc. That is not to say that large-scale global guiding companies like Adventure Consultants, IMG, or AAI don't turn a healthy profit. But in each case, the business is largely propped up by peaks far lower and less complex than Everest.

The more likely explanation is that getting clients to the top of Everest is more intoxicating for a certain subset of climbers than reaching the summit themselves. Guiding not only requires a different set of skills than climbing, its rewards come from an entirely different place, one that has little to do with first ascents or pushing one's own physical limits. Guides need to have the leadership skills of a military general; the stamina, strength, and agility of an Olympic triathlete; the patience of a preschool teacher; and the cool head of a bomb squad technician.

More often than not, guiding is a thankless pursuit. When clients don't make the summit, their top three excuses tend to be "shitty guide, shitty guide, and shitty guide." It's not uncommon for clients to tell their guides exactly how they feel about being turned around with a slew of defiant insults. Some clients have even sued their guide for the dishonor. Other, more likely, considerations for not making the top, such as "I didn't train enough," "The weather is unpredictable," and "We used all our strength and resources to save someone's life and we had nothing left for a second attempt," typically fall much lower down the list than "It was my guide's fault."

While some Everest clients in the early 1990s wondered whether they might simply be funding their guides' Everest dreams, for most good Everest guides, personally summiting has always been an after-thought. "My big revelation was discovering that I got more pleasure, or more satisfaction, from seeing another person achieve something than I did achieving it myself," explains Steve Bell. "You have this sort of incredible vicarious glow—you've given something to someone. Or, rather, it is a gift that you've enabled them to receive. There is something very special about sharing a mountain with a client, with somebody who would otherwise never be able to go there." So perhaps the rewards of guiding on big mountains is akin to catching a wave on a surfboard: rare, but so powerful when it happens that it erases all memory of the hours spent flailing around in an angry ocean. It's a lopsided suffering-to-satisfaction ratio, and that might be the point.

"When you facilitate someone doing something they never thought was possible—or a lifelong dream like climbing Everest—it has a huge impact on their life," reflects Jimmy Chin. "It could change somebody's life and I think there is a real draw to that."

"Why guide? It is a very good question," says the pioneering Himalayan guide Bernard Muller in his thick French accent, choosing his words carefully. Muller has been bringing clients to the top of Himalayan mountains since the late 1980s. "First, it is about the challenge of bringing people who are not considered specialists, to help them live their dream. Climbing is often about being first, but guiding is a shared experience. There is the technique and then there is the psychological experience. When you're with your clients on a big mountain in the Alps, with some danger, you are sharing a big experience. In the Himalayas, it's even bigger. This human dimension is more important for me than the technique."

"Of course, I myself wanted to spend time in the wilderness," explains Heather Macdonald, an early IMG guide. "But there was also a really deep interest in taking others into the wilderness. And don't forget, this was a time when Everest was still wilderness. I got asked all the time why I wanted to go up the same mountains over and over. But it's not the same thing when you're with different people, and especially when you're with people seeing it for the first time."

Phil Ershler, the cofounder of IMG, feels not enough people understand the difference between a good climber and a good guide. "I know some climbers who are incredible—amazing athletes—but I wouldn't trust them to walk my mother across the street," he says. "Nobody's going to remember Phil Ershler as a great climber—that won't be on the epitaph—but I think they will talk about the fact that I was a pretty fucking good guide."

Ershler—like so many other guides who became influential on Everest and made the industry's growth possible—credits one man for setting him on the path to this future: Lou Whittaker. "Lou didn't teach me much about mountaineering, but he taught me everything I know about guiding," he says.

·   ·   ·

Lou Whittaker and his twin brother, Jim, were born in Seattle in 1929 and began climbing around Rainier as teenagers. The six-foot-five Whittaker boys got into college on a basketball scholarship but preferred putting their athleticism to use in the mountains. The twins soon became indispensable members of the Rainier National Park search and rescue. Occasionally—and unofficially—they also guided people up Rainier.

After being drafted into the army in 1952, they pushed for an assignment training special forces soldiers in mountaineering and skiing for alpine warfare, which they did as part of the famous Tenth Mountain Division, based at Camp Hale near Leadville, Colorado. In 1955, Jim became the first full-time employee of REI, the Seattle-based outdoor gear company, which his friends, climbers Lloyd and Mary Anderson, had started out of their home.

In 1962, a year before the first REI store finally opened on Pike Place in Seattle (and nine years before the first Starbucks opened a few blocks away), Lou and Jim were offered pole position on an upcoming Everest expedition, in an effort to become the first Americans to summit. However, the expedition was structured in a way that only one brother and one Sherpa would be in each summit team, which meant that, if successful, either Jim or Lou would make the first ascent, but not both. Just two weeks before they were set to depart, Lou broke the news to Jim that he wasn't going. The expedition would take up to three months, and Lou, who was a father, said he didn't want to be away from home that long. Jim became the first American to summit Everest on May 1, 1963.

Jim returned a reluctant hero and national symbol of adventure. A self-described introvert, the only guiding he did after that was on rare exceptions made for high-profile people, like his friend Robert F. Kennedy, who appeared on the cover of *Life* magazine in his down jacket atop Mount Kennedy in Canada, thanks to Big Jim's guiding work. Jim took sponsorships and speaking engagements, and in the mid-1960s, he became CEO of REI, a position in which he remained for the next twenty-five years.

Lou took his own path. In 1969 he founded his guiding company, RMI, and started the business of taking people to the top of Rainier. Though it's only the fifth-highest peak in the lower forty-eight, at 14,411 feet, it's an active volcano rising 13,246 feet above the land around it, making it by far the most prominent. On a clear day you can see Rainier perfectly from downtown Seattle, sixty miles away as the crow flies. (You can also see it from Portland, Oregon, more than one hundred miles away.) Additionally, it's the most glaciated mountain in the contiguous United States, which is why it is riddled with more crevasses than any American peak outside Alaska, and is a great training ground for the Himalayas. Its lines aren't delicate and feminine like the Matterhorn, or symmetrical like Mount Shasta; it's more like Denali in its scale, appearing almost as its own mountain range, rather than as a single peak. The weather that comes off the Pacific Ocean and heads straight for Rainier, with not a single other mountain in the way to slow it down, makes it one of the most dangerous mountains in the world, too. Rainier is the peak that makes American mountain guides.

Among Lou's first hires at RMI were Phil Ershler, George Dunn, Eric Simonson, and Joe Horisky. During the climbing season, the young men lived together in a rustic barnlike building on Rainier's south slope in an area called Paradise.

"Lou hired me as a seventeen-year-old, without much climbing experience," says Horisky. "I lived at Paradise for eighteen seasons and got all my training on the job. You'd come off the mountain and, in the late seventies, there was nowhere to go except the bar at the Paradise Inn." Horisky and the others would often move on from the bar after last call to the huge stone fireplace in the grand lobby, and swap stories all night beneath the timber beams. "I think that's where we all started to talk about Everest," he says.

Simonson climbed Rainier in 1970 at age fifteen. "That climb was a pretty momentous occasion for me," he remembers. By twenty he got himself hired as an RMI guide and was making $325 a month working for Lou. Simonson was known to have a one-track mind when it came to climbing, with a "tough love" guiding style that could make him seem insensitive at times. But he also had remarkable intuition when it came to looking after people in the mountains. "It's hard to find people who can see everything, every possibility, and cover themselves and everyone around them, the way Eric could," says Dunn.

"There weren't many climbers back then, so we'd just hire healthy people who were in top shape," Lou says of the early days. "Some of them had started climbing a little, but, at that time, none of them had guided before. I'd always start by asking them two questions: Do you like being outdoors in the rain and snow? And do you like people?"

On his brother's recommendation, in the early 1970s, Lou hired the talented Nawang Gombu Sherpa—Tenzing Norgay's nephew, who had been by Jim's side on the Everest summit in 1963, and became the first person to summit the mountain twice, in 1965. Nawang Gombu led Rainier climbs alongside Simonson, Ershler, Dunn, and the others throughout the 1970s and 1980s, which made RMI the first Western guide service to hire Sherpas to guide in the United States.

Women were also aiming to break barriers in the early 1970s at RMI—a company that, at the time, was rife with *Mad Men*–type sexism and reductive hierarchies. Lou did hire women, but only as "cabin girls," whose primary duties were housekeeping and cooking. One of the best gigs for a cabin girl with an interest in guiding was cooking at Camp Muir, because it required a four-hour climb to get there. That's exactly how Marty Hoey started demonstrating her talents in 1970. "I think Lou hired her for the sheer number of times she'd been up and down the mountain," says Horisky. By 1975, Hoey was leading climbs, and she soon became one of the first women to lead Denali expeditions as well. Lou came to refer to her as the heart of the guide service. Hoey and the other RMI guides were workhorses, sometimes spending three weeks guiding on Denali in the spring, then summiting Rainier twenty times in a single summer.

In 1978, Lou's guides—numbering a dozen or so by then—grabbed their sleeping bags and duffel bags and migrated ten miles down the road from the Paradise bunkhouse to Ashford. The no-stoplight town of about five hundred people located just outside the national park was where Lou himself lived with his wife and children.

Lou bought properties in Ashford to accommodate his growing family of guides. They could either stay at the "Ranch" or the "Estate," depending on whether they liked to get eight hours of sleep or not. The Ranch—a forty-acre spread with a main house and a few outbuildings—was known for its parties.

"I took a little eight-by-ten chicken coop and put windows in it and a potbelly stove, and that's where I lived," remembers Lou's son Peter, who set himself up at the Ranch and started guiding for his father's company when he was just sixteen. "We worked hard climbing the mountain, but played really hard, too. I mean, it was bonfires and combat roles, getting drunk and being a little stupid. It was a real fraternity."

When Hoey died on Everest in 1982, it was a huge loss for the company. But new guides, like Dave Hahn, continued making their way to RMI and joining the unique community, training under Lou.

Hahn first encountered RMI as a client when he climbed Rainier after college in 1985. "I'd never seen anything like it, proportions like that on a mountain," he says. "I vividly remember looking up at it, and only seeing parts of the mountain through holes in the clouds. Then I'd see another part way over there and say, 'Wait a second, that can't be right—how can that go on at that angle, that long, that high up in the sky?'"

After spending a few days with Dunn and another guide named Greg Wilson, Hahn says, "I was swept off my feet. Just watching them work, seeing their confidence . . . I was totally caught up in it. I knew what I wanted to do for the first time in years."

He got hired by RMI and started training. "I lived at the Estate— we went climbing on our days off," he says. "Guides that lived at the Ranch were great partiers."

Another climber who showed up on Lou's doorstep was Heather Macdonald. A young woman from the Pacific Northwest, she was inspired by Hoey's story and in 1990 came to Rainier with something to prove.

"I was twenty years old and I was going to Reed College in Portland, Oregon," she recalls. "One day, I just decided to drop out, drive down to Joshua Tree National Park, and climb. I lived in a cave at the end of a hidden valley loop with a bunch of other climbers. Then I drove from Joshua Tree to guide tryouts in Ashford. When I arrived at Mount Rainier, I just knew I was meant to be a guide. It was just a deep, intuitive knowing. I immediately felt connected to Phil and Eric because I already felt somehow connected to Marty Hoey. She was my inspiration."

There were still less than a half dozen women guiding for RMI at the time—among about fifty men—but Whittaker and the other guides eventually looked past gender, for the most part. "They were actually mentors," Macdonald explains. "It wasn't just guiding to them, it was the art of guiding." And Macdonald says that when the men were inadvertently—or overtly—sexist, she and the other women guides were never afraid to set them straight.

Macdonald learned quickly. "Right after I had started at RMI, Eric would just kick me right out front: 'Your rope team is leading!' he would say. And I'm like, 'Wait, what?!' I realized later that a big part of how I learned climbing was having to teach it."

Simonson, Dunn, and Ershler had asked Lou for his permission to create IMG in 1987, and since it was an international guiding business that wouldn't compete with RMI, he obliged. "Lou didn't begrudge us going off and guiding in these places as long as we'd come back and work for him in the summers," says Simonson. But when the promise Lou had long been dangling in front of them—that the three would eventually be given part ownership in RMI—still hadn't materialized by the mid-1990s, they decided to take matters into their own hands. They severed ties completely and set up IMG headquarters two miles up the road. IMG started looking into getting its own licenses on Rainier and Denali.

"Yeah, I lost some of my best guides," Lou remembers with characteristic indifference. "But I had plenty by then. That's just how it goes; we can still have a beer with each other and enjoy the memories."

RMI remained the leading guide company on Rainier, and one of only a handful on Denali, before eventually branching out to international trips in the 2000s. (It even ran Everest expeditions between 2009 and 2015, but had trouble gaining traction among the more established companies.) And in the end, whereas Jim holds a significant spot in Everest's history, Lou became the more influential figure in the story of Everest thanks to the guides he trained.

At ninety-two years old, Lou still owns RMI and still lives a few miles from Mount Rainier, though his son, Peter, is a co-owner and does most of the management. Lou speaks in a way that reminds people of simpler times. And while his take on why people choose a life of guiding may seem trite, most Everest guides today would agree that he's right. "There's a satisfaction in helping people to achieve something they wouldn't normally be able to," he says.

As RMI and other companies groomed young climbers into guides for the long term, the Everest guide pool grew. The ballooning number of Everest clients were being well taken care of by guides who may not have had many Everest summits yet under their belt, but who were willing to accept the risks of looking after others on the world's highest mountain, which a climber like Conrad Anker had no interest in doing. Talents like Vern Tejas, Guy Cotter, and Pete Athans were helping to increase the summit success rate of Everest clients. Astonishingly, they did it without incident. The safety record they and the others were putting together seemed almost too good to be true.

8

The BIG FIVE

Incredibly, by the end of the fall 1995 climbing season, one guiding industry first that had not been claimed on Everest was a client fatality. (One twenty-two-year-old AAI Sherpa climber died in 1995 in a fall on the Lhotse Face, after forgetting or choosing not to clip into the safety rope.) The business was humming along. Around 150 people had paid for a guided attempt up Everest to date. A third of those had reached the summit. The percentage of expeditions on Everest that were guided had gone from zero in 1989 to about forty in 1995.

The challenge, then, as the client numbers grew and the pipeline to recruit new guides matured, became refining the experience of the climb. The company at the forefront of this evolution was Himex, thanks to the particularly obsessive thinking about safety and detail of its owner, Russell Brice.

Brice had been coming to the Solu-Khumbu since 1974, when he'd helped Edmund Hillary build a hospital there. As a climber, he steadily built his own résumé up to a career high in 1988, when he completed what is still considered one of the boldest climbs in Everest history—

traversing what are known as "the Pinnacles" on the north side, and spending a harrowing night above 27,000 feet in the process. That climb was the apotheosis of his interest in pursuing aesthetics and style over summits—he didn't summit that year, and wouldn't for nine years more. However, as a guide, it was a very different story.

In the 1980s, Brice and Nick Banks co-owned a guide firm in New Zealand together. They went their separate ways; Brice ended up living in the United Kingdom, Chamonix, or wherever he was climbing or guiding at the time, and in 1994, he simultaneously launched an Alps-based guiding company called Chamonix Experience and an Asia-based company, Himalayan Experience.

Brice set up his operations on the north side of the mountain in the spring of 1994 and quickly established the suitably militaristic and official-sounding Himex as the tightest operation around. He instrumented and refined safety systems and ensured that others used them as well.

"I myself never really had any ambition to climb Everest, until it came along as part of the job," says Brice, who favored jeans, a ball cap, and sunglasses around base camp instead of fleece and down. "And, even then, I was much more interested in dealing with the logistics of how to guide Everest safely. Guiding here felt like we were trying to achieve something that hadn't really been done before."

His overbearing style earned him the title of "mayor" on the north side, but his influence quickly spread to the companies guiding from Nepal as well. Himex became so rapidly successful and fundamental to the industry that within a year of its launch it was operating on par with, if not beyond, Adventure Consultants, AAI, IMG, and Jagged Globe. Collectively, these companies had established themselves as what could be called the Big Five.

Regardless of whether they were operating from the Nepal or Tibet side, the Big Five guided expedition leaders were developing familiar rhythms and routines that could be transplanted across the border and repeated from one season to the next. Hired Sherpa climbers and porters would arrive months before the trekkers and client climbers to prepare for the season ahead. Base camps would be erected (from scratch each year), and then Sherpas, working along-side Westerners, would prepare and secure sections of the mountain with fixed rope. Team leaders would come together to discuss the weather, how to pace their clients, and where it made the most sense to establish the higher camps. They would also join in strategizing about how to minimize trash and human waste and clean up the decades' worth of garbage from expeditions past, recognizing that their financial futures depended on a certain amount of stewardship. "Clean-up" expeditions became ubiquitous around this time and were largely effective (signing up for one also became an easy way to jump the queue for a permit).

But as much as they cooperated, the companies also still competed, particularly when it came to attracting the best clients. The Big Five tried to differentiate themselves from each other in hopes of standing out in what was becoming a crowded field.

"We all competed with each other mightily for customers," says Eric Simonson. "But there was respect." Simonson was still operating IMG on the Tibet side, where he was happy to stick to his blue-collar guns, offering the sort of no-frills, less expensive expeditions he him-self was used to taking as a young Himalayan climber. In 1995, IMG charged $40,000 per client—$25,000 less than Adventure Consultants. Simonson had top guides and knew how to keep people safe, but he felt strongly that climbing Everest was not supposed to be easy or com-fortable. He hoped that keeping prices lower with a more bare-bones approach would also keep his business healthy. This meant fewer West-ern guides and more Sherpa oversight, which alarmed the other guides at first. But in the long run, he ended up with a larger number of more experienced climbing Sherpas than other companies, while maintaining an enviable success and safety record.

"When Simonson went with Sherpa-led climbs, I was really upset about it," says Todd Burleson, whose clients at AAI were paying $60,000. "Nonguided up there?! It sounded insane. But it started working. And it wasn't killing people."

"Eric's model appealed to the ego of the person who didn't want to be guided, and he leveraged that," says Guy Cotter, who in the wake of Gary Ball's death had become Rob Hall's top guide at Adventure Consultants. "It was a successful business model—we even considered it—but just couldn't justify it, the idea of putting Sherpas up high to look after moderately or inexperienced climbers. That IMG model brought a lot of people to the mountain."

"Rob's advice was to always bring good comfort food," says Cotter. "And we were quite famous for it. We took a Kiwi approach: little parties when it was time to have fun, and typically more female clients." For their $65,000, Adventure Consultants' clients got raised cots in their tents, benches padded with Tibetan rugs, and proper toilet seats in their makeshift restrooms, along with top-notch guiding.

Brice went in a similarly cushy direction with Himex. His attention to detail extended to making Everest as comfortable as possible for his clients, and he is considered to have kicked off the arms race among companies of trying to have the most comfortable setup in base camp. "Russell was always proud of his big tents," Simonson says of his friend, whom he got to know well on the north side in 1994 and 1995. "He had his tent and a fax machine and he made sure that you knew about it."

As Brice describes it, though, his reasons were all about effective guiding. "We made a point of having fresh vegetables and fresh meat," he says. "It wasn't about luxury. We were making it safer—this made the clients stronger. Yaks were carrying the equipment on the north side so we didn't need to be light. We could now have some creature comforts, which made us safer and more successful."

A perennial challenge when it came to intercompany cooperation was deciding who was responsible for fixing rope—the process of putting rope, ladders, and snow and ice protection hardware along a section of the route. Nonguided climbers had always loosely shared the responsibility, but the budding guiding companies were loath to be the ones to spend the time and money preparing the route for the others. This was a particularly acute issue on the south side of the mountain, where the dangerous crevasses of the constantly shifting Khumbu Icefall required an intricate system of ropes and ladders to be installed and maintained before clients went anywhere near it. Shouting matches broke out often, whenever a guide arrived with clients at a section that was supposed to have been fixed the previous day, only to find it naked and exposed. Higher up, the lack of proper advanced rope-fixing could kill up to an hour of precious time in the death zone. And when guides whose employees had done the rope-fixing tried to get other companies to chip in, it typically didn't go over well.

One oddball entrepreneur who saw this as a gap in the market was Henry Todd. Todd, a Scotsman, started his own small guide company, Himalayan Guides, with a similar ethos to Simonson, believing that Everest expeditions could be both affordable—relatively speaking— and safe. He was even able to undercut IMG's price by $5,000 for his primary expedition type, while still hiring top guides. At the same time, he innovated by allowing clients even more self-direction and control than IMG, leaving it up to them to decide if they wanted to have less oversight for an even lower cost. The fact that his trips were almost always at capacity signaled a growing market for his vision. For a variety of reasons, not everyone was comfortable with his way of doing things.

"Boy, Henry was a piece of work," remembers David Breashears.

•   •   •

Henry Todd's commercial debut on Everest was in 1994, though while he had been the one to secure the permit, the expedition was led by Burleson and AAI. The next year Todd got Himalayan Guides up and running in earnest. He brought nine clients to Everest and hired one of the greatest alpinists and guides in the world, Anatoli Boukreev of Kazakhstan. Seven of Todd's clients summited.

The way Todd really made a name for himself, though—and made good money—was by refining an approach to organizing rope-fixing in the Khumbu Icefall that had first been tried by a woman named Pasang Lhamu Sherpa in 1993.

Pasang Lhamu was making her second attempt at Everest that year. Her all-Sherpa team fixed the icefall themselves and then went around collecting a few hundred dollars off the other teams for the effort. It made sense, but she took it a step too far when she stationed several of her team members at the entrance of the icefall to bar any climber who had not paid. Pasang Lhamu summited that year, becoming the first Nepali woman to do so, but died in bad weather during her descent.

Todd heard about what happened, and correctly surmised that while chipping in to fix the icefall made sense from an organizational standpoint, the Western guides were not comfortable leaving this extremely important task to climbers they did not know—particularly Sherpa climbers. When he came to Everest in 1994, Todd rallied the other expedition leaders to let him develop a similar fee system to the one Pasang Lhamu had attempted, but in which only trusted and trained Sherpas who were affiliated with the guide companies would contribute man-hours and share the work. Of course, Todd would volunteer to handle the money side.

"The Nepalese government had a meltdown," remembers Simonson. "They said, 'We can't have some Westerner running a business like this on Everest.'"

Then, in 1995, a local Khumbu government agency called the Sagarmatha Pollution Control Committee (SPCC) attempted to take control of the icefall preparation, overseeing an all-Sherpa group that soon became known as the Icefall Doctors. According to Wally Berg, a Canadian with significant experience in the Himalayas who had started guiding for Burleson at AAI in 1993, the moniker was a reference to Lhakpa Gelu Sherpa, a man known by the nickname "Doctor Icefall." Berg says that in the early days of the SPCC taking over management of the icefall, "Lhakpa Gelu Sherpa was the guy who liked to work in the icefall and who became most engaged and directive with foreign climbers about route decisions."

The SPCC trained the Icefall Doctors in the necessary rope and ladder skills and added a fee to the climbing permits to cover the costs. But it seems that they didn't actually take control quite so quickly. "To be clear, we didn't hand the icefall over to the Sherpas completely until the late nineties," remembers Berg. He says that until then, egos were still colliding over who controlled what. "There were some pretty epic fights about finances and the logistics of moving equipment and fixing rope. Whoever it was that bought the ladders and got the icefall route up, they kind of had the king-of-the-hill status that year, and then could charge other teams. Henry Todd liked doing it, and he would then even arrange for lines to be fixed up the Lhotse Face."

Todd had made himself indispensable. And even when the SPCC's Icefall Doctors took over the icefall fixing completely, he continued to profit by supplying them with the sturdy imported aluminum ladders they needed.

"The ladder that became popular on Everest was what firemen call an attic ladder—narrow enough to fit between two roof joists, sixteen inches apart," explains Simonson. "They're narrow and much lighter than, say, a ladder you might buy from Home Depot, but it makes them a little scarier to walk on."

Todd was the chief importer of such ladders to the Nepal side of Everest. He provided them at a markup, of course.

That Todd was hanging around Everest base camp at all in the early 1990s was quite a surprise, considering where he'd been a decade prior. Born in Dundee, Scotland, in 1945, Todd was the son of a high-ranking Royal Air Force officer. He was tall and athletic and he began climbing as a teenager with dreams of scaling the big walls of Yosemite. After dropping out of Cambridge University, he worked in Paris as a photographer, and bummed around Europe before returning to the United Kingdom and picking up odd jobs, including as a nude model.

By the late 1960s, the psychedelic flower power movement was in full swing in Britain, as bands like Pink Floyd and the Who led a youth revolution. A new hallucinogenic drug called LSD was already everywhere in the United States and gaining popularity in the United Kingdom. The younger generation held a sympathetic attitude toward the drug, with its connotations of enlightenment and self-awareness, and Todd saw an opportunity to get in on the ground floor. The only indication he himself was part of this counterculture was his bushy hair and beard, framing a prominent nose, deep-set eyes, and long chin that made him look like an eighteenth-century British king. He spoke in soft benevolent tones—unless you crossed him. Evidence suggests that within a few years, Todd was producing 90 percent of the LSD in the United Kingdom and a large percentage of the global supply. He had a sharp mind for elaborate planning, a talent for evading surveillance, and an attachment to the good life that came with his new occupation.

One reporter who followed the LSD trade in mid-1970s Britain appropriately described Todd as a "man's man, a bon viveur, who enjoyed mountain climbing, paying lip service to the ideals of the LSD counterculture, more interested in profit than revolution." Allegedly, Todd began diluting the LSD in order to create twice as much product for the same cost. To his chemist partners, it was disgraceful and they called

him a mercenary, before severing the partnership entirely. Todd didn't
flinch at the prospect of going it alone. He collected rare stamps, had a
château in France, and kept safe-deposit boxes all over Europe.

He was also making regular trips to the Alps to link up with climber
friends at the International Mountaineering School in Switzerland. He
even once sent an underling to scout the big walls of Yosemite, which
sent the police, who were watching his every move, on a wild goose
chase and left them scratching their heads. Indeed, Todd had been
under surveillance for years, as part of what was known as Operation
Julie, which led to one of the most famous drug busts in history.

On the evening of March 26, 1977, more than a dozen bobbies
and detectives burst through Todd's front and back doors, ripping his
telephone from the wall so Todd could not call and warn his business
partners. As he stood in his living room in handcuffs, he asked the
police if they had come to give him the Queen's Award to Industry.
(The British band the Clash wrote the song "Julie's Been Working for
the Drug Squad" about the bust the following year.) At thirty-two years
old, Todd was sentenced to thirteen years in prison. He spent seven and
a half locked up before being released on parole in 1985. That's when he
decided he needed to go climbing again.

Todd did some winter mountaineering in Scotland and attempted a
larger expedition in Patagonia. Then, in 1989, he attempted Everest. He
joined an extremely strong, mostly Polish team that was trying a challenging route up the west ridge and Hornbein Couloir. Todd left the
trip before any real climbing began. "It was a very difficult expedition,"
he later said. "It was not terribly well run and, afterwards, I decided I
wasn't going to go on any more big expeditions if I wasn't the leader. I
felt they needed to be properly managed." His instincts were right. Six
people ended up dying during the climb.

Todd returned to the Himalayas over the following years and did
some increasingly challenging climbs, though not on Everest, before

setting up his guiding business and icefall-fixing operation. When the Nepalese government moved in on the icefall-fixing, Todd identified another opportunity: oxygen bottles.

Few things are at the center of more controversies on Everest than these beaten-up, bullet-shaped metal cylinders, and nothing makes a bigger difference between life and death. Found oxygen bottles have made climbers cry with joy at times when they believed all was lost, and an empty oxygen bottle is the last thing many people see before they lose consciousness.

Because of how much oxygen bottles weigh and how integral they are to guided climbing, moving and storing them became the most expensive and logistically challenging part of the hired Sherpas' work. A single client climber required up to five bottles. (Sherpas typically used about half the oxygen client climbers did.) Each bottle weighed just under six pounds. For a Sherpa climber carrying his own bottles and those of one client, that's roughly fifty pounds that needed to be transported from camp to camp—usually starting at Camp Two—and then brought back down (though the bottles were about one-third lighter when empty). The bottles were reusable and worth hundreds of dollars each.

In 1991, the Soviet Union was dissolving into a loose alliance of corrupt and bankrupt countries that needed to figure out how to survive without Mother Russia as quickly as possible. Once the AK-47s, missiles, tanks, and MiG fighter jets that the Soviet Army had left behind were sold, people began digging for anything else that could be valuable. One such item was the Poisk oxygen system of lightweight bottles and regulators used by Russian fighter pilots. "It felt like they weren't there in 1990 and then all of a sudden they were there in 1992," recalls Wally Berg.

Their presence would become only more ubiquitous thanks to Todd, who visited the factory in Saint Petersburg and figured out the fastest pipeline to deliver them to Everest each year. Many expedition leaders began contacting Todd to facilitate their oxygen orders.

The value of the bottles made them a target for unscrupulous climbers or, on rare occasions, desperately poor Sherpas. One year, AAI's entire supply went missing, which threatened to upend their season. They were later discovered stacked in the shape of a table beneath a tablecloth in a Russian mess tent.

Simonson sourced his own oxygen instead of going through Todd. "I just wasn't comfortable putting all my eggs in the basket of some Russian company that might not be there six months from now," he says. Instead, he found a company based in California, which he still uses today. He was never protective of his access to the new systems but, as he puts it, he also "wasn't exactly proactive in sharing."

While Todd's entrepreneurial ventures were central to the rapid evolution of the guiding industry, his criminal reputation couldn't escape him, and his demeanor rubbed many the wrong way. Some even saw him as a grifter. There were often breathless accounts of faulty equipment on his climbs, and some felt that he was more profiteer than pioneer. But most agree these criticisms were overblown. He was successful not only in getting his company, Himalayan Guides, up and running, but keeping it going strong over the years.

"I always felt Henry was a really genuine, bighearted guy," says David Hamilton, a Jagged Globe guide. "I've seen him do an awful lot of philanthropic stuff for people not expecting anything in return. Sure, okay, he has a short fuse and a temper if people rub him the wrong way. But he's done an awful lot of good on Everest."

Regardless of what anyone thought of Todd, it's undeniable that he played a huge part in the guiding companies' being able prove that they could get clients to the top affordably *and* safely—despite the fact that, to this day, Todd has never summited Everest himself. After his attempt in 1989, he focused on running his ladder and oxygen businesses and overseeing expeditions year after year.

The Big Five were proud of what they'd proved themselves capable of by the end of 1995. Then, after so much hard work and triumph over the previous four years, the entire guiding industry came to be defined by a single horrific day in May 1996. It felt like it happened in the blink of an eye—but the day would hang around the neck of the industry for decades.

9

The IMPERFECT STORM

*O**utside*** magazine editor Brad Wetzler remembers feeling a surge of adrenaline after he hung up the phone with the writer Jon Krakauer. It was the winter of 1995 and Krakauer had just called in the middle of a trail run near his home outside Seattle to give an update on his thinking about his next assignment. "He was out of breath and a bit excited," remembers Wetzler.

"I've started training," Krakauer told him. "If I'm going to do this, I'm going to do it right."

"Jon is a very righteous man," says Wetzler today.

Krakauer, a regular contributor to *Outside* with one bestselling book already under his belt, *Into the Wild*, had agreed to embed himself with a group of client climbers on Everest during the 1996 spring season. His intent: to peel back the layers of the growing guiding industry. Krakauer had originally been indifferent about climbing the mountain himself, and had initially planned to go only as far as base camp. His editors were happy with that—anything more seemed too risky. But Krakauer was telling Wetzler that after a lot of thought, he'd decided that he would go for the summit. He was a very good mountaineer, after all—a frequent climbing partner of Conrad Anker's—and uniquely positioned to reveal the inner workings of a guided Everest climb, especially high on the mountain.

"When he told me about wanting to summit, I actually got quite serious and I think I told him to please knock it off," says Mark Bryant, *Outside*'s editor-in-chief at the time. Bryant was not only Wetzler's boss, he and Krakauer were good friends.

"Personally, I wasn't really that worried about the idea of him wanting to go to the summit," says Wetzler, who handled the day-to-day contact with Krakauer for the story. "Jon is such a competent guy. Even if he didn't know how to fly a plane, I might trust him to fly me somewhere."

The decision to go for the summit while reporting was an audacious one, but it fit the bill for *Outside*—the publication that had elevated adventure journalism to high art. It had become the sort of *Rolling Stone* of outdoor magazines, which was in fact exactly how it was conceived. In 1977, drafting off the success of *Rolling Stone*, its publisher, Jann Wenner, had launched *Outside*. Wenner was an avid skier and an armchair adventurer. He hired William Randolph Hearst III as editor, siphoned big-name writing talent from *Rolling Stone*, and immediately racked up 250,000 readers. But spending severely outpaced profits and, after about a year, the magazine began to feel like Wenner's vanity side project. That's when a trust-fund playboy with an adventurous spirit named Larry Burke, who had launched an outdoor magazine of his own in Chicago called *Mariah* shortly before Wenner founded *Outside*, stepped in and bought Wenner's publication. Burke merged the two magazines under the glitzier *Outside* name and brand, but kept his headquarters in Chicago.

The publication did well throughout the 1980s, winning several National Magazine Awards and turning a profit. As the 1990s approached, Burke looked for ways to bring in even more readers. "We want to drive the product upscale," he told the *Chicago Tribune* in 1989. "In the sixties and seventies baby boomers were going out with sixty pounds on their back. Now those same people maybe want a baby on their back and hike hut-to-hut in the Sierras or Europe."

"We were all living in downtown Chicago, trying to be *The New Yorker*," recalls Wetzler. "Very few of us were really that outdoorsy, but there used to be an adventure travel show in Chicago and an entire adventure travel industry that grew out of *Outside's* [readership and culture] in the late eighties and early nineties. We had run stories about outlandish guided trips to exotic places that had gone bad. We were making fun of it and shaming it at the same time. But we were also aware on some level of how much we were the ones popularizing the outdoors."

As the Everest guiding industry kicked into gear in the 1990s, *Outside's* writers and editors did indeed strike a skeptical tone in their coverage of it (despite having been the ones to publish Burleson's groundbreaking ad in 1989, which helped launch the industry). Of the evolving guiding phenomenon, Bryant says, "I recall kind of rolling my eyes and saying, 'Well, this is asking for trouble.'"

In 1995, Greg Child, a respected Australian American climber and writer, summited Everest as part of an expedition to assist the first man with an artificial leg, Tom Whittaker (no relation to Lou and Jim Whittaker), to the summit. Afterward, Child wrote an article for *Outside* that was presented like the famous *Harper's Magazine* Index. The piece included plenty of zingers based on his firsthand observations and research about the guiding industry, including:

Number of people camping at Everest's two base camps: 600
Number of climbers attempting to summit vs. number who did: 276: 73

Number of people who attempted vs. summited, between
  1954–1994: 5,000: 547
Number of espresso machines: 2
Average cost per person to climb the less difficult Nepalese side:
  $20k
Per capita annual income in Tibet: $300
Number of lawsuits against climbing guides by clients who
  failed to summit: 5

"In the sixties, we thought Everest was a real test of a climber,"
says Child today. "It used to be something that you had to dig deep in
yourself to do. For anyone in our sport who felt this was a measure of
something—perhaps even our sense of self-worth—when people who
never climbed anything get up Everest, we wondered if we were delud-
ing ourselves. You can't help but wonder if Everest was special in the
first place."

Overcrowding and overcoddling had become the greatest sins of the
Everest guiding industry to purists like Child. Though the business was
still very new, the reputation had been building already for years.

"There was a small gridlock as rope teams had to wait for others
to leave the summit before they could ascend," the *Los Angeles Times*
reported all the way back in 1991.

"It is becoming so that you can go to the beach for your holiday or
climb Everest," Edmund Hillary told the London *Times* in 1992. Hillary had become particularly outspoken in scoffing at just about anyone
who climbed Everest under easier conditions than he did.

Elizabeth Hawley, a Kathmandu-based American reporter and the
founder of the Himalayan Database, which recorded every climbing
expedition throughout the Himalayas, said Gary Ball had told her he

had never been so scared in his life as when he was caught in a traffic jam at the Hillary Step during Adventure Consultants' first guided Everest trip in 1992. He said that four members of an Indian border patrol had grabbed at his clothing to use him as a handhold to ascend. "I could see myself falling down the southwest face tied to four Indians," he'd told her. She also reported that some Spanish and Dutch climbers threw stones at each other in contention over space at base camp.

To Yvon Chouinard, the crowds of inexperienced climbers were proof that the fundamental philosophy of the sport of climbing was being sullied. He and his band of Yosemite big-wall merry pranksters would often talk about what they called "clean climbing." Chouinard even wrote an essay on the subject that was published in one of Patagonia's early catalogs. As an inventor of gear, Chouinard was focused on equipment that would allow climbers to adhere to a leave-no-trace ethic. He felt strongly that once climbers completed a route, there should be no evidence they were there. "I believe people should have the freedom to do whatever they want, as long as it doesn't negatively impact other people," he explains. "On these rock climbs today, you're not even looking at the rock, you're looking for bolts, or the next anchor, or the next chalk mark. I did this really beautiful route in the Tetons and now it's got bolts on it. It absolutely doesn't need any bolts. Someone has turned this great thousand-foot rock climb into a 'sport crag.'" Whereas bolts do not make a rock climb any easier, like mountain guides on Everest, they widen the safety margin.

Chouinard came of age on the ethos of self-reliance, so it's no surprise this highly supported type of climbing bothers him. "The big trend is to just democratize everything and take the risk and the adventure out, to make it easier for the next person," he says. "Fishing guides are using drones to spot the fish; surfing a wave pool is like playing a video game. And it's not much different on Everest these days, where you're mindlessly following the guide. That is where you lose all the gains of adventure. You gotta be awake—if the guide and you get into trouble in a storm, you don't know how you got there. The guides have made themselves indispensable, which is why I called them enablers."

The name-calling he references was done in a Patagonia-produced documentary called *180 Degrees South*, in which Chouinard also made a pithy statement about people who used guides to reduce the risks of mountaineering. "If you compromise the process that much," he said, "you're an asshole when you start out, and you're still an asshole when you come back."

To some, these comments reveal a bitter undercurrent of sour grapes and elitism. In the case of Hillary, many believe what underlined his finger-wagging at the Everest guiding industry was a fear that his own accomplishment was diluted each time someone else stepped on the summit. In the case of Chouinard, many point out that Patagonia has profited greatly from the expanding pool of amateur adventurers.

Part of the distaste Child, Hillary, Chouinard, and other thoughtful climbers had for the Everest industry was rooted in the way it was upending their ability to make sense of the sport they loved. This was something that a twenty-five-year-old philosopher-climber-skier from Bolivia named Lito Tejada-Flores had foreseen when he wrote a now iconic 1967 essay titled "Games Climbers Play." It ran in the first-ever volume of the Sierra Club Mountaineering Journal, *Ascent*, in May of that year.

Climbing, Tejada-Flores wrote, is fundamentally meaningless, so humans apply ethical rules to the endeavor to disguise that. The rules are "designed to conserve the climber's feeling of personal (moral) accomplishment against the meaninglessness of a success that represents merely a technical victory." Satisfaction in climbing is all about preserving the sense of having overcome a true challenge. The "game" of climbing is to choose which set of rules to use for the particular type of climb you wanted to do.

The less risky the climb, the more rules climbers need to apply in order to feel they've accomplished something. For example, self-imposed handicaps—like choosing a difficult route to the top even if there was an easier one, or completing what is normally a three-day climb in one day—are used to increase the challenge and up the uncertainty of success.

Tejada-Flores went on to unpack and identify the types of games that climbers tended to play based on what discipline of climbing they were pursuing, such as "the Alpine Game" and "the Bouldering Game." In "the Expedition Game"—which at the time he was writing, Tejada-Flores said was the only one that could be played by those looking to summit Everest—no additional rules needed to be applied to make the climb harder. Summiting would be impossible with any challenges beyond those encountered on the mountain itself. Survival was enough.

Tejada-Flores published his essay eleven years before Peter Habeler and Reinhold Messner first summited Everest without oxygen, and twenty-five years before AAI and Adventure Consultants first successfully guided it. However, he correctly speculated that, of all the disciplines, it would be the Expedition Game that would eventually go extinct. Innovation and technology would allow for an accomplishable ascent of Everest and pretty much any other mountain in the world. The challenge would be gone, and the victory would be only a meaningless, technical one.

In 1971, well before he summited Everest, Messner wrote a famous and similarly prophetic essay of his own called "The Murder of the Impossible." In it, he decried what he saw as the heresies of modern climbing. "The [newer] generation has thoughtlessly killed the ideal of the impossible," he wrote. "Anyone who doesn't oppose this makes [themselves] an accomplice of the murderers."

By the early 1990s, the most serious Everest alpinists were already applying new rules to make their climbs harder. Some, like Messner, climbed without oxygen. Some stopped using rope. Others stopped using multiple camps, and would make their summit bids in one continuous push. But this type of climb was for the elite and far outside the realm of possibility for the typical Everest client. The guide companies carried on inviting as many people as possible on their expeditions and refining a by-all-means-necessary approach to shuttle their clients to the top. While the successful guides of the early 1990s—all of whom were serious climbers themselves—were aware that they were enabling a shift on Everest that bothered people like Hillary, Chouinard, and Messner, they didn't believe that meant they were spoiling the mountain. It meant they were sharing it. The climbers they were bringing might be inexperienced, but they were there for as good a reason as anyone else, and for them, reaching the top was a challenge, no matter how much help they got. Mountain guides contended that to hold climbing against some philosophical standard of purity was, at best, missing the point, and, at worst, elitist.

As a climber and writer, Krakauer always had notoriously inflexible ideas of right and wrong. His writing shows a particular disdain for narcissism. He declined to be interviewed for this book, and he declines almost every interview that has to do with Everest or *Into Thin Air*, telling friends he's "just tired of talking about it." He also says that all his thoughts on the subject are on the page, which is mostly true.

He wrote that he initially wrestled with whether or not to go to Everest, wondering if staying off the mountain would be a form of protest that fortified his integrity. In the end, as he candidly admits, the pull was too much. "I had a secret desire to climb Mount Everest since I was nine years old," he writes in *Into Thin Air*—kept secret, presumably, because he felt that real climbers, like Messner and Chouinard, were not interested in Everest. They were attracted to the B sides and rarities of the alpine world.

"Most of us were purists, too," says Bryant of his *Outside* editorial staff and writers at the time. Like many of the readers of his magazine, Bryant wasn't even a climber, but that didn't stop him from being swept up by the romance of climbing: solitude, self-reliance, just a climber and the elements.

Once Krakauer decided he was going to try to summit Everest, and Bryant approved, Wetzler got to work finding an outfitter that would be willing to significantly reduce its guiding fee and allow Krakauer to tag along for an entire eight-week expedition. Steve Bell at Jagged Globe couldn't believe his luck when *Outside* reached out to him first. But the magazine's editors quickly withdrew their interest when they realized Jagged Globe would be climbing on the less popular—and less crowded—north side in 1996. Wetzler next contacted a guide named Scott Fischer, who after years of preparation was finally launching his first guided Everest expedition and would be on the south side.

Fischer, a well-liked Seattle-based climber with a scraggly mane of blond hair and an endearing bravado, had long dreamed of establishing the premier guide service on Everest. He was a beast at altitude and had already come to the Khumbu several times to gain experience. At last, his company, Mountain Madness, had the client list and permits to run a guided Everest trip. Fischer was thrilled by the prospect of getting coverage in a popular magazine, and struck a deal to take Krakauer in exchange for a combination of cash and credits toward ads in *Outside*'s Active Traveler section (where Burleson had advertised AAI's inaugural guided Everest trip).

In February 1996, however, before guides and clients headed to Nepal, Wetzler called Fischer to let him know that they would instead be sending Krakauer with Adventure Consultants. Rob Hall had once again charmed the pants off a client. Fischer was devastated. In fairness, Hall had been running the most professional guided climbs on the mountain for four full years, and he had delivered more clients to the summit than anyone else (thirty-nine, to be exact). Like Fischer, Hall was happy to cut his guiding fee for Krakauer—in this case, from $65,000 to $10,000—and make up the rest in free advertising. When Krakauer asked Hall why he was so eager to have a writer along, Hall replied, "I'm not—I'm eager to reach the American market."

As he got set up at base camp in the spring of 1996, Krakauer encountered the familiar face of David Breashears, whom he had gotten to know in the Colorado climbing scene when both men were living in Boulder. The two had become friends, and Krakauer would later write the foreword for Breashears's Everest book, *High Exposure*.

It was Breashears's tenth time on Everest, and he knew all the main players on both sides of the mountain. "I remember all the guided teams in ninety-five and ninety-six," he says. "On the north side, you had Russell bringing the big geodesic dome, the bar, a big TV. Everyone had a banner. In 1996, on the Nepal side, I remember Mountain Madness had a Starbucks banner, being from the Northwest. But it still just seemed improbable that you could turn it into a business and make money."

Though Breashears was hoping for his third summit, of more importance to him was completing a project culminating his years as a high-altitude cameraman. He was attempting to capture the mountain he knew so intimately on a new type of film that could be projected onto movie screens up to three times larger than a regular one.

One of the early IMAX champions, a filmmaker named Greg MacGillivray, had reached out to Breashears in 1994 asking if he would like to help capture the first-ever IMAX footage from the summit of Everest. The hope was that it would allow an elementary school teacher from Ohio or a sixth-grader from South Africa to experience Everest themselves, without having to wear so much as a hoodie. "It would be a celebration of the mountain and its glory—the place that holds a spot in our imagination. And, at that time, it still held a wonderful place in our imagination," said Breashears. For him, the mountain had not been spoiled in the years since he'd climbed it with Dick Bass. It was also fitting that the man who had helped the first average Joe summit Everest was on a mission to allow anyone who had enough money to buy a movie ticket to step onto the top of the world.

Breashears enlisted a small team of climbers, camera operators, and Sherpas to assist with his IMAX film. "The camera's a monster," he says. "It uses six feet of film per second—about ten pounds of film in ninety seconds—and it sounds like a lawn mower." The people helping him lug it up the mountain would include America's 8,000-meter maestro Ed Viesturs, who was joining up with Breashears after having spent the past two seasons as a lead guide for Adventure Consultants; Robert Schauer, a German climber-cameraman; two women climbers, Araceli Segarra from Spain and Sumiyo Tsuzuki from Japan; and Jamling Tenzing Norgay Sherpa, Tenzing Norgay's eldest son. "I wanted a team that represented the world," Breashears says. "Not just a bunch of white guys."

In addition to Todd Burleson—back for AAI's record sixth guided expedition—Hall, and Krakauer, Breashears was happy to see his friend Scott Fischer living out his dream. In base camp that year, Fischer famously declared that he and the other guides had built a "yellow brick road" to the top.

One of the only unknowns that remained was the weather. The guides were nearly as accurate as meteorologists at predicting the weather on Everest, and, unfortunately, neither group was very good. Each day, the fax machines at base camp would spit out vague forecasts that offered a comically wide margin for error. Hall had become known for his superstition that May 10, the day he himself first reached the top in 1990, was the perfect one to summit on. "Rob had this thing about summiting on May tenth," says Guy Cotter, who was not on Everest but guiding Adventure Consultants clients on nearby Pumori that year. "And because of previous success, it sort of reinforced this as good decision-making. There were no proper weather forecasts, so you had to go on something."

Krakauer immersed himself in the Adventure Consultants experience, and over the weeks he spent with the guides and clients, he grew close to some of them. Doug Hansen was one of his favorites. The mailman had attempted Shishapangma with IMG in 1993, saved up and remortgaged his house to attempt Everest in 1995, and after having to stop short of the summit that year was now back with Adventure Consultants for another shot. Hansen was not some rich guy coming to the mountain on a lark, and Hall was resolute about doing everything he could to get him to the top in 1996.

From the start of Mountain Madness's expedition, Fischer was under strain. He and his superhuman but stoic Kazakh guide, Anatoli Boukreev, were at odds over whether their clients needed five-star treatment or not. Boukreev was with Fischer after having successfully guided Everest for Henry Todd the year before. He was tough as nails—but not a fan of hand-holding.

Fischer's team was first thrown off-balance after a rotation up to Camp Two. One of the Mountain Madness Sherpas succumbed to altitude sickness, and when Fischer was told he would likely be in a coma indefinitely, he became preoccupied with the financial problem that would create for the Sherpa's family. Nonetheless, the Mountain Madness team reconvened at base camp and set off for their summit push on May 6. Adventure Consultants' team left base camp on the same day.

As the groups ascended, the weather did what it usually does on Everest: blow in fiercely and then disappear. It was routine enough for the climbers to keep moving higher. Fischer, though, was derailed yet again by having to escort an ailing client back down to base camp, and then turn around to catch up with his team, which sapped his energy.

On May 8, as members of the two client teams were ascending the Lhotse Face toward Camp Three, they encountered Viesturs, from Breashears's IMAX crew. "We're headed down," Viesturs told Boukreev. "The weather is too unstable, so we're going to hang back for a few days."

Fischer's and Hall's teams pushed on, and Viesturs later recalled feeling a little sheepish about coming down. Yet when they arrived at Camp Four on the South Col on May 9, it was a hellscape of wind, with gusts so powerful the groups decided to erect fewer tents than they had planned, and to pile more people into each for extra warmth and to weight them down. As the afternoon progressed, the wind only got worse.

In his book *The Climb*, Boukreev recounts consulting with Hall about the weather, the two screaming to be heard over the wind. Boukreev expressed concern but Hall wouldn't have it. "My experience is that often it is calm after a squall like this," Hall said, according to Boukreev. "And if it clears in the night, we will make our summit bid." That would be the tenth—Hall's magic day.

Around seven thirty p.m. on the ninth, the wind stopped dead. Among Hall's group, concern quickly turned to elation, with Krakauer calling Hall's instincts uncanny. Indeed, Hall's lucky weather window was opening right on cue. Fischer decided to take his team to the top as well.

When the climbers first stepped out of their tents late that night in preparation for their summit bid, the sky was an otherworldly ink black, plastered with brilliant stars. It would have been hard not to feel that Hall had a sixth sense on Everest. The climbers began sipping hot tea and putting their boots and crampons on by headlamp. By one a.m. on the tenth, they were all on the move.

By this point, Hall's and Fischer's teams had more or less become one. The clients began to spread out according to who was faster and fitter, rather than which company they were with. By four a.m., the slowest clients had already turned around, but for the most part, the climb was going well. Krakauer was moving quickly, seemingly propelled by the same dream of summiting that was driving Hansen and the others who were still going up.

The first challenge of the day came when the guided teams arrived at 28,000 feet and a series of rock steps above the so-called Balcony to find that ropes had not been fixed in advance by other teams, as they had been led to believe they would be. The sun was already rising. The guides and Sherpas got to work fixing the route. In total, thirty-three climbers from various climbing parties were on that part of the mountain and, just like that, the rock steps above the Balcony became a bottleneck. The climbers were falling behind schedule.

A strict turnaround time had become a vital part of the Everest formula. With the right mixture of weather intuition and discipline, guides believed they could avert most disasters by simply setting a turnaround time and sticking to it. This was usually around one or two p.m. That day, Hall had announced it to be two p.m. for his Adventure Consultants team. Fischer had talked about a "two o'clock rule" with a journalist a couple of months before leaving for Everest.

Some climbers were on schedule. By 1:45 p.m., Boukreev and Krakauer, along with a Mountain Madness client, Martin Adams; a Mountain Madness guide, Andy Beidleman; and an Adventure Consultants guide, Andy Harris, were standing on the summit.

Boukreev had summited without supplemental oxygen. Conventional wisdom in the guiding world is that even if you do not feel you need oxygen, you always guide with it. But Boukreev's strong-man philosophy was that the sudden and unexpected loss of oxygen from a defective or empty bottle—which was still worryingly common and could cause a climber to pass out—was a bigger danger than not having a bottle at all.

The problem was that most of the other climbers were still spread out along the southeast ridge, many as far back as the Hillary Step, and still trudging upward. As the climbers who had already summited were steeling themselves for the hard return to Camp Four, Hall, Hansen, and two other Adventure Consultants clients, Beck Weathers and Yasuko Namba, carried on, blinded by ambition. Also still headed up and even farther behind were five Mountain Madness clients—Sandy Hill Pittman, Charlotte Fox, Tim Madsen, Lene Gammelgaard, and Klev Schoening—as well as several Sherpa climbers charged with looking after them. Fischer, their expedition leader, was so far back, owing to his serious fatigue, that he was basically climbing completely alone.

Around 2:30 p.m. the team of Pittman, Fox, Madsen, Gammelgaard, and Schoening arrived on the summit and, by all accounts, had very little energy left for the descent.

Minutes later, Hall, along with Mike Groom, an Adventure Consultants guide, and Yasuko Namba arrived on the summit. Beck Weathers, overcome by snow blindness, had asked to remain behind, so Hall had left him in a safe spot below the summit. Hansen was behind the group but still on his way up. Hall radioed to base camp saying they had summited and that he would head down as soon as Hansen made it— he couldn't see him, but assumed he was close. Fischer was still down there somewhere, too. At 3:40 p.m., more than ninety minutes past his own stated turnaround time, Fischer finally arrived at the top. He was suffering from altitude sickness but tried to remain upbeat and radioed to base camp to report that he and his entire roster of clients had summited. There was still no sign of Hansen.

During Hall's and Fischer's summit calls, base camp notified the teams of an incoming storm, which was now moving more quickly than they had originally thought. Fischer began descending solo. Hall's client group descended, too. However, Hall remained alone on the summit waiting for Hansen. As soon as Hansen was close, Hall walked down to meet him. He put his arm around Hansen to begin helping him inch upward. They finally stood on top together a little after four p.m. and, almost immediately, turned around to descend.

Just about the only thing the many people who have written about this day agree on when it comes to what happened next is that eight members of Hall's and Fischer's teams didn't make it off the mountain alive. The specifics of how and why are lost to the disorienting, blinding time warp of the storm.

The best evidence suggests that Fischer was about thirty minutes ahead of Hall and Hansen on the way down, but still well behind his clients and in bad shape. Fischer's lead climbing Sherpa, Lopsang Jangbu Sherpa, who had remained at the back as a sort of sweeper, came across Fischer at the top of the Balcony and found him sitting down. According to Lopsang, as recorded in Boukreev's book, Fischer said to him, "I am very sick . . . Lopsang, I am dead."

Then the storm that everyone had prayed would dissipate suddenly dropped down on the climbers like a piano on a cartoon character. Hall indicated to base camp that he and Hansen were probably in a bit of trouble, with night falling and Hansen—who had run out of oxygen at the top of the Hillary Step—in desperate shape.

By six p.m., about a half dozen of the strongest climbers—including Krakauer, Boukreev, and some of the other guides—reached the safety of Camp Four, where they joined the client climbers who had given up on the summit hours earlier. But the rest of the climbers remaining on the mountain were spread out along the southeast ridge in the worsening whiteout, as if floating in the middle of the ocean in a hurricane. It was what climbers call being stuck inside the Ping-Pong ball.

Boukreev made a dash upward to try to find the stranded Mountain Madness clients and Fischer. In his first attempt, he couldn't locate them and returned to the tents. But he went out again and, this time, spotted a headlamp. It was Madsen, one of his clients, and he was with Pittman and Fox. Namba was also spotted by Boukreev and guide Neal Beidleman around this time, but she was lying in the snow and presumed dead. Weathers, Boukreev learned, had wandered off alone and was also presumed dead. Pittman and Fox were barely alive, but Boukreev and Madsen managed to carry the two women to safety. Because Hall, Hansen, and Fischer were still trapped in the death zone, their destinies had more or less been determined. Boukreev and Lopsang, who was assisting in the search as well, continued looking for Fischer relentlessly. They finally found him dead, just below the Balcony. His down suit was unzipped, and he was missing a mitten.

Just a little higher up, past the point Boukreev and Lopsang searched, were Hall and Hansen. They had been forced to bivouac just below 29,000 feet and Hansen died in the night. Early the next morning, Hall was fading.

Eventually, other teams on the mountain became aware of what was going on above them. Those at Camp Two, including Burleson and Pete Athans, mobilized a rescue and, at first light, began climbing the Lhotse Face, carrying oxygen toward the South Col. So did Breashears and some of his IMAX film crew, who dropped everything and headed up to assist.

Hall, still stuck in place beside Hansen's body, unable to move, spent the day waiting, at first for rescue, and then for death. In one of the most heart-wrenching moments in Everest's history, Hall's base camp manager, Helen Wilton, managed to contact Hall's pregnant wife, Jan Arnold, in New Zealand and relay the call through their base camp radio to Hall's personal radio as the sun was setting on the eleventh. She cried as he said goodbye. "Sleep well, my sweetheart," Hall told his wife through the radio. "Don't worry too much." These were his last words.

Four members of the Adventure Consultants team had died: Hall, Hansen, Harris, and Namba. (In total, eight people died on Everest that day as a result of the storm, including three independent Indian climbers on the north side). Miraculously, Weathers was found alive, and survived. From Mountain Madness, Fischer was dead. His family requested he not be moved from the mountain, and his body remains there today.

10

The WORLD'S WORST
SELF-HELP BOOK

Mark Bryant remembers the terrible hours of uncertainty during which he waited for news about Krakauer. "At first, I was reminded by colleagues that if this had to happen to anyone, Jon's the journalist you want there," he says. "But our own website reported Jon missing or unaccounted for, and I actually remember chewing someone out to get to the bottom of it. I said, 'What do you mean missing and unaccounted for?!'"

His relief at finally learning that Krakauer was safe was enormous, but he barely had time to take a breath. When Bryant arrived at the office he had seventeen voice messages from people looking for information and commentary. While Bryant wanted to keep things low key in the wake of the disaster—he didn't want the magazine to come across as opportunistic—*Outside*'s owner, Larry Burke, had other ideas. "Don't be a snob about this," Bryant remembers him saying. "It's blowing up and we should really get some publicity out of it."

Krakauer initially seemed in no state of mind to take part. He arrived home in a dark place. "I think at one point *People* magazine and some of the papers were parked out on his front lawn," Bryant says. Bryant told him to forget about writing the article, to wait until he had more time to process the experience, to let wounds heal and gather some perspective.

But Krakauer convinced himself he had a journalistic duty to record what he'd experienced as soon as possible. He spent the rest of his summer buried under interviews, notes, and Everest stats, while suffering flashbacks and bad dreams. "He filed something like seventeen thousand words over twenty days," says Bryant.

What came pouring out was not what he had planned. Despite his genuine commitment to objectivity, Krakauer has, in so many ways, acknowledged that he went to Everest with a suspicion that the purity of mountaineering was being eroded or at least watered down by the guiding industry. Then he ended up in a situation where that very impurity nearly killed him. There were too many inexperienced people on the mountain. Too many mistakes made. The hubris of the industry was no longer just amoral, it was deadly—and here was the proof.

In September 1996, *Outside* printed Krakauer's ten-thousand-word story, titled "Into Thin Air." Bryant called it "the most powerful piece the magazine had ever published." It won the National Magazine Award for reporting that year.

At first, Krakauer didn't have any interest in turning it into a book. "Jon's fame and reputation were riding pretty high because of *Into the Wild*," remembers his publisher at Random House, David Rosenthal. "We had been discussing what his next book might be, but there was no plan for this to be it before he went to Everest. It was in the media within twenty-four hours, so we knew about it. But all we were thinking was, 'Oh God, I hope Jon is okay.'

"There was a lot of emotion involved in this project, even before tragedy struck. Jon was a climber, he was very close to the Sherpas and many of the other climbers on the mountain. But Jon is very strong willed.

When he says he doesn't want to do something, he's not just being cute. I had moved on from it—just thought it wasn't going to happen.

"Then he called one day and said he wanted to write the book."

Less than a year after coming back from Everest, Krakauer's book of the same title as his article was on the *New York Times* bestseller list.

Writing *Into Thin Air* required him to embark on a huge journalistic undertaking in which he attempted to untangle the knot of what exactly happened on Everest that season. "He felt there were people who shouldn't be there—as a journalist and as a mountaineer," says Rosenthal. "He was horrified by it. And Jon went through hell."

There is very little disagreement that the deaths of the five clients and guides were primarily the result of a series of poor decisions by Rob Hall and Scott Fischer. In an interview with the *San Francisco Chronicle* in 1997, Krakauer was clinical in his criticism. He blamed the accident on the "failure to fix ropes ahead of time, which created a bottleneck, and the lack of firm, preset turnaround times," all of which should have been under the management of the guides.

Guy Cotter, who took over Adventure Consultants after Hall's death at Jan's request, doesn't disagree. Reeling from the shock of what happened, he wished that he or Ed Viesturs had been there with Hall on summit day, believing they could have steered him to make more measured choices. "If either Ed or I had been there that year, I'm pretty confident the outcome would've been different," he says. "Rob had way more experience than I did back then, but Ed and I were often in charge of the decision-making on summit day—we were his strong lieutenants—and this was the first year he didn't have us. Either of us would have drawn that line in the sand. His assistant guides that year were great, but inexperienced at eight thousand meters. Just a year prior, Rob and I turned back at the base of the Hillary Step."

As to why he agreed to take over the company and keep going back to Everest, Cotter says, "I didn't want the events of 1996 to be the final

history of New Zealand guiding in the Himalayas. I considered changing the name. I carried on using it out of respect for Rob. I wanted his
legacy to carry on."

Some people have suggested that Krakauer's presence on Everest
that year, and the desire Hall and Fischer both would have had to be
depicted in his story as successful guides, had something to do with the
poor decisions they made. "Competition is incredibly powerful," says
Steve Bell. "But I don't think that's what killed Rob. I reckon I might
have done exactly the same, but it would have had nothing to do with
what somebody would write about me afterward."

"It would have purely come down to the fact that I'm there with
one client, who I turned back the previous year," explains Bell. "Rob just
didn't want to disappoint Doug Hansen."

Henry Todd, who was at Camp Two during the disaster, expressed
a similar sentiment. "Rob was a friend," Todd said, just days after Hall's
death, while decompressing in a teahouse in Pangboche, where he
agreed to be interviewed on camera by a member of his own expedition.
His loss is fresh and, in the footage, he is clearly despondent. "Rob felt
he owed Doug so much. He had Doug in the same place the year before.
Doug had worked nights sorting mail to pay for the trip."

While Breashears was unsparing in his assessment that his friends
Hall and Fischer had made poor decisions, his *Everest* IMAX film,
released in March 1998, about one year after the publication of *Into
Thin Air*, also served as a powerful counterweight to Krakauer's narrative. Though he and Krakauer had documented the same climbing season,
whereas Krakauer felt it was his duty to denounce guided Himalayan
climbing in the wake of what he saw, Breashears pushed back on the
notion that guides were irresponsible, unscrupulous, and greedy; that people who hire guides to help them climb Everest are narcissistic, hapless,
and full of hubris; that certain people belonged and others didn't on the
highest mountain in the world. To that end, Breashears had carried on

with filming in 1996 even after the disaster, and returned the following year to summit and complete his love letter to Everest. The film showed the beauty of the mountain and the joy of reaching the top safely.

The movie grossed nearly $130 million, making it the most successful IMAX film to date. One of Breashears's first stops on the talk show circuit to promote it was with Charlie Rose. Breashears was still dashing at forty-three, with salt-and-pepper hair, and he spoke with quiet confidence.

"We had to prove Everest is not a death sentence," he explained to Rose. "I've enjoyed every minute I've been on Everest over eleven expeditions."

Breashears admitted to Rose that in returning to the summit after the tragedy, he dreaded the fact that he would have to pass the frozen bodies of Fischer and Hall.

"Are you angry that they would have been alive if not for the amateurs?" Rose asked.

"No," Breashears said quickly. "I felt like they had let us down. They let their guard down. I couldn't understand how these two titans of Himalayan mountaineering could get caught out like that. And make those mistakes.

"I sat next to [Rob's body] for a half an hour. I was mostly bewildered. He was such a talented man. He stuck with Doug. He did what we would have all expected him to do. How could this have happened to you—such an organized and dedicated guide."

Though he and Krakauer were in agreement on this point, one of the many characterizations of Krakauer's that Breashears took serious issue with was his portrayal of one of Scott Fischer's client climbers.

"What do you think of Sandy [Hill] Pittman?" Rose asked, referring to the socialite mountaineer who had been a client on Fischer's team. After being depicted in a harsh light in *Into Thin Air*, she had become the Everest client everyone loved to hate.

"Wonderful woman and incredible climber," Breashears replied. He praised her dedication to preparation and training, and said, "She's an easy target, an easy villain in a story where we need heroes and villains."

In 1996, Sandy Hill—referred to by the last name Pittman in *Into Thin Air*, as she was still legally married to Robert Pittman, a media executive and cofounder of MTV, at the time of her climb—was making her third attempt at summiting Everest. Breashears had climbed with her on the rarely visited east side in 1994 (and she had attempted Everest from the south side the year before with AAI). In her Mountain Madness group, she was the only Western climber besides Fischer and Boukreev to have been on the South Col route before. She had also already climbed six of the Seven Summits and was on the verge of becoming the sixth woman in the world to complete them. To Krakauer, this only proved that she climbed for all the wrong reasons. In his eyes, she was the most vivid example he could have asked for in showcasing to readers what was wrong with Everest clients.

Hill and Krakauer spent very little time together on the mountain. But her personal life provided a well he could pull from for his book. Introducing her as a "millionaire socialite-cum-climber" in *Into Thin Air*, he went on to tell the story of how Hill arrived at her going-away party for Everest, held at a trendy Manhattan restaurant, wearing her 8,000-meter down suit over her dress. He described her opulent lifestyle back home and her flamboyant antics in base camp, including her infamous "espresso maker."

To be fair, it was the phrase Hill herself used to describe the apparatus, but Krakauer allowed his readers' imaginations to run wild in picturing what was essentially a simple coffee maker. What many assumed to be along the lines of a professional-style cappuccino machine was in actuality one of those ubiquitous aluminum coffeepots, about ten inches tall, with an octagonal base. It did little more than sit on a stove and pour coffee. But on Everest, the pot gave her an opportunity to be creative and fun-loving in a way that connected to childhood memories.

"When I went camping as a kid, we'd bring canned ham, present it on a rock, and then see how fancy we could make it feel," she says. "So at base camp I would bring this Indian dried milk that has fat in it. I'd put it in a Mason jar and shake it really hard to get it frothy and then pour the coffee into the Mason jar. I'd pretend we were at a fancy hotel and ask Scott or Neal or whoever if anyone would like a cappuccino."

Hill is in fact quite proud that her little coffeepot reached such unexpected levels of notoriety, and keeps a twin of the original in her home office today as a token. She also doesn't think it's so wrong to have done things that made her stand out while living on a cold, barren glacier. "My birthday is April twelfth, so I often celebrated at Everest base camp. Sometimes we'd even do costume parties with whatever we had with us, like a turban made from long underwear or something. I had a new device called a Walkman and a little pair of speakers. The Sherpas had never heard Michael Jackson. We would have a dance party, wearing our turbans and banging the pots and pans."

Krakauer did not write about the fact that Hill was in the early stages of divorce proceedings when she arrived at Everest in 1996. (He may not have been aware of the fact, and if he had, perhaps he would have understood her better.) Though Hill would end up with a large settlement in the end, she hadn't received it yet and funded a portion of her climb by doing the same sort of fundraising in her social network as many other Everest clients. "I had been served with divorce papers in September of 1995," she recalls. "And I had a fourteen-year-old child. I was concerned that there would be some custodial issues, so I wasn't in a position to just write a check." Hill also helped offset some of the cost of the trip by filing live dispatches throughout her expedition for NBC and working on a feature for *Vogue* magazine. Just like Krakauer, Hill summited in 1996. Unlike Krakauer, she survived a harrowing night in the death zone to make it back.

Still, she understands why Krakauer would highlight her story in his book in the way he did, and accepts that he got some things about her right. "I actually did put myself in the public eye," she acknowledges today. "It was somewhat well intentioned, but I also see where I went wrong." She recognizes the ways that she represented how much things had changed in the rarified world of Himalayan mountaineering. "But Jon never even called me when he was writing his book," Hill notes. "Instead, he just buried me with innuendo.

"I'm not sure he was really suited to be on a mountain like Everest," she adds. "In his book, all he talked about was how cold it was and how thin the air was."

Given Krakauer's own horrific experience in 1996 and subsequent grieving process for the friends he'd lost, it's understandable that he would lash out at those he felt played a part in the degradation of climbing. Yet the fact is, you'd be hard-pressed to find an Everest guide who is a fan of *Into Thin Air*, and it has little to do with self-preservation. To them, his view of climbing is far too narrow, and he doesn't get what guiding is about. He caricatured Everest clients too simplistically, and encouraged people to judge their motives and actions from afar.

Dave Hahn has known Krakauer for more than thirty years and counts him as a friend, but says they bicker. After getting his start at RMI, Hahn began working for IMG and soon became one of the best mountain guides not only on Everest, but throughout the world. Hahn's grace on steep snow and ice and distinct physical features—tall, with a pronounced nose and chin, and huge hands—make him seem larger than life. He likes to tell stories and is known for his subtle one-liners and self-deprecating sense of humor.

The *Nova* documentary "Mountain of Ice" is a fascinating window into Hahn's dynamic with Krakauer. The film is about a team of climbers on Mount Vinson in Antarctica in 2001, of which Krakauer, Hahn, and Conrad Anker were members. On camera, Krakauer becomes frustrated with Hahn for suggesting a safer route that will allow the less experienced documentary crew to continue ascending with them. Krakauer says that it may be time to just leave the crew behind. "I've been on one guided expedition in my life and it was the biggest mistake I ever made," he says, referring to 1996. "I've seen what happens when very good guides make one bad decision with clients who don't have the skill or experience to look after themselves. I swore I would never be in this position again."

But Anker is in charge, and defers to Hahn, who held the record for most summits of Vinson at that point as well as of Everest, among Western climbers. They all end up summiting together as a group.

"Dave was right, it worked," Krakauer later says to camera. "It was a remarkable bit of guiding. I came away with a great deal more respect for him after seeing what he did."

He might have respected Hahn, but he hadn't changed his mind about guided clients. Those who hired Hahn because they didn't have the experience to ascend and descend a slope safely on their own were still a problem, in his eyes.

"I just never thought that Jon understood guiding at all—despite the fact that he'd written the bestselling book about guiding," says Hahn today. "He didn't view it as legitimate, he didn't view guided clients as climbers, didn't even view guides as climbers. I do go into less danger-ous settings than Jon, or, say, Conrad, but I'm happy to do it regularly, with novices, and depend on their abilities and my abilities. I was once a client."

Something else that Krakauer didn't—and perhaps couldn't have—understood was the effect that *Into Thin Air* would have on the Ever-est guiding industry. He assumed his story would serve as the ultimate cautionary tale about the mountain. So did David Hamilton, a Jagged

Globe guide who had not been to Everest yet but was guiding often on 7,000- and 8,000-meter mountains in Pakistan when *Into Thin Air* came out. "I remember thinking nobody was going to want to go to Everest now—and that I'll probably never get to guide Everest. In fact, I remember Steve Bell saying, 'Welp, I guess we'll just have to focus on the six other Seven Summits.'"

But Eric Simonson—who was not on Everest but with clients on Cho Oyu in the spring of 1996—immediately recognized what was coming next. It was Bass's *Seven Summits* book, times ten. "I knew our Everest business was about to go through the roof," he says.

Simonson understood a crucial, uncomfortable fact: the specter of death is not a deterrent—it's what makes many people want to climb Everest in the first place.

Heather Macdonald was with Simonson when news of the disaster hit. She says Simonson told her, "You can't buy better advertising."

"Eric is a smart man," she adds. "In that moment, I knew Everest was about to change."

That was right. And yet, the surprising fact is that even taking the disaster into account, Everest was statistically safer than ever in 1996. Eight people total had died on the Nepal side, of the 398 climbers who went above base camp. That's a rate of 3 percent, meaning 1996 had come out slightly ahead of the average climbers-to-fatality number to date, by 0.3 percent. With eighty-four people summiting that year, it also came out far ahead of the fatality-to-summit ratio, which dropped from an average of one death per four summits in years past to one in seven in 1996.

But it was the public perception that mattered. And for the guiding industry, a sprinkle of danger to go along with the impressive safety record was catnip for people with an inclination for alpine adventure. To the potential clients, the possibility of death was an opportunity for rebirth. An eight-week Everest expedition was the perfect time to work through a divorce, a midlife crisis, or the loss of a loved one.

"All our trips filled up after that," says Burleson. "I felt like I could sell a penny-size Everest rock for fifteen grand."

Hamilton says, "I guess even if ninety-nine percent of the people who read *Into Thin Air* vowed to never go near Everest and the other one percent said, 'Wow, I can pay to go to Everest?'—that was enough to fill commercial trips for the next twenty years. Nineteen ninety-six was the best marketing Everest ever had."

"To me, *Into Thin Air* was the story of a train wreck," says Hahn. "But people seemed to be pretty inspired by that train wreck. I was amazed. For a lot of people, *Into Thin Air* was a how-to book."

Krakauer's megaselling book proved that there was an audience of people who were morbidly curious about Mount Everest beyond the climbers who would actually consider scaling it. The surge in interest in the mountain was coinciding with technological developments that suddenly made it possible for audiences to follow Himalayan expeditions in real time. The internet age was dawning on Everest, and early dot-com entrepreneurs were seeing opportunities to feed an adventure and adventure-sports market hungry for news about the mountain.

It was an Australian sailor named John Bertrand and a couple of his techie partners who first got in the game with a website they'd launched in 1995 called Quokka. Initially, they focused on daily dispatches, photos, and live video of sailing races, but soon they branched out into other action sports including mountain biking, skiing, snowboarding, and climbing.

In 1996, another group of entrepreneurs decided that the world of climbing and mountaineering had enough drama to support a website completely devoted to it, and started MountainZone.com. Peter

Potterfield, an author and journalist, was hired as the founding editor, and he recognized that Himalayan climbing—and Everest, in particular—would be red meat for his audience. "I lived in Seattle so I knew everyone—Todd Burleson, Pete Athans, Scott Fischer," Potterfield remembers. "I was hired just as news of the 1996 disaster was coming in, and it took a few days for us to learn Scott had died. News was still traveling out of the Khumbu Valley pretty slowly."

Over the subsequent years MountainZone sought ways to speed up its coverage of Everest to an audience that believed—almost hoped, it seemed—that each climbing season would bring similarly compelling events to 1996. "In Namche Bazaar, we'd get a room in a teahouse that faced south," says Potterfield. "We'd set the sat phone up in the window—trying to get the best angle on the Indian Ocean satellite—and we'd make our dispatches. And, eventually, we were doing the same thing from Everest base camp. People were amazed—we were reporting things that had just happened on Mount Everest minutes earlier."

The technological advances and devotion to Everest paid off for MountainZone in a big way in 1999. That year, Potterfield convinced his bosses to give Eric Simonson $50,000 in exchange for exclusive access to Simonson's needle-in-a-haystack search for George Mallory's body, which had presumably been buried since he went missing in 1924. Dave Hahn and Conrad Anker were recruited by Simonson to the team, along with a local aspiring high-altitude worker named Phunuru Sherpa, who was just sixteen years old. On May 2, 1999, Potterfield got a call from Simonson, who was reporting via sat phone from Everest base camp on the Tibet side. "Are you sitting down?" Simonson asked.

Within minutes, MountainZone had posted audio of Simonson's call, announcing that the team had in fact found Mallory's body. "I had sold sponsorship to Lincoln, and the people at the ad agency were popping champagne," says Potterfield. Hahn stayed up all night uploading a high-resolution picture of their discovery and, by morning, the photographic evidence pinged from one continent to the other in time to make hundreds of morning news broadcasts.

In the end, like so many other dot-com-era startups, neither MountainZone nor Quokka lasted. In early 2000, Quokka bought MountainZone for $25 million. Two years later, Quokka went bankrupt. But these now-obscure businesses heralded the age of hyperconnectivity on Everest.

"It wasn't Dick Bass or Jon Krakauer that ruined Everest," says Russell Brice. "It was Al Gore, if you believe his claim that he invented the internet."

By the end of the 1990s, "sat phones" were as ubiquitous as oxygen tanks, and dozens of the climbers lounging around base camp at any given time were filing their own personal dispatches through websites, personal blogs, or the expedition journals for the guiding companies' flashy new websites. Their accounts were often bombastic and error filled. It didn't sit well with Potterfield. "Motivations changed," he says. "The guide services obviously wanted to make themselves look like the best, and the climbing teams that weren't associated with the guide services had their own agendas." As the Everest record keeper and founder of the Himalayan Database Elizabeth Hawley noted even as early as 1997: "It is clear that instant reporting about Everest developments is quite unreliable and also sometimes irresponsible."

By the 2000 spring season, *Wired* magazine reported that Everest base camp had become a "multimedia hub" and that "the flood of technological innovations has revolutionized the Everest experience." That same season, Henry Todd allegedly punched a journalist, Finn-Olaf Jones, after learning Jones was sending daily dispatches full of disparaging base camp gossip.

In 1953, it had taken four full days for the world to learn that Edmund Hillary and Tenzing Norgay had made the first ascent of Everest. A half century later, on the fiftieth anniversary of that climb—during Hall and Ball's 1990 climb—Edmund's son, Peter, called his father from the summit using a phone that was roughly the size of a walkie-talkie. Edmund had jokingly asked Peter whether he'd had trouble with the Hillary Step. Ten years after that, it seemed that half of the clients and guides on Everest had a personal blog going about their trip. The posts were written, photos were uploaded, and electronic dispatches went live, immediately—and all from the comfort of a dome tent.

11

The IMMORTALITY PROJECT

As more client climbers were arriving on Everest in the mid- and late 1990s without a clear sense of why they were really there, it was often up to the guides to figure it out for them. Heather Macdonald was one of the best at that. In fact, she was so intrigued by what motivated people to come to mountains like Everest, she left guiding altogether in the late 1990s to seek the answers. Macdonald pursued a career in clinical psychology and today has a practice in Seattle. She is one of a tiny handful of therapists in the world who have guided on 8,000-meter peaks.

"People always remark about how my new career is so different from guiding," she says. "No way—sometimes I feel like *all* my clinical skills came from guiding."

In considering the mystery of why so many amateur and hobbyist mountaineers sign up for Everest climbs, she often thinks back to a question she was asked on a sunny afternoon her first time guiding the mountain for IMG. It was 1994, she was twenty-three years old, and they were climbing from the Tibet side. She'd just led IMG clients on a rotation to Camp One and back. As they approached base camp, IMG's head cook, Pemba Sherpa, greeted the weary climbers with tea. Macdonald and Pemba sat together on a rock. "Heather, why is it Westerners come to Everest looking for something they did not lose here?" he asked.

Climbers—whether experienced or amateur—have never been known for having incisive answers to questions like these. When George Mallory was asked in 1923 why he wanted to climb Everest so badly, he famously replied, "Because it's there." Macdonald, however, has some deeper notions. For one, she believes people *are* drawn to the possibility of meeting and overcoming mortal danger. "One definition of heroism, globally, is to have survived the unsurvivable," she explains. After 1996 and the publication of *Into Thin Air*, she says, "people were very aware that Everest had just massacred eight people [including the climbers on the north side] over two days. But they also believed deeply that they could go there and survive. Surviving Everest after what happened in 1996 actually magnifies that heroism. People believe that climbing Everest could possibly undo any vulnerability they feel about themselves. It has been suggested that the visible dead bodies on Everest reinforce the heroism of climbing it further, as the stakes are literally staring you in the face at times. And like the guys in the trenches in World War I that would run blindly toward gunfire, they think it will never be them—that it will always be the guy next to them that gets killed."

Macdonald isn't claiming to have invented this theory; she credits an American cultural anthropologist named Ernest Becker, who, in 1973, wrote a book called *The Denial of Death*, which itself was a continuation of the work of Freud and others. Becker's book won the Pulitzer Prize for nonfiction (awarded to him, ironically, two months after his own death) and is required reading in many university psychology departments.

In his book, Becker cites the ability to be heroic as one of the primary defense mechanisms we use to process our mortality and diminish our anxiety around it. As with Macdonald's World War I example, Becker says we want to believe practically everyone else is expendable except ourselves. But in the peaceful period immediately following World War II, Western society suddenly lacked outlets for heroism. That was a problem, in Becker's account.

"The need for heroism is not easy for anyone to admit," he wrote. "There's the rub. . . . To become conscious of what one is doing to earn his feeling of heroism is the main self-analytic problem of life. Everything painful and sobering . . . revolves around the terror of admitting what one is doing to earn his self-esteem. This is why human heroics is a blind drivenness that burns people up."

Becker goes so far as to say depression is the result of feeling that one's "immortality project is failing." It helps explain why the phones started ringing off the hook at the guiding company offices after 1996.

"I think everyone who wants to climb Everest should be required to go through a year of therapy first," says Macdonald, only half joking. If you ask her, or her former boss, Eric Simonson, it is perfectly okay to turn up at base camp in the midst of a midlife crisis, having spent $65,000 on a guided expedition instead of a sports car, so long as you've come to terms with what's motivating you. "We definitely tried to get into our clients' heads a little," says Simonson. "Like a coach might with an elite athlete."

"There are basically three different types of Everest client," Macdonald says. "The first are those looking to awaken something they feel might be dead or dying inside them. The second are clients looking to discharge something, some built-up negative energy or tension from something that happened to them or from something they are going through. Finally, there are the people who just need a new experience to help them reorganize their life a little.

"Spend some time trekking with clients up to base camp and I guarantee you'll see they each fit into one of those three categories."

Unfortunate, then, is the fact that client climbers on Everest are often the type of people who think they have all the answers, yet too many have no idea why they're there. David Hamilton says, "I think one of the main subtleties of guiding on Everest is that you often have clients who are overqualified but underconfident, and then others in the same group who are underqualified and overconfident."

Macdonald points out that many Everest guides show up with just as much baggage as their clients, herself included. Hopefully, as it did for her, this makes guides more empathetic toward their clients, and accepting of the contradictions and foibles that make them human beings and not villains.

The first wave of people who signed up for guided ascents of Everest included a remarkably high number of dentists and doctors, followed closely by lawyers and investment bankers—almost all of them men. Climbing was still a very male-dominated sport in the 1990s, and these were the people with the requisite amount of disposable income.

"We used to call them the 'Dentists from Dallas,'" an IMG guide, Lisa Rust, once told a reporter when asked about the typical Everest client.

Collin Fuller—a cardiologist who attempted Everest in 1990, drafting off the skills of an Iranian American Exum guide named Hooman Aprin during one of the early client-funded trips—has unique insight into what might draw doctors, in particular, to the mountain beyond having room in their budget and a type A personality. "They say doctors make poor pilots because we take risks," he explains. "The inventor of the angioplasty learned to fly, bought himself a twin engine, and flew it into the side of a mountain. I figured a better way to get my mind off work was to go *climb* a mountain."

By the late 1990s, the typical Everest client was becoming more reflective of global society. Guiding companies continued to build a bigger and more inclusive tent, welcoming people from different socioeconomic and ethnic backgrounds as well as experience levels. The companies openly applauded those who chose to step out of their routine or comfort zones to climb the tallest mountain in the world. Says Wally Berg, "This idea that some people don't belong has always been a massive oversimplification and assumption. The mountain takes care of people who don't belong. Believe me. It is eight weeks, and people who don't belong go home after two or three weeks. And the people who are still there at the end—you know what? They belong."

However, every experienced guide still agrees that as the mountain became safer, and the net was cast ever wider for people with more diverse backgrounds and less technical experience, client vetting became even more crucial. It also became more complex. Everest applications always asked prospective clients to describe their previous climbing experience. Some people began leaving this section completely blank. "I've always been an advocate—and I still am—that you should have climbed another eight-thousand-meter peak before you go to Everest," says Russell Brice, who, like most reputable outfitters, steered prospective Everest clients to easier peaks first. "But people can always make themselves look good on paper."

This often resulted in guides having to use their best judgment, and sometimes losing out on business by erring on the side of caution. Hamilton points out: "But then we'd see the same client we turned away at base camp with another company.

"A really interesting development from this time was the increase in attempts to be the first man from this country, first woman from that country," he adds. "So, within all the guided groups, ten or twenty percent of them would be people who just want to become professional adventurers, and summiting Everest was an achievement that might get you in the news in some countries, or even launch a career. That's what Jaime Viñals came for."

Jaime Viñals is from a place where climbing tall, snowy mountains is a novelty. "I have a pretty big name in Guatemala," says Viñals today. "When I climbed Everest in 2001 it was such a big deal here—there was a welcome parade for me, there are chicken restaurants with my face on them, there are napkins with my face—I became a little famous. Now I am a motivational speaker."

In Guatemala, the average year-round temperature is about 80 degrees and the tallest mountain is a lush volcano called Tajumulco that reaches an impressive, but still very terrestrial, 13,789 feet. In the 1960s there was a national climbing club, but it later disbanded. When some of the old-timers resurrected it in the 1980s, the young Viñals joined one of their climbs and became hooked. "I loved it," he says. "Then I climbed all thirty-seven volcanoes in my country, then some of the higher peaks in Mexico and in the Andes and, eventually, some trekking peaks in the Himalaya." By 1993, Viñals, at age twenty-seven, was determined to be the first Guatemalan to climb the Seven Summits.

He got a little ahead of himself, though, when he signed up for an Everest expedition with Himex in 1994. "It was a total failure," he says of that trip. "I was not mature enough for Everest yet. I was the youngest on the trip and I just couldn't manage all these emotions. I got scared. Everest doesn't require skilled climbing. But you do need to be very stable in your feelings and understand why you are there."

He went back to try again five years later, now with five of the Seven Summits under his belt. Again, he left early. The expedition report, which is filed at the end of each climb, simply says Viñals was "terrified of the icefall and went home."

Perhaps this second failure was a wake-up call, as the very next year, in the spring of 2000, Viñals signed up with Jagged Globe to climb Cho Oyu in Tibet, which is often touted as a smart dress rehearsal for Everest. He summited Cho Oyu, claiming his first 8,000-meter peak. The following year he returned to Everest with Himex, and this time, he summited.

"I was feeling so good because I was not afraid of Everest anymore," says Viñals. "I felt it—I felt something inside of myself, that I would summit. I had a sense that I was ready."

But was he? "Jaime caused a pretty big problem for us," says Brice. "Our guide Andy Lapkass lost his toes looking after him," which was the end of his high-altitude guiding career. Viñals admits that his summit day was brutal, though he doesn't mention any of the specifics of what it cost his guide. In reality, Viñals was struggling so much after summiting that Brice begged Lapkass to leave him behind and save himself. Lapkass chose instead to spend the night in the death zone with Viñals, and it was a minor miracle they both survived. Only Lapkass is in a position to decide if what he went through that day falls under the typical job description of an Everest guide. But he says he prefers to leave that between him and Viñals.

Viñals's story introduces a question often discussed by guides: What makes a "good" or "bad" Everest client?

"I once got sued by a French client because he got frostbite," says Brice. "He was going way too slow and I kept telling him he's got to turn around. He kept refusing. Eventually, we did get him to turn around, but, of course, by then he had frostbite. He sued me because he lost a finger. It's very, very hard to turn people around on Everest."

"When someone showed up without the experience, but also without the arrogance, they could learn," says Hamilton. "Somebody approaching the mountain humbly was somebody who could also turn around when it made sense."

"We were very judicious about the kinds of people we brought on expeditions," says Macdonald. "But I remember very clearly a client who began to concern Eric and me after a couple weeks on the mountain. He'd been giving us problems all along. One day he's walking out of base camp with trekking poles stuck to the side of his pack, sticking up quite high. We had just had our puja ceremony—a Nepalese ritual asking the mountain gods for safe passage—so we had the juniper burning, had the prayer flags all strung up. This guy walks right into the prayer flags, gets them all tangled up in his poles, and tears down the entire puja setup. Eric just looked at me and said, 'We're sending him home.' Eric isn't even really a very spiritual person, so you knew it was bad.

"So, the real question is: Should that behavior have consequences? I think it should. And did I judge whether or not he was a 'good' or 'bad' client? I did, because he was a liability and people's safety was at stake. Even though we're all just working it out big-time on Everest, emotionally, you have to ask yourself whether you working it out could have consequences."

Guides broadly agreed that being a good or bad client had very little to do with climbing experience. What it came down to in the end was self-awareness. A lack of it could make a client come across as an asshole in base camp, which was one thing, but not having self-awareness in the death zone was potentially fatal.

In the rare but always tragic situation in which a stubborn, ill-prepared client lacking in self-awareness does die on Everest, it's the guides who get the blame, regardless of culpability. It can even put a top guiding company out of business.

In the spring of 1999, Out There Trekking was poised to finish the decade on a high note. While not quite at the level of the Big Five companies in terms of influence or size, it had been successful throughout the 1990s. "OTT had had a lucky year on Everest," says Hamilton of

1997. "They made some money and thought, 'Hey, let's double the size of this.' Then it all kind of collapsed."

Among OTT's sixteen clients in the spring of 1999—a record-high number for the company—was an ambitious twenty-two-year-old stockbroker from London named Michael Matthews, who, despite his age, already had a reputation as an alpha male on the trading floor. The year prior, a friend and colleague had thrown a magazine down on his desk. It was an issue of a snarky men's publication with an article playfully suggesting Everest was the sort of difficult-but-doable challenge that could be accomplished on a lark. Less than a year later Matthews was trekking to base camp.

Matthews was what the Brits refer to as a toff. He was the heir of a millionaire race car driver turned hotelier and socialized with a class of cool kids who were not used to hearing no. The Matthews family remains well known in Britain today, as Michael's younger brother, Spencer, made a name for himself on the reality show *Made in Chelsea*, and his older brother, James, married Pippa Middleton, the sister of Catherine, Princess of Wales.

OTT had a great reputation for summit success and safety. While still in base camp, however, OTT clients became alarmed when they learned that many of the expedition's regulators, the apparatuses that control oxygen flow, did not fit the oxygen bottles OTT had been supplied by Henry Todd. The OTT guide team reassured the clients it was not uncommon to have to make some adjustments to oxygen systems in the field, which was true, and which they were able to do in this case successfully.

Then, when the team arrived at Camp Four on the South Col, ready for their summit push, Jon Tinker, the team leader and OTT's co-owner, had a minor stroke and was told by a doctor in base camp to descend immediately. That left the OTT clients in the care of two guides, Nick Kekus and Mike Smith. The reshuffling unsettled the clients further, and animosity grew between the guides and their clients, who were soon being asked by Kekus and Smith to descend all the way back down to base camp to regroup and contemplate their next move.

Expedition members recall Matthews being particularly frustrated at being asked to descend. Matthews, along with another client, ignored Kekus's request and remained at Camp Four for the night in hopes that others would return soon. Eventually, the conditions forced him down to Camp Two, and, after repeatedly being asked by Kekus to descend all the way to base camp, he finally relented and rejoined the group there. Then the guides decided to rev up the summit engine once again and begin pushing up toward the higher camps.

Matthews once again made it up to Camp Four, but he was in far worse shape this time, tired from previously spending so much time up high and now making the climb a second time. The team got some rest in the afternoon and awoke to a beautifully calm and clear night. Most teams leave from Camp Four for the top between ten p.m. and one a.m. Matthews was reinvigorated enough to gear up and start his summit push.

The climb was long but went smoothly for most of the clients, who summited around nine a.m. Matthews, however, had fallen way behind, and was still heading up at midday. Meanwhile, as often happens later in the day, whisps of lenticular clouds and light snow blurred visibility. Lhakpa Gelu Sherpa, an OTT employee who had summited Everest five times by then, was on his way down from the summit when he encountered Matthews. In no uncertain terms, he told Matthews to turn around—that continuing on would be suicidal.

However, Matthews was only four hundred feet from the summit, and it was later reported that when Smith encountered Matthews, the guide agreed to help him get to the top. Matthews became the young-est Briton ever to summit Everest, breaking the record of the twenty-three-year-old Bear Grylls from the previous year. Smith and Matthews began their descent in worsening weather conditions.

Suddenly, they found themselves feeling their way through a whiteout. Matthews was spent and was having trouble just keeping up with Smith in the deepening snow and deteriorating visibility. At one point, Smith decided to push ahead so he could pull the fixed rope up out of the new snow before it disappeared. The next time he looked back, Matthews was gone. With frostbite creeping into his extremities, Smith had an anguishing decision to make. He would have remembered Rob Hall facing the exact same dilemma three years earlier. Smith understood that Doug Hansen would have perished had Hall stayed with him or not. He felt he had no choice but to get back to Camp Four as quickly as possible to save his own life. Smith had to have one of his toes amputated. Matthews's body has never been recovered.

It was a tragic end to a dysfunctional climb. OTT guides and clients left the Khumbu Valley sad, angry, and splintered. Whereas death is always a part of mountaineering, so is blame. But grieving family members can't sue the weather. Within a year, the Matthews family was suing OTT, Mike Smith, *and* Henry Todd.

David Breashears, who had always been one of the more inclusive and welcoming people toward Everest clients, was startled by what he was seeing. A sort of dangerous obliviousness appeared to have become the norm. "We had set up a system on Everest that made it so the client climbers really didn't understand the peril they were placing themselves in," he says. Many guides were as frustrated as they were saddened by the Matthews story, questioning whether he should have been on the mountain at all.

Ironically, Sandy Hill—so often judged for being the wrong kind of Everest client—had her own idea of who belonged on the mountain and who didn't. "I believe any person who attempts Everest should be made to solemnly swear that they understand they could spend the night out there," she says, meaning high on the mountain.

The mental and emotional reserves required to sustain an under-equipped person in the death zone until sunrise are not skills you can learn, necessarily, but to acknowledge the possibility and state a readiness to do it would say a lot about a person.

Hill will forever be questioned and doubted by some people, but her memories of her time on Everest remain her own, and they speak volumes. "There's nothing like camping on the Lhotse Face," she says today. "Sitting and watching the sunset, and the light off Pumori. Scott would be out there smoking a joint, we'd be watching the golden light—these were some of the most wonderful, wonderful times of my life."

12

The BIG TOP

While a sudden influx of inexperienced climbers like Michael Matthews concerned old-school Everest climbers like David Breashears, the guides relished the challenge. The Big Five and other companies had installed so many redundancies and systems, co-opted so much technology, and hired such an increasingly talented and well-trained Sherpa workforce, that they believed they could get just about anybody to the top of the mountain. Clients were excited to take them up on the challenge and arrived in droves in the early 2000s.

Between 2000 and 2005 there were 2,346 climbing permits issued for the mountain across the Nepal and Tibet sides—up 75 percent on the previous five years—and the climbers using them were coming from more than seventy countries. In total, 1,400 people summited in that span, more than 90 percent of them being client climbers and Sherpas ascending in support. Guiding clients on Everest via the South Col route was becoming an almost paint-by-numbers operation. Henry Todd—who was banned from the Nepal side for two

years by the Ministry of Tourism after allegedly punching the journalist Finn Olaf-Jones—had the audacity to simply base himself on the
Tibet side in 2002, while his guides, clients, and Sherpa team climbed
on the Nepal side, and lead his company's expedition by radio. Four of
his clients and two Sherpas summited. Even Dick Bass returned for
a second shot at the north side, in 2003 at seventy-four years old—
though he cut the expedition short after his back went out on him in
base camp.

"Things were working really well," remembers David Hamilton,
who was racking up ascents guiding for Jagged Globe—four of them
between 2000 and 2010. "I can't overstate how much the Western
guides and expedition leaders cooperated—guys like Russell Brice and
Henry Todd. They all said to me, 'Hey, we just want you to be safe. We
want your clients to have a great time—if you have any questions, just
come and ask.' We were all in it together. We were each other's rescue service; we used the same radio frequencies. And the accumulated
knowledge of all these groups is what allowed for the success rate to
really improve."

"As a climber, I know that *not* being successful is a big part of forming character," Brice says. "To be successful all the time, you don't really
appreciate the amount of heartache and effort you put into it. But we
were also trying to make sure people were as successful as they possibly
could be, for the huge amount of money and time they put into coming
to Everest."

The guiding outfits were further buoyed by a major legal victory. Michael Matthews's parents spent hundreds of thousands of
dollars in legal fees in hopes of destroying the men they felt were
responsible for their son's death. The family won a civil settlement
that eventually bankrupted OTT and sent its co-owner Jon Tinker
into a dark period of his life, according to his friends. But, in a 2006
criminal trial, the three defendants—Tinker, the OTT guide Mike

Smith, and the oxygen supplier Henry Todd—were acquitted of manslaughter charges. Smith cried when the judge read his verdict to the courtroom. The ruling echoed loudly throughout the Everest guiding community.

"It is not the purpose of the criminal court to stifle the spirit of adventure or inhibit personal ambition," the judge said. "All the evidence shows that this was a tragic accident. Mr. Smith deserves the greatest understanding and least condemnation. In his anxiety about Michael, he put his own life at risk."

"By the mid-2000s, I never really felt Everest was a sketchy place," says Dave Hahn, who was putting up bigger numbers than any other Western guide, primarily for IMG. (After 2008 he started guiding on Everest under Lou and Peter Whittaker's RMI banner, as the company was trying to expand its operations, but while Hahn was a star guide during those years, RMI never became a major competitor on the mountain.) He would summit nine times as a guide between 2000 and 2010, and fifteen times total over the course of his career (a record for Western climbers that stood until a British guide, Kenton Cool, surpassed him in 2022).

"Of all the places in the world I was guiding, Everest was pretty well organized, in terms of the information and the resources I had to run a safe trip. I never really felt that we were putting people at much risk. It's true there were some close calls, but at that point we were really well equipped to deal with those.

"It got to a point where I had a better chance of getting a client up Everest on a given trip than getting them up Denali," he says. "We knew what rock to anchor rope to, we knew exactly where the route went, where to put the camps, what food to eat—we had it pretty figured out."

Hahn also points to advances in weather forecasting as having had a big impact on success and survival rates. In large part, that was thanks to technology that allowed the guide companies to finally outsource the forecasting to experts, such as a Seattle-based meteorologist named Michael Fagan, and a European company called Meteotest. Later, Mark Dekeyser, a Belgian meteorologist who holds a position with his country's Royal Meteorological Institute, started doing forecasting on Everest as a side job, and he attracted many guiding companies as clients. "I couldn't make a living off the mountains alone," he says, adding, "It's a job you can probably only do for a couple years before you get fed up with mountain guides—they are not the easiest to deal with."

Dekeyser took particular pride in being able to accurately identify weather windows during the mountain's busiest weeks, which could allow a team to sneak up to the summit before others, or, conversely, have the confidence to wait until the crowds had subsided. But he also felt the weight of the responsibility of the work. "It was frightening the first few seasons," he recalls. "I was trying to figure out which forecast sources to use, which graphics were best. But it's great when we nail that keyhole. For example, there's almost always a window at the very end of the season—but, while all the other groups are going up, your clients have to trust you."

"Knowing we could wait for warmer, more stable weather meant we never had to force it," says Hahn. "We had moved on from that whole May tenth idea from the 1990s—that Rob Hall formula—and it became easier to convince clients and guides to wait it out."

The Khumbu Icefall remained the most dangerous and unpredictable part of the mountain, but even that was exaggerated by the magazines and newspapers of the time. "It's actually surprisingly safe," Brice says. "The number of man-hours that people spend in the icefall is astronomical—statistically, the icefall should be killing many more people."

Other developments in place by the mid-2000s were a well-equipped medical facility at base camp run by the Himalayan Rescue Association (Everest ER, as it is known), and a new pothole-free, FAA-approved asphalt runway at the airport in Lukla, where most climbers and trekkers land to begin the journey on foot to Everest. Furthermore, a man named Tsering Gyaltsen Sherpa had embarked on his mission to bring Everest base camp fully online by creating the highest Wi-Fi hot spot in the world, called Everest Link.

"People still think climbing the southeast ridge is an adventure," Pete Athans told *Outside* magazine. "It's more of an adventure figuring out the New York subway system."

Tragedy had fueled media coverage of the mountain since 1996 and, suddenly, bad news was hard to come by. Instead, media outlets went snooping for a different angle. They discovered a rich vein in what became known as the Everest Circus, and in doing so, swapped danger for twisted comic relief.

Every May, *Outside* magazine published its "Everest Special" edition, which was always a bestseller. The coverline across the top of the 2001 issue read: "Base Camp Follies: Sex, Death, and Bad Behavior at 17,500 Feet." Among the articles was a profile of Henry Todd headlined "The Toddfather" that was heavy on the ex–LSD dealer's backstory and light on Todd's innovations in refining the icefall-fixing routine early on, sourcing oxygen, and offering affordable but quality guided climbs. There was also an oral history called "Base Camp Confidential" in which Chris Bonington recounted whisky-fueled poker games and Todd recalled Guy Cotter "swinging from the mess tent rafters like a chimpanzee," dangling above a table covered in empty glasses.

Without question, base camp had become unrecognizable from the relatively sparsely populated sea of moraine Bass and Breashears camped on in 1985. By the early 2000s it sprawled across nearly a mile of ice and rock, with brightly colored tents set up like battalions, and impressive stone shelters built by the Sherpas—who had a thousand years' worth of experience erecting instant villages—acting as mess tents, cooking stations, or impromptu casino-saloons during downtime, of which there was plenty.

By 2004, clients and guides could get a good cup of coffee, a fresh croissant, and a massage before ice climbing class, and perhaps still have enough time left in the day to play horseshoes or take in an art exhibit before joining happy hour at sunset. "Sitting around base camp, knocking back cans of beer, I don't particularly regard as mountaineering," derided Edmund Hillary.

That was on the Nepal side. On the north side, Himex was reputed not only for its impeccable record of safety and success, but also for having one of the first massive geodesic dome tents, at about fifty feet across, sometimes referred to as the "pleasure dome," other times as the "tiger dome" for the huge faux skin rug on the floor.

"Russell was famous for his supply of hard alcohol and afternoon drinking sessions," says Hahn. "We often joked that if you visited Russell's tent at the wrong time of day you could get really hammered by accident. Personally, I was usually too obsessed with staying healthy or busy playing horseshoes to drink much before the climb." Brice's ability to hold his whisky was a thing of legend, as for all but a pickled few, one beer feels like three at 17,000 feet.

"That was all part of us trying to live normal lives in that environment," Brice explains. "That social outlet for the team was a big part of the way we ran our trips." Most of the other major guiding companies, especially those owned by Kiwis, took a similar approach to Himex in making their clients comfortable and showing them a fun time.

There were rumors of more scandalous entertainments elsewhere on the north side. "Hell, I heard they eventually had whorehouses over there," says Hahn. "The Chinese liaison officers were running a bit of a racket. There were Sherpas losing entire seasons' worth of wages gambling."

The guides were understandably defensive about the bad-mouthing in the press. "We were communicating constantly, talking about how to make the mountain safer," says Willie Benegas, a guide who worked for Mountain Madness before launching his own company, Benegas Brothers Expeditions, with his brother Damian. "Everest base camp wasn't a circus, it was a community—we all really loved each other. That whole Burning Man image was driven by writers looking for drama."

That was nothing new, of course. Drama was always one of Everest's chief draws, and in 2004, Hollywood came calling to see if the greatest drama in the mountain's history to date might have box-office appeal. One of the most renowned film directors in the world, Stephen Daldry, visited Nepal, trekked to base camp, traveled through the Khumbu Icefall—twice—and even spent a day at Camp Two, all for the purpose of researching a potential *Into Thin Air* movie.

At forty-four years old, the English filmmaker had already received Best Director Oscar nominations for *Billy Elliot* and *The Hours*. His frequent producing partner, Tim Bevan, was the founder of Working Title Films, and the two were obsessed with the 1996 tragedy. Bevan had been one of the first to make a play for the rights to Krakauer's book at the time of its publication, but he'd ended up being outmaneuvered by Sony, which then squandered its victory with a widely panned TV movie that came out on ABC in 1997. Bevan and Daldry were undeterred.

Daldry's visit to Everest affected him the way it does just about everyone. "It was a major moment in my life," he says. "I loved it. I loved the icefall, the fact that it's not stable. It changes and you don't know what's going to happen. You can feel it moving as if it's alive—like you're climbing a monster."

On his scouting trip, he was looked after by David Breashears and Ed Viesturs, both of whom had witnessed the 1996 disaster. "David had this incredible emotional, almost *guilt* about the incident," recalls Bevan. "He seemed obsessed by it and wanted there to be a film that honored Rob Hall. His obsession rubbed off on us."

Passionate as Daldry, Bevan, and Breashears were about the project, as happens with so many Hollywood films in development, the pieces failed to come together and the production went into hibernation. Meanwhile, in 2006, a seventeen-person production crew embedded with Brice and Himex to film a reality show for the Discovery Channel. The early working title was "Everest: No Experience Required," but it was released as *Everest: Beyond the Limit* and ran for three seasons. The show charted the full gamut of Everest experiences, from clown-car climbs to inspirational ascents. Brice made for good TV.

For *Outside*'s 2007 Everest special edition, the magazine sent the writer Kevin Fedarko to the south side to—as announced in the headline of the piece itself—"spend a month at the world's most exclusive party town." Fedarko enjoyed solar-powered showers, padded toilet seats, and surprisingly fast internet. At the camp of a super-rich American client climber, he was offered gourmet snacks and access to a vast DVD library. He witnessed a former Playboy bunny from Poland getting the Sandy Hill treatment from fellow climbers and saw the Sherpa Icefall Doctors getting drunk—a lot. A twenty-five-year-old Sherpa stood on the summit naked for several minutes (not to set a record, he claimed, but for world peace). Though Fedarko wasn't there at the time, there was also a rock concert at base camp in 2006 featuring members of 1980s relics like the Alarm, the Stray Cats, the Fixx, and Squeeze.

Yet, for all of that, Fedarko—who was not a climber—discovered a more wholesome favorite pastime, which was telling of the tenor of the much more balanced than alarmist story he ended up publishing. He made a ritual of stopping by Everest ER for happy hour with the Idaho-based doctor Luanne Freer and her team, who had turned their facility into an indispensable resource on the mountain, with a rotating staff of volunteer doctors from around the world. People like Freer showed Fedarko that a less cynical side of Everest still very much existed.

"It was a story about the Renaissance fair that Everest base camp had become," Fedarko says of the article he published. "But I also showed it to be a marvelously human place, swimming in all kinds of human contradictions. The base camp that I encountered was so different from the base camp that I was led to believe I would encounter."

He praises his editors for allowing him to color outside the lines of the narrative that the magazine had stuck to for years, that Everest was beyond redemption. "I didn't have a very strong ethical or moral framework about what I thought Everest should or shouldn't be," he says. "I didn't have a sense of rules or principles of altruism that I thought Everest was somehow violating."

Part of the genuine enthusiasm Fedarko sensed among those who worked in the guiding industry had to do with a change in culture underway on the Khumbu Glacier. The Big Five were still dominant operators, but their owners, along with many of the other early pioneering guides, were stepping back from micromanaging. Brice was the only one of the five still returning to the mountain each year. Todd Burleson, Eric Simonson, Steve Bell and Simon Lowe, and Guy Cotter had long been letting their talented guide staffs lead on the ground so they could focus on growing their global companies.

Coming up at base camp in their place was a new generation of ambitious guides, who had their sights set on one day running Everest companies of their own. They, like Fedarko—and even many of the clients coming to the mountain at the time—were not shackled to nostalgia, nor were they under any illusions that Everest was a place to commune with nature. They understood that an Everest climb was a matter of logistics and endurance.

Mike Hamill, Garrett Madison, and Ryan Waters were three young American guides eager to begin absorbing a decade's worth of Everest wisdom from their forerunners. All had gotten their training at, and worked for, RMI. Hamill had since become one of the lead guides for IMG. "I was guiding for IMG two hundred and fifty days a year," he says. Madison got his first opportunity to guide an 8,000-meter peak with IMG as well, taking clients up Cho Oyu with Hamill in 2003, when he was in his midtwenties. Three years later, Madison took his first shot at guiding Everest for a smaller but highly respected American guide firm called Mountain Link. Shortly after that, Madison was poached by AAI, where he began making a name for himself as one of the most competent young guides on the mountain—a reputation he would leverage in due time.

Waters first went to the Himalayas in 2003 as a customer, signing up with an outfit called Summit Climb, owned by an American named Dan Mazur, to scale Pumori. Waters used the trip as research. The following year, he joined Mazur to take on Everest, and he summited. Mazur noticed Waters's talent, and Waters was soon leading Everest and Cho Oyu climbs for him. Though Waters continued working with Mazur from time to time, by 2005, he had already established his own guide firm, Mountain Professionals. In 2008, Waters worked as a guide on Cho Oyu for his former employer RMI.

These young guides were falling in love with the Everest industry at a time when it was so often being ridiculed. They simply didn't understand why there was so much derision. The diversity of people showing up to base camp, and the fact that so many of these people were making it to the summit—people who fifteen years earlier nobody could have imagined even having a shot—seemed worthy of admiration.

"Sometimes you would look over and see someone and think, 'Huh, that's funny that this person wants to climb Everest,'" says Waters. "But, you know, that's what we were there for, to take less experienced people up the mountain safely. Even if you had some wealthy client from Aspen—some stereotypical beautiful socialite that no one takes seriously as an alpinist—they actually usually knew their shit. They were also pretty cool—they could be dirtbags on the mountain and just blend right in." ("Dirtbags," in this case, being the accolade an outdoorsy person could earn through length of time spent between showers.)

In 2006 alone, Mark Inglis, a double amputee from New Zealand, summited, and seventy-year-old Takao Arayama from Japan became the oldest person to reach the top. The first Filipinos summited. There was a team of climbers representing eight separate religions and a team of disabled veterans. Despite Everest's increasingly bad reputation as a desecrated dump, crowded with egos, the young guides remained optimistic, and the guiding business was growing. "It was much different than what was reported in the media," says Waters. "I often had clients tell me they heard Everest was a circus and I always told them, 'No, it's actually an amazing expedition. The dead bodies, the trash—it's all overblown.'"

Many climbers from the old guard, however, didn't take the same cheery view of the increasing number of average Joes summiting the mountain. Yvon Chouinard, for one, admits that when people come up to him and proudly tell him they've climbed Everest, he doesn't give them the response they're probably hoping for. The last time it happened was at a gas station in Montana. "This woman recognized me," he recalls. "She came up and told me she was, like, the four hundred and eightieth woman to climb Mount Everest or something. I just said, 'Well, good for you.' That's all I said—I probably sound like an old fart."

Chouinard also wasn't fond of the seemingly endless claims of records being set or broken. "I've never liked the idea of claiming first ascents like first blue-eyed dentist, or whatever," he says. He will forever abide by climbing's strictest definition of "first." As in first *human*. Period. "It's all egos—it's just a way for people to delude themselves into thinking that they're doing something greater than what they actually did," he says.

For his part, Hahn doesn't see the expanded claims of firsts as a bad thing. He conceded that Everest was getting crowded, but also insisted that many of the people in those crowds were "darn good folks."

"If you can't appreciate that a blind man reached the summit [in 2001], that's your loss," Hahn wrote in 2004. "If you missed the significance of the first ascent this last spring of an African Black man, then maybe your view of climbing has too much to do with rocks and too little to do with humanity."

While the talented young guides and the impressively low fatality rates were helping foster a more uplifting narrative on the mountain, death and drama had not lost their appeal in the press. It had been nearly ten years since *Into Thin Air* was published; perhaps the guiding industry was due for another morality and mortality audit. During the same season in 2006 that Fedarko was reporting his nuanced account of Everest, two other writers focused on a few tragic mishaps that provided clear evidence to them of rot under the industry's surface.

Michael Kodas, a Connecticut-based journalist and climber, was climbing from the north side in the spring of 2006, on assignment for his city paper, the *Hartford Courant*. Instead of writing only an article, Kodas came away with enough material to write a book, which he called *High Crimes: The Fate of Everest in an Age of Greed*. It made the oft repeated case that the Everest industry had become morally bankrupt. The story is "not a journey to the top of the world, but an investigation into the underworld that has spread beneath it," Kodas wrote.

The so-called leader of Kodas's expedition was a Romanian-born, Connecticut-based mountaineer named George Dijmarescu. Unknown to Kodas when he left for Tibet, Dijmarescu was somewhat notorious around base camp on the north side. He was married to a Sherpani climber named Lakpa Sherpa, who in 2000 had become the first Nepali woman to summit Everest and survive. Before Kodas got started on his climb, he received a note from Russell Brice warning him about Dij-marescu. Dijmarescu was apparently known for having troubling, public domestic disputes with Lakpa. According to Kodas, these often turned physical. Kodas's expedition with Dijmarescu ultimately fell apart in dramatic fashion—devolving into feuds, theft, and death threats.

But, while still on Everest, Kodas also learned of the deaths of two client climbers who had seemingly been left by their guides. One of them, David Sharp, had been based just a few yards away from Kodas on the Rongbuk Glacier. There was a rumor swirling that after Sharp had become incapacitated high on the mountain, he was ignored by dozens of climbers as they ascended toward or descended from the summit. The company that had organized his climb was a Sherpa-owned outfitter called Asian Trekking. Asian Trekking was in fact the very first Nepali-owned company to offer guided climbs, and 2006 was its inaugural year of doing so. Unfortunately, controversy overshadowed the momentous occasion.

As a boy, Asian Trekking's owner, Ang Tshering Sherpa, attended a school that was built by Edmund Hillary's foundation, and he helped his yak-herder father porter for trekking companies. In 1982, just shy of his thirtieth birthday, he bought a small trekking agency called Asian Trekking, and fairly quickly built it up to be one of the most success-ful in the Himalayas. Until 2006, the company was one of a handful of Nepali-owned outfits that served as back-end logisticians for Western guiding companies and private expeditions, without offering guided trips of their own.

Ang Tshering and his Belgian-born wife had a son, Dawa Ste-ven Sherpa, who hung around the Asian Trekking headquarters in Kathmandu as a child, meeting all the Western guides as they passed through. "Our family took over the Hotel Gallery in the Thamel neigh-borhood," he recalls. "And that's where most of the climbers would stay.

So I grew up around a lot of mountaineers." Burleson, Simonson, and Brice were all regulars there. For Dawa Steven, it was like hanging out with a bunch of cool uncles.

Once Dawa Steven graduated from Heriot Watt University in Edinburgh, Scotland, with a degree in business, he got more involved in his father's company. He and his father worked to expand beyond the back-end-only model of other Nepali-owned companies and break into the guiding business.

"When I first arrived on the scene, everybody knew me. I'd go to Russell's camp and he'd be like, 'I remember you when you were this big and now you're running the company!'" Dawa Steven says. He proved to be a well-liked, popular figure who other guides say had humility as well as a flair for leadership and a passion for mountaineering.

Nepalis always had an advantage when it came to permit fees, as the government charges lower rates to its citizens, so Dawa Steven and his father planned to pass along the savings to their clients and hoped that the affordability of their expeditions would set Asian Trekking apart from other companies. To their regret, David Sharp's death resulted in the company initially being known for something other than bargain prices.

David Sharp was a tall, wiry, thirty-four-year-old climber from the outskirts of London. When he signed up with Asian Trekking in 2006, it was his third attempt on Everest in four years. He'd made his first try with a group that included guides but was not strictly guided, and he'd left with severe frostbite and no summit. The next year he'd attempted to climb unguided, and was frostbitten and unsuccessful once again.

Sharp told friends that his 2006 attempt would be his last, even if he didn't reach the top. The trip was sold as a guided ascent; however, Sharp was well aware that his particular climb was extremely affordable

Elite climber and guide Marty Hoey on the 1982 Lou Whittaker–led expedition to the north side of Everest, which was Dick Bass's first-ever Himalayan climb. JIM WICKWIRE

Dick Bass and his Seven Summits partner Frank Wells on the south side of Everest in 1983, for their second attempt at the mountain. RICK RIDGEWAY

Bass became the first to climb all Seven Summits when he reached the top of Everest on April 30, 1985. DAVID BREASHEARS

Bass and David Breashears celebrating their historic success with a toast at Nepal's Everest ba[se] camp. DAVID BREASHEARS

In 1987, Jagged Globe cofounder and former Royal Marine Steve Bell was accumulating Himalayan experience by joining British military expeditions. SIMON LOWE

American guide Scott Fischer (pictured here in 1989) founded Mountain Madness in the late 1980s with the intention of creating the leading Everest guide service. WALLY BERG

THE ACTIVE TRAVELER

◊ DIRECTORY OF EXPEDITION & ADVENTURE SERVICES ◊

A small ad placed by Alpine Ascents International (AAI) in the August 1989 issue of *Outside* magazine was the first publicly marketed offering of a guided Everest climb.
OUTSIDE

In 1990, AAI brought four clients to Everest's north side, including Bob John, seen here marrying his second wife at base camp (with guide Vern Tejas playing fiddle in the background). BOB JOHN

AAI founder Todd Burleson (*bottom center*); AAI lead guide Willi Prittie (*top center*); AAI client Mike Gordon (*bottom left*); and star guides Martín Zabaleta (*top right*) and Peter Habeler (*bottom right*), on a bus in Tibet. TODD BURLESON

Preparing the route through a particularly tricky section of the Khumbu Icefall in the early 1990s, using nine separate aluminum ladders, tied together with rope. TODD BURLESON

New Zealander Russell Brice was climbing on the north side of Everest in 1991, four years before he launched his company, Himalayan Experience (Himex). ERIC SIMONSON

After two previous attempts (in 1982 and 1987) IMG cofounders Eric Simonson and George Dunn summited Everest together in 1991. ERIC SIMONSON

Eric Simonson during IMG's inaugural 1991 Everest expedition from the north side. ERIC SIMONSON

In 1992, twenty-six-year-old Lakpa Rita Sherpa (*bottom row, third from left*) joined the AAI team and remained with the company for thirty years. TODD BURLESON

Todd Burleson and AAI guide Peter Athans in 1992 during the first successful guided expedition.
TODD BURLESON

Burleson (*foreground*) guiding on the southeast ridge during AAI's 1992 climb.
TODD BURLESON

Burleson (*center*) and Lakpa Rita (*right*) summited Everest for their first time in 1992, alongside AAI clients.
TODD BURLESON

In 1992, Adventure Consultants cofounders Gary Ball (pictured here in 1993) and Rob Hall successfully led the first clients to the summit of Everest alongside AAI's guided group.
GUY COTTER

Adventure Consultants' go-to Everest guide was Guy Cotter (*left*), pictured with Gary Ball in 1993.
GUY COTTER

In her quest for the Seven Summits, Sandy Hill (pictured here near Camp One) signed up with AAI to climb Everest in 1993. WALLY BERG

Former Everest summit record holder Apa Sherpa and AAI guide Wally Berg in 1993. WALLY BERG

IMG guide Dave Hahn carving a stone memorial in 1994 for Australian climber Michael Rheinberger, who died high on the mountain's north side that year.
ERIC SIMONSON

In 1995, IMG guide Heather Macdonald—seen here on Cho Oyu—was one of very few women guides in the Himalayas.
HEATHER MACDONALD

Scott Fischer's guided 1996 Mountain Madness team, before the infamous tragedy, which killed eight, including Fischer.
MOUNTAIN MADNESS

British expedition leader and guide company owner Henry Todd decompresses in a Khumbu Valley teahouse after the events of 1996. BRIGITTE MUIR

This photograph of a smiling Rob Hall, taken by David Breashears as they passed each other below Camp Three in 1996, is the last known image of Hall. DAVID BREASHEARS

In 1999 a team led by Eric Simonson, which included Dave Hahn and Conrad Anker, found the body of early British Everest explorer George Mallory; Simonson is seen here notifying the press and his sponsors, from base camp. ERIC SIMONSON

In 2001, *Outside* profiled the first "rock star" Sherpa climber, Babu Chiri. OUTSIDE

Dave Hahn on the Khumbu Glacier in 2002, with remnants of Edmund Hillary and Tenzing Norgay's 1953 base camp.
ERIC SIMONSON

Adventure Consultants sirdar (Sherpa team leader) Ang Dorjee Sherpa in 2003. ALAN ARNETTE

Altitude Junkies' British-American owner and guide Phil Crampton in 2008. ALAN ARNETTE

Dan Mazur (*bottom, second from right*), owner of Summit Climb, and some of his Sherpa guides and employees during their puja ceremony, in which climbers are blessed ahead of their expeditions, in base camp in 2013.
MONIKA WITKOWSKA

New Zealand's best and brightest Everest guides, joined at base camp in 2013 by mountaineering royalty Austrian Reinhold Messner; from left to right: Ang Dorjee Sherpa, Lydia Bradey, Reinhold Messner, Guy Cotter, Mike Roberts, Dean Staples, and Mark Whetu. GUY COTTER

Pro climbers Ueli Steck of Switzerland and Simone Moro of Italy arrived at Nepal's Everest base camp in 2013 upbeat and excited to attempt a new route. SIMONE MORO

Serial client climber and preeminent Everest chronicler Alan Arnette in 2014, honoring his late mother, Ida, atop K2. ALAN ARNETTE

Guy Cotter (*left*) was hired in 2014 to act as a technical advisor and safety consultant during the production of the 2015 film *Everest*, which starred Australian actor Jason Clarke (*right*) as the late Rob Hall. GUY COTTER

Jennifer Peedom, director of the documentary *Sherpa*, with cameramen Nima Sherpa (*left*) and Nawang Sherpa (*right*) in 2014. JENNIFER PEEDOM

Longtime Himex sirdar—and onetime Everest summits record holder—Phurba Tashi Sherpa, photographed in 2014 during the production of *Sherpa*. JENNIFER PEEDOM

Sherpa cameraman Renan Ozturk gives a thumbs-up as he captures Russell Brice in damage-control mode after a devastating avalanche in 2014, boarding a helicopter bound for Kathmandu. JENNIFER PEEDOM

Steve Bell with British alpinist Kenton Cool in 2017; Cool is the current Everest summit record holder among Westerners (with seventeen as of 2023). ROSSY REEVES

Mountain Professionals owner Ryan Waters (*top*) with clients and his lead guide, Tashi Riten Sherpa (*bottom left*), in the Khumbu Valley after a successful 2018 Everest climb. RYAN WATERS

Khumbu Climbing Center (KCC) founder and esteemed American alpinist Conrad Anker with elite Himalayan guide and fellow North Face–sponsored athlete Dawa Yangzum Sherpa in 2018. CONRAD ANKER

Climbing the Seven Summits (CTSS) founder Mike Hamill and IFMGA-certified guide Tendi Sherpa at a puja ceremony in 2019. MIKE HAMILL

Nepal's Everest base camp in 2022. MIKE HAMILL

Apa Sherpa (*left*), at sixty-two, and Dawa Steven Sherpa, at thirty-eight,, at base camp in 2022. DAWA STEVEN SHERPA

Pioneering Sherpani guide Maya Sherpa, who has summited eight-thousand-meter peaks seven times, on Makalu in 2022. MAYA SHERPA

Lance Corporal Nirmal "Nims" Purja with his MBE (Member of the Most Excellent Order of the British Empire; awarded for an outstanding achievement or service) at Windsor Castle in 2022. GETTY IMAGES ENTERTAINMENT POOL

In 2023, Garrett Madison and his sirdar, Aang Phurba Sherpa, successfully guided Madison Mountaineering clients on Everest, Lhotse, and the elusive Nuptse, shown here behind them. GARRETT MADISON

Imagine Nepal owner Mingma G. (*right*) with employee Lakpa (Sona) Sherpa, who summited Everest three times in the spring of 2023. MINGMA GYALJE SHERPA

IMG lead Everest guide Phunuru Sherpa in the spring of 2023 on the summit of Everest for the eighth time. PHUNURU SHERPA

CTSS is among the modern-day Everest guiding companies that offer maximum comfort and convenience at base camp for a premium, including a "coffee shop" and games, as shown here in 2023. MIKE HAMILL

precisely because he would not actually have a guide or Sherpa climber beside him during the entire climb. Simonson's IMG, Todd's Himalayan Guides, Dan Mazur's Summit Climb, and a handful of other companies had already begun experimenting with offering options in which clients could choose for themselves how much support they wanted. However, Sharp paid Asian Trekking the shockingly low fee of $20,000 to facilitate his climb, which was less than half of what even IMG and Himalayan Guides were charging. Sharp told his mother not to worry about him, saying to her that "no one is ever alone on Everest."

On summit day, Sharp was climbing so slowly that people who were watching him from the north side base camp feared they knew what would happen. "He was still going for the summit at nightfall," remembers Brice, who could see Sharp's headlamp through his telescope, and who had the *Everest: Beyond the Limit* reality show camera crew following him at the time. "Then I couldn't see any sign of him in the morning."

As it came to be understood, Sharp had run out of steam just shy of 28,000 feet. There were many other climbers nearby on the North Ridge, but he did not indicate to any of them that he was in trouble. Instead, he sat down and huddled inside a small cave—often referred to as Green Boots Cave, for the Indian climber Tsewang Paljor, who had died there during the 1996 storm. Climbers headed to the summit from the north side had to pass through the cave. As Paljor's body was slowly entombed in ice and snow, his green mountaineering boots remained visible.

"Unfortunately, the route passes really close to this cave and everyone has to step over these boots," said Brice. "We've tried to move Green Boots, but we can't, because he's frozen to the ground. It would be a huge job to get him down." Sharp took his last breath beside Paljor. (In 2014, Paljor's body was finally relocated by a team of Chinese climbers to a less conspicuous location, though not off the mountain altogether.)

Most who knew Sharp—or got to know him on the mountain—could tell he was in over his head. "I knew David before he got himself killed up there," says Phil Crampton, a British expat and former New York City bar owner turned Himalayan guide, who launched a company called Altitude Junkies on the north side in 2008, after working for Mazur's Summit Climb for several years. "David was showing up without enough Sherpas, no proper gear—he was just hell-bent on climbing Everest. The first attempt he lost fingers to frostbite, the second time he lost toes, the third year he died."

Kodas was not the only one reporting on Sharp that year. Upon learning of Sharp's death, the editors at *Men's Journal* magazine sent a journalist, Nick Heil, to Nepal to learn more. Heil—a former Everest correspondent for *Outside*—dove deep into the story for the magazine. He then spent nearly two years interviewing people and writing a book of his own, *Dark Summit: The True Story of Everest's Most Controversial Season*, which was published in 2008. Like Kodas, Heil was struck by what he saw as the overall erosion of ethics throughout the Everest guiding industry. "[In 2006] Everest displayed a weakness much more dangerous than death to humankind—lack of compassion, selfish ambition, and silence," Heil wrote. According to his reporting, as many as forty climbers had passed the dying Sharp without helping.

The year after Sharp's death, Brice, who has affection for Dawa Steven, and who cares very much about the reputation of guiding on Everest in general, asked his sirdar, Phurba Tashi Sherpa, to climb up to Sharp's body and see if he could find anything that could help definitively determine what happened. Phurba Tashi moved Sharp's body out of the cave and retrieved his backpack. He found several potentially lifesaving items in it, including an unused shot of dexamethasone, an altitude drug that can be administered in an emergency. To some, this was proof he could have been saved by fellow climbers; to others, it was proof that Sharp had all he needed to save himself but had pushed beyond his ability to retrieve and administer the drug.

Brice, for one, wasn't even so certain that climbers had seen Sharp in trouble and chose to ignore him. "There's all these people that say they saw him there, but I'm not sure that they did," he insists. "They're in their down suits, oxygen masks, and goggles, walking by headlamp—it's pretty claustrophobic. And, honestly, when people see Green Boots, the natural reaction is to sort of turn the other way." Brice made a special trip to the home of Sharp's parents in the United Kingdom, at his own expense, to help offer some closure about the incident. Sharp's mother made a statement saying she did not blame anyone for her son's death.

Understandably, people were still concerned by what had happened to Sharp. "Asian Trekking had these huge client teams with not enough Sherpas," says Crampton. Others chimed in with questions about the company's client-selection process.

"It was coming from both sides," says Dawa Steven, who felt pinned by the double bind his detractors were presenting. "Companies were getting criticized for charging a ton of money and inviting clients that are not qualified, with people saying it's all about greed. Then, if you are charging less and inviting more-experienced people, like David Sharp—who had been to Everest twice before—you get criticized for not taking good enough care of your clients. After that, though, I did want to take things to a higher level, to try and match the level of service the Western companies were providing. That's when I started going on the expeditions myself."

That Asian Trekking was being held up as the prime example of greed, incompetence, and of the so-called Everest circus was problematic. Asian Trekking was not the only company offering a stripped-down guided Everest climb; it just happened to be the only Nepali-owned one. Meanwhile, an ever-growing number of Western clients were crowing about their success on the mountain, while minimizing the role Sherpas played in their climb, whether via the base camp infrastructure that Sherpas had set up for them, the extra oxygen Sherpas had hauled for their summit day, or any of the countless other things Sherpas did to make their climbs possible.

Many Sherpas rightly felt that despite indisputably being the backbone of the industry, they were too often marginalized and too rarely celebrated by Westerners. This was nothing new. For eighty years, Western mountaineers had been coming to the Himalayas and hoisting stereotypes onto the backs of their hired local support in addition to climbing gear.

13

The WEIGHT *of* HISTORY

E ven today, the word "Sherpa" is too often used to describe an occupation instead of a people. It means "person of the east," and is also
used as a sort of surname across the ethnic group. Most first names for
Sherpa men and women alike are the words representing the days of the
week on which they were born: Dawa, Mingma, Lakpa, Phurba, Pasang,
Pemba, Ngima.

To say you'll "hire a Sherpa" is like saying you'll hire a Norwegian, not a porter or guide. "I feel like every time a reporter calls
me I have to start by just explaining what a Sherpa is—that it is
an ethnic designation that has nothing to do with mountaineering,"
says Pasang Yangjee Sherpa. Originally from Pharak in the southern
Khumbu, the doctor of anthropology now lives in Vancouver, where
she is the assistant professor of lifeways in indigenous Asia at the
University of British Columbia, and is a leading voice in dispelling
misconceptions about Sherpa culture. "A lot of good has come out of
the mountaineering industry. But this idea of who a Sherpa is in the
West does not necessarily reflect who we are as a people—we didn't

create this idea, and now it feels like we cannot do anything about it," she says.

Sherpas began migrating across the Himalayas from Tibet in the 1400s and settled in the Solu-Khumbu region. Solu refers to the lower foothills of the area in which Everest sits; Khumbu refers to the steep-sided valley that funnels right up to the toe of the glacier that leads up to the mountain itself. The most recent census information shows that of Nepal's 30 million people, less than 150,000 are Sherpas, with about 100,000 living in the Solu-Khumbu region below Everest. There are also Sherpa populations in neighboring countries like Bhutan and India. Darjeeling in India is one community hub, largely as a result of Sherpas beginning to migrate there in pursuit of work in the 1920s, when the city was a popular place for the British and others to organize their early Himalayan expeditions.

The basic nature of the arrangement between Western climbers and Sherpas was a harsh, colonialist one from the start. From the early 1920s all the way up to the 1990s, Westerners assigned such demeaning titles as "coolies" and "cook boys" to low-ranking Sherpas, and Sherpas regularly referred to white expedition leaders as "Sahib," which basically means "master." On the first British Everest expedition in 1922—of which, George Mallory was a member—seven local porters were killed in a single avalanche, in what remained the worst disaster on the mountain for decades. The message sent out from the expedition about the accident read "all whites are safe."

Not every British climber was so callous about the loss. At least one of the expedition's members, a surgeon named Howard Somervell, was disturbed by the ethical and moral lines his compatriots had drawn between themselves and the Sherpas. "I would gladly at that moment have been lying there dead if only to give those fine [Sherpa] chaps, who had survived, the feeling that we shared their loss, as we had indeed shared their risk."

The author Wade Davis, who wrote what many consider the definitive account of Mallory's early Everest attempts, *Into the Silence*, once
said "the reason that the deaths of the seven Sherpas happened in 1922
was because of the vanity of Mallory." That vanity remained unchecked,
but after the avalanche, Mallory did realize how indispensable Sherpas
would be to his future attempts on Everest. They would need to have
basic rope- and ice ax–climbing skills to be effective expedition members, so Mallory began teaching them.

Portering has always been one of the most common low-ranking
roles on expedition teams, and it is backbreaking work. Sherry Ortner, an American anthropologist who spent significant time in the
Khumbu Valley in the 1980s and 1990s studying the mountaineering industry and its impacts on Sherpa culture, emphasizes that portering jobs are considered low-ranking not only by Westerners, but
also within Sherpa culture itself, which has a robust class system. "In
Sherpa society doing something like ferrying loads up and down the
Khumbu is something poorer Sherpas might do for wealthier Sherpas," she explains. Though portering for Westerners can be relatively
lucrative for Sherpas, it doesn't erase the class implications and subtle
humiliation of the work.

Throughout the first half of the century, Sherpa workers of all
types carried small books that served as a sort of report card about how
they'd performed on previous expeditions. The Western climbers would
write in the Sherpas' books, cataloging their strengths and weaknesses,
and Sherpas would use the entries to prove their worth while seeking
employment again the following year. These books, as well as many early
Everest expedition journals written by Westerners, would often describe
the Sherpas as loyal, tireless, and beaming with positivity—stereotyped
traits that were self-serving to those applying them and remain sticky
to this day. Early Western expedition members also implied that Sherpas were primitive, uncivilized, and not particularly intelligent. Ortner

points out the racist implication of the depiction of Sherpas as simple and happy—in other words, "childlike."

"People often talk about how we always smile, even when a situation is hard, and how it must be because we are Buddhist people," Pasang Yangjee explains. "Imagine being an angry person in the mountains and having to survive all by yourself. That's just not going to work. Practically speaking—whether you are a Sherpa or not—to survive up in the mountains, you better behave and you better know how to take care of each other and maintain harmony in the group. How do you do that? Sometimes you just have to smile."

There was never any question as to whether Sherpa workers had the *ability* to summit Everest. Scientific studies have proved the long-held assumption that Sherpas have a genetic advantage at altitude, which makes sense given theirs has long been one of the highest-dwelling cultures in the world. The reasons they hadn't chosen to climb the mountains around them during the centuries before the arrival of Western expeditions were cultural and religious. "In Nepal people worship the mountains, just like a god," Anil Sigdel, a political scientist specializing in Nepalese policy, explains. Sigdel is originally from the outskirts of Kathmandu but now lives in Washington, DC, where he founded a nonprofit called Nepal Matters for America. "This Western idea of climbing them did not fit into their frame of mind, at all—they have never liked it. But over time they got used to it and it was bringing money."

In sharing the honor of being the first person to summit Everest, Tenzing Norgay demonstrated the strength of his people to the world and changed the trajectory of the Sherpa culture's relationship to the mountains. He became one of the most important historical figures of the twentieth century, and was featured on the cover of *Life* magazine, profiled in *The New Yorker*, and cowrote a popular autobiography for a major American publisher called *Tiger of the Snows* with one of the most well-known adventure writers of the 1950s, James Ramsey Ullman. (Other accomplished pioneering Sherpas of his time, however, such as Lakpa Chedi Sherpa and Ang Tharkay Sherpa—who had at least as much expedition experience as Tenzing—remain relatively anonymous in Everest's history.)

In the decades that followed Tenzing Norgay's accomplishment, more and more Sherpa cooks, load carriers, and support staff distinguished themselves to Western expedition leaders and were recruited as climbing Sherpas. Climbing Sherpas were those with just enough rope-management and crampon skills to navigate more technical or steep terrain. Western mountaineers often spoke about the "brotherhood of the rope" they shared with these climbing Sherpas. However, what the Western climbers typically forgot, or ignored, is that their Sherpa brothers were scaling mountains to feed their families, not for fun.

That doesn't nullify the fact that there were real relationships and bonds that formed between Western climbers and Sherpas, even in the early days. Though some charged that Edmund Hillary and Tenzing Norgay's friendship was mostly for the cameras, Tenzing Norgay was said to be truly close with another climbing partner, Raymond Lambert, of Switzerland. Lou and Jim Whittaker were close with Nawang Gombu, who guided in the United States at RMI in the 1970s and 1980s. After summiting Everest together in 1983 and 1985, David Breashears and Ang Rita remained best friends.

Yet the truth remained: there was a cultural and economic imbalance in these relationships, and, in the vast majority of cases, the reasons Westerners and Sherpas were climbing mountains remained very different. "I would say ninety-five percent of Sherpas working in the mountaineering sector in the nineties and early two thousands were doing it just to make a living," says longtime AAI guide Lakpa Rita. "There were no other opportunities. Maybe a few were climbers and just loved the mountain. But then they are probably coming from a wealthier family and don't even need to go work on a mountain."

Tenzing Norgay's motivations were clear. He came from a humble background, and after summiting Everest, he did not continue climbing. He returned to his home in Darjeeling, where he lived a quiet life. He discouraged his children from pursuing a career in climbing. When his eldest son, Jamling Tenzing Norgay, asked him for permission to follow in his footsteps in 1983, his response was achingly protective: "I climbed Everest so you don't have to."

Given the economic opportunity, though, the draw for Sherpas to work on expeditions was significant. The frustration in the 1980s was primarily that the work was hard to come by. Western climbers at that time were mostly coming to Everest to take on the mountain without Sherpas' help, consciously rejecting the siege mentality of large teams and well-stocked camps that had characterized Himalayan mountaineering in the times of Mallory and Hillary. Nick Banks, Russell Brice, Reinhold Messner, and others would show up to base camp with one or two climbing partners and a couple weeks' worth of supplies. They would move all their own gear up the mountain and fix ropes as needed. For the most serious climbers, summiting with Sherpa support wasn't even really considered summiting. Some feel that way to this day.

The emergence of the guiding industry in the early 1990s and its explosion by the time of the early 2000s changed all that. Talented Sherpas were suddenly in high demand.

"In 1989, I think we had two Sherpas working for us," remembers Burleson. "In 1990, maybe it was three or four. Then in 1992, I think we had something like thirty-five."

The Big Five and other companies were building infrastructure for the long term, looking for dependable Sherpa teams that they could work with year after year. They snatched up raw talents like Lakpa Rita, Ang Jangbu, and Ang Dorjee, who were all in their teens or early twenties when they were first hired in the early 1990s by AAI, IMG, and Adventure Consultants, respectively. Russell Brice met Phurba Tashi in 1997, and they worked together at Himex from that point forward. Eric Simonson met Phunuru in 1999 and hired him to work for IMG, where he's remained ever since. All these elite Sherpas eventually earned the title of sirdar at their companies—the bosses of the Sherpa teams, responsible for managing and in many cases recruiting and hiring all the other Sherpas.

"When I first met Lakpa Rita I thought the Nepali trekking agency I was using was screwing me," recalls Burleson. "He was tiny and looked like he was way too young to be on Everest. Then I saw that guy run up and down the mountain. Man, to watch that guy climb."

"Lakpa Rita is among the best guides in the world," says Hahn. "And that's not to be confused with somebody who just carries loads."

Cotter feels the same way about Ang Dorjee. "In 1993, the year after I summited with Ang Dorjee, Adventure Consultants hired him as climbing sirdar," he remembers. "He shot up in everyone's estimation because he was still quite young. He became boss of all of these older Sherpas because he just had so much tenacity, skill, and ability."

Lakpa Rita, Ang Jangbu, Ang Dorjee, Phurba Tashi, Phunuru, and a small handful of other Sherpas became part of the fabric of the companies they were employed by, working side by side with Western mountain guides—and summiting with them—year after year.

Grateful to have improved their stations in life by working in the Everest industry, they, like most Sherpas at the time, were reluctant to rock the boat.

One Sherpa climber and guide forged a different path.

When Eric Hagerman, a writer, went to Everest in 2000 to report on a rising star in the guiding industry for *Outside*, his subject wasn't any of the people the magazine's readers might have heard of or expected. Hagerman spent three weeks huffing and puffing around the Solu-

Khumbu with Babu Chiri Sherpa, an incredibly experienced mountaineer and longtime sirdar for OTT. The resulting thirteen-page feature
in the April 2001 Everest special issue sported a huge coverline that
read, "True Everest: The Untold Story of Babu Chiri—the Mountain's
Greatest Climber." The headline of the piece within the magazine's
pages was "He Ain't Your Sherpa."

Babu Chiri, at thirty-five, was courting fame, fortune, and independence in a way that challenged the fixed notions many Westerners had
of Sherpas. "Babu wanted to be the first rock star Sherpa," Hagerman
says. Before going to Nepal, Hagerman met Babu Chiri at the Outdoor
Retailer trade show in the United States, where a startup gear company,
Mountain Hardwear, was unveiling him as its newest sponsored athlete.
During a trip to California in the late 1990s, Babu Chiri had walked into
the Berkeley-based gear manufacturer, asking if they would make him
a special tent that would allow him to become the first person to stay
overnight on the summit of Everest. The Mountain Hardwear crew was
so impressed with him they sponsored the climb and offered him a spot
on their athlete team, for which they paid him $5,000 a year. Babu Chiri
succeeded in his mission and spent the night atop Everest—twenty-one
hours, to be exact, without supplemental oxygen—in the spring of 1999.

"We sponsored a couple of high-altitude mountaineers—Robert
Link and Ed Viesturs—and we thought it'd be really cool to have a
Sherpa climber on the team as well," says Mountain Hardwear's marketing manager at the time, Paige Boucher. "It was Berkeley—it just
seemed like a good and fair thing to do. The Sherpas were the ones getting the climbers and their stuff up the mountain."

The sponsorship Babu Chiri received from Mountain Hardwear
was on top of the $4,000 or so he made working for OTT during the
climbing season. He also earned money working in the Mountain
Hardwear warehouse during his regular trips to the United States. It
didn't add up to much by Western standards—especially considering

that high-profile Western mountaineers like Link, Viesturs, and Anker were being paid anywhere between $20,000 and $30,000 per year as sponsored athletes at the time—but it was a lot back home, where the annual per capita income by then was a little more than $200.

By the time Hagerman met him, Babu Chiri had summited Everest an astounding ten times. His father had been a porter on the 1953 Hillary-Norgay climb, and he'd always felt destined to work on the mountain, though he didn't necessarily look the part. "He was a big guy, big tummy," says Willie Benegas, who was one of Babu Chiri's closest friends. "He would put his arm over his tummy and use it as an armrest. He had what we called the double-decker smile, because he smiled to his eyes. He was always on his feet." On his first few expeditions, Babu Chiri surprised his climbing partners by performing like a machine. He summited Everest on his very first attempt in 1990, at the age of twenty-five, with the notoriously fast and fit Frenchman Marc Batard. He made ascents without supplemental oxygen—sometimes twice a year—throughout the 1990s. And he broke the Everest speed record in 2000, climbing in just under seventeen hours.

"There was this contradiction between our understanding of revered Sherpa culture—or of the 'poor Sherpas' and their Buddhist faith—and what Babu was doing," Hagerman remembers. "They were so often portrayed as passive victims, and then here's this guy saying he's going to set a bunch of records and get sponsored and make money. As far as I knew, he was the first Sherpa climber who'd done anything like that."

Though many Sherpa climbers had set serious records, to this point they'd done so quietly. In the 1980s, first-time national ascents of Everest—such as by Martín Zabaleta for Spain and Arne Naess Jr. for Norway—made front-page news, while Ang Rita had summited *five times* by 1990 to little fanfare. By 2000, he, along with Babu Chiri and another popular climbing Sherpa, Apa Sherpa, had summited ten times; Ang Dorjee had summited nine times; and Lakpa Rita had racked up six ascents. And yet Babu Chiri is the only one who went after the kind of name recognition outside of the Khumbu Valley some Westerners had who climbed the mountain only once or twice.

In her seminal 1999 book, *Life and Death on Mount Everest*, Sherry Ortner writes, "Himalayan mountaineering was originally, and still is, for the most part, defined by the international mountaineers. It is their sport, their game, the enactment of their desires."

Pasang Yangjee explains, "When a Western client returns home after summiting Everest, they gain social merit. It's something to brag about; some client climbers even become brand ambassadors. But the Sherpas who took that person to the summit, they return to their village and just try to see if they can get a job again next season."

Dawa Steven puts it more bluntly: "A foreign client climber might be up at Camp Three and shit his pants because he's too sick or too tired to get out of the tent in time—and the Sherpa climber is there helping him clean up the mess. Then the client goes home, and he's a hero . . . the [Sherpa guide] is thinking, 'Shouldn't I be celebrated in that same way?'"

Babu Chiri was on a mission to do just that. He wanted to snuff out the creaky notion that no matter how skilled Sherpa climbers were, they would always be supporting players. He made a business card with his name and photo front and center, which sported a catchy slogan: WHO BETTER TO GUIDE YOU TO THE TOP OF THE WORLD? Despite his strong alliance with Jon Tinker, OTT's owner, who called Babu Chiri "a world-class quarterback," he was more interested in trying to prove to young people in his community that the seemingly out-of-reach goal of attaining a level of success on Everest that resembled that of the Westerners was possible. As Hagerman learned, creating a better life for the Sherpa people writ large, including his six daughters, was even more important to Babu Chiri than his reputation. He sent his daughters to school in Kathmandu and used his money and clout to support school projects closer to home in the Khumbu Valley. Whereas Tenzing Norgay had filled subsequent generations with a sense of their own strength and capability, Babu Chiri wanted to fill them with hopes and dreams of independence and upward mobility, whether that was on Everest or elsewhere. "I want Sherpa kids to have options," he told Hagerman. "If we can be more famous or rich, and we get that opportunity, we'll take it."

"He wanted something bigger, he wanted to shine," says Hagerman. "He wanted whatever his version of glory was."

Though Babu Chiri was proving that Sherpas could break out of the mold they'd so often been cast into on Everest in *certain* ways, there remained a rather large elephant in the room until the mid-2000s that posed a huge challenge to their further development in the guiding industry. Broadly speaking, the skills Sherpas had gained were crucial—but not the ones that make someone a mountain guide. They had strength at altitude and an understanding of the contours and weather patterns of Everest; they were setting records and accompanying the seemingly endless parade of guided clients to the top; and thankfully, things were going right most of the time. However, being a guide means knowing what to do when things go wrong. Most Western guides working in the Everest industry, whether officially certified or not, had been very thoroughly trained on how to avert disaster, and when that failed, how to mount a rescue and save a life. Sherpas had not.

Benegas remembers Sherpas calling him to action whenever a complex rescue was required. "I'd hear 'Willie Dai!' or 'Dave!' Or 'Pete!'" he says, referring to Dave Hahn and Pete Athans. "If someone fell into a crevasse, the Sherpas would be shouting for help."

Benegas happened to be an internationally certified guide; however, certification was not the main way Everest guides learned their skills. Many Western guides, including Hahn, Hamilton, Tejas, Mazur, and Crampton, were not certified. Yet, at RMI, Genet Expeditions, and elsewhere, they'd had opportunities to undergo long and intensive training of the type that Babu Chiri and other even very experienced Sherpas had not.

Cotter remembers many instances of the Sherpas on his team making consequential miscalculations as a result of lack of training. "I remember saying once to the Sherpa climbers, 'We need six hundred more meters of rope,' and they're going, 'No, it's only four hundred.' I'm going, 'No, no, six hundred!' And, sure enough, we needed the six hundred."

Brice had similar experiences. "I've seen it time and time again, Sherpas fixing rope, and the first thing they do is get the rope in a tangle. And now you've got to untangle it in the freezing cold and wind before you can even start fixing it."

It may sound nitpicky, but guides have a mantra: small mistakes can have grave consequences in the mountains. In the event something does go wrong, technical and precise rope skills are some of the most important for guides to have. Up to six able-bodied, knot-savvy people are needed to bring a single injured climber down through the icefall. Retrieving an injured climber from a crevasse requires the quick construction of a very specific and complex system of ropes and gear. Training in snow stability and risk assessment—in other words, avalanche training—is also crucial. Avalanches have killed more Sherpas on 8,000-meter peaks than any other single hazard. Far fewer would have died had they received proper training.

Sherpas also faced a cultural challenge that, when some Westerners were being frank, made them wonder if Sherpas had what it took to be guides. The subtlest but perhaps most important skill a guide must have is the ability to get a client to turn around. Burleson explains the deficit Sherpas were facing in that area in no uncertain terms. "Sherpas are the greatest climbers in the world, but they could never say no to a

Westerner—that's how the client *and* Sherpa die," he says. "By not being able to say no to a client, they were dying with clients that should have been turned around. Or, if a client was too far gone, they should have just been dumped and the Sherpas come down themselves. The Sherpas were instead staying with them, and sometimes dying with them."

Only a few Sherpas were able to get a technical mountaineering education before the mid-2000s. Lakpa Rita was one of them, and he had to leave Nepal for the opportunity. "Todd [Burleson] brought me over to the US for training," he says.

"I learned navigating with a map and compass, crevasses rescue, Leave No Trace camping—before I went, I didn't even know what that was. I'm very strong—I could always get clients up and down the mountain safely. But before getting training, if a client broke a leg or fell into a crevasse, I would have had no idea how to get them out or down the mountain safely. We didn't know anything about medical things, like splinting, or injecting dex [dexamethasone], or how to set up a crevasse rescue. Even by the end of the nineties, there were only a few really good Sherpa climbers."

For Sherpas looking to get technical training at home, the only ones who could reliably access it were the Icefall Doctors. The powerful local organization they were under the management of—the Sagarmatha Pollution Control Committee—sponsored trainings for the exclusive few members of the team, who learned the knots, rope skills, and subtleties necessary to navigate the Khumbu Icefall.

There was another important local organization that was supposed to train Nepalis in basic mountaineering skills and regulate the industry, called the Nepal Mountaineering Association (NMA). But Lakpa Rita says that it was not very effective in this area. By the early 2000s, the NMA's foremost accomplishment was to have created a "book" system in which as a Nepali climber's status increased, they could trade up from a black book, for low-altitude workers, to a blue book, for climbing

Sherpas, and, finally, to a red book, given to experienced climbing Sherpas and sirdars. Lakpa Rita says progressing through the books often had less to do with climbing ability or technical skills and more to do with seniority or a simple endorsement from a trekking or climbing company.

"A lot of the local trekking companies would require you to have a red book to work as a sirdar," says Lakpa Rita. "I have my red book somewhere, but after I had been working for AAI for a while, and then immigrated to the US, I didn't care about that red book much."

Others did continue using the books, however, and many even still do today. Whatever their faults, they're considered beneficial enough to Nepalis to maintain, because they at least provide an entry point for getting work in the mountaineering and trekking industries.

When *Outside* published its profile of Babu Chiri in April 2001, readers were shown a very different side of Everest—perhaps a glimpse into the future of the mountain. However, Babu Chiri's success didn't erase the fact that foreigners owned the Everest guiding industry. Babu Chiri was a maverick, but there was little collective momentum behind the broader struggle for Sherpas to break out from stereotypes and pre-assigned roles, so few Nepalis heard about him or the goals he was pursuing.

Another more overtly political struggle, however, was underway beyond Everest that Nepalis were talking about. Less than two months after the Babu Chiri profile was published, something happened in Kathmandu that would escalate discussions about equity to an entirely new level.

14

An INSURGENCY
in WAITING

O n a typical morning in central Kathmandu, the ancient royal palace grounds of Durbar Square heave with jet-lagged tourists, tchotchke vendors, cavorting teenagers, and dreadlocked Hindu holy men who will pose for a photo for a few rupees. Thousands of motorbikes flow through the surrounding commuter streets, the vehicles packed so tightly they appear as one giant organism. Incense smoke drifts through the small, atmospheric alleys. But things were not at all typical on the morning of June 1, 2001. The city woke up to a nightmare.

Police and government officials had been gathering since well before dawn at Narayanhiti Palace—the contemporary home of the reigning royals—a short walk north from Durbar. Strewn over the cold tile of the palace's parlor and the concrete of the adjacent outdoor courtyard were the bodies of nine members of Nepal's royal family. They were riddled with bullet holes, lying in a congealing pool of their own blood. There had been no struggle. The executions were sudden and unexpected.

Like a lot of climbers, Eric Simonson is a very early riser. On that morning he was at the seventy-room Hotel Tibet on the outskirts of

Kathmandu, which had become a fixture on the IMG Everest itinerary thanks to its affordability, cleanliness, and quiet location—close to the airport but far from the energy-sapping hustle and bustle of the city center. He had finished his spring expedition and was scheduled to fly to Bangkok that day and then to his home near Seattle. At three a.m. he turned on the bedside lamp and felt around the sheets for the remote control, ready to start his day. He flipped on CNN.

"Holy shit," he said to himself as he took in the gruesome early reports. "I knew immediately this was really bad and that it was going to get worse," he says today.

Thankfully, all of IMG's clients had already left the country, but Simonson still had a team of guides and a film crew with him at the hotel. He began making room-to-room calls and banging on doors. Their scheduled flight wasn't until two p.m., but he knew he needed to get his group to the airport early enough to ensure they were on the first plane out of the country. They piled into taxis and managed to secure seats on the flight. As their plane took off and banked south, Simonson could see the sun rising over the Himalayas. He couldn't help but wonder when, or if, he'd be back.

Later that morning, martial law was declared in Kathmandu and all flights in and out of the country were canceled. Foreigners were told to stay put in their hotel rooms. Many couldn't leave the country for days; some couldn't get out for weeks.

This tense reaction to the royal slayings had everything to do with Nepal's recent Maoist uprising, which most Westerners knew little about, but came to mind immediately for Nepalis. The Maoists, as the interrelated Communist political groups were collectively known, had been pressuring the government to put an end to the monarchy for years. The assumption was that the royal murders were a ghastly ratcheting up in that conflict.

It was only a matter of days before an official inquest determined that the shooter was not a Maoist terrorist after all, but in fact Crown

Prince Dipendra himself. He was said to be despondent over being forbidden to marry his true love. Twenty-nine years old and an avid gun collector, Prince Dipendra was reported to have excused himself from a family gathering earlier that evening, walked up to his bedroom to change into military dress, walked back downstairs, and shot his entire family, before turning the gun on himself. The *New York Times* cited eyewitness accounts of a "drunken, drugged crown prince, in a frenzy." Dipendra survived for three days in a coma, during which time he was crowned king, before he passed away.

While the royal massacre was not committed by Maoist insurgents, the killings did shine a spotlight on the dysfunctional state of the monarchy and create more general civil unrest, which elevated the Maoists' cause to a hot topic of conversation and debate among Nepalis. The center of Maoist activity was in Kathmandu and other large cities, but the conflict was soon felt everywhere, including in the remote Solu-Khumbu region. In late 2001, Maoists attacked government facilities in the Himalayan foothills, killing upward of thirty policemen and members of the army, and losing approximately two hundred people of their own.

Kathmandu did not remain on lockdown for long, and most of the established Western Everest guiding companies were prepared to come right back in the fall of 2001 and spring of 2002. But there were noticeable, and sometimes concerning, changes. "I remember these militias had set up a roadblock on the bridge between Lukla and Phakding, on the way to Everest," says Simonson, who returned with clients in the spring of 2002. "Trekkers had to pay money to cross, but they'd get a receipt so that when you were stopped again farther up the trail by another group of Maoist rebels, you could just show your receipt to get through."

The BBC reported on several mountaineering teams traveling in the Makalu region, which is only about twenty-five miles southeast of Everest as the crow flies, being asked to "donate" to the Communist cause—robbed, basically. The fact that they were able to negotiate how much money would be stolen and were also given a receipt took the edge off the experience. But the Maoists were far harder on the locals.

"Thankfully, the violence was never aimed at foreigners," Simonson says. "But for a lot of the business owners and people in Kathmandu there were threats of violence. One of my longtime cooks had his house and farm taken over by the Maoists—they took all his food, all of his livestock, they cleaned him out. The Maoists were a huge problem for years, but it was something we were able to work around." Burleson says one of his cooks was kidnapped for ransom, which he paid.

"The Maoist leadership was very aware of the importance of tourism in Nepal," says the political scientist Anil Sigdel. "Throughout the ten-years-long insurgency [from about 1996 to 2006] the Maoists literally didn't touch a single tourist. Considering the nationalistic rhetoric of the Maoist movement—and its sharp rebuke of foreign influence—in theory, they would have gone berserk, taking hostages, saying, 'This is our country,' and ending everything. Absolutely not. I remember instances where my friends were camping in the mountains right next to Maoists who were trying to hide from police."

As a result, Western climbers weren't particularly deterred by the royal massacre or the broader Maoist uprising. They still saw the Khumbu Valley as a wonderful escape from the woes of the world. In 2002, Everest client summits were up more than 30 percent from the previous year. Between 2001 and 2004, they nearly doubled.

The Sherpas of the Khumbu Valley largely remained apolitical. They were extremely disciplined in pursuing their goal of bringing prosperity to the region, and they felt staying out of the fray was the best way to do that. However, there's no doubt that some of the deeper issues that the Maoist conflict represented—struggles of class, power, and inequality across Nepal—resonated with Sherpa communities at a time when the Everest guiding industry was still entirely Western owned.

.   •   •

Just three months after the royal massacre, in the fall of 2001, Babu Chiri was on Everest, coguiding a group of OTT clients. The team was on a rotation up to Camp Two. Climbers typically cluster together and spend more time in their tents once they get to this point, fighting off the symptoms of altitude sickness. Not Babu Chiri.

"He was taking pictures," recalls Willie Benegas. "He had this really expensive Nikon camera, which wasn't really something Sherpas had back then. Taking pictures was just completely irrelevant for most of them."

"It wasn't just a job for him—I mean, here he was, doing photography on his own," says Paige Boucher, Mountain Hardwear's former marketing manager. "I think he did love it."

Later that night, Benegas remembers he was having trouble sleeping. "I was tossing and turning," he says. "And then I hear a group of Sherpas screaming."

Babu Chiri hadn't returned from his photography session. Some of the other Sherpas had gone looking for him, and discovered a hole punched through a layer of snow, which led into a huge crevasse. By headlamp, the Sherpas could make out some worrying limb-like shapes deep inside.

Benegas suited up and recruited a climber, Sandy Allan, to help with the rescue. They set up a pulley system and Benegas prepared to be lowered into the chasm. "It was the middle of the night so it was pretty terrifying," he recalls. "With my headlamp I could see all these icicles hanging like swords. Then I could see a bare foot. When Babu broke through the snowbridge, all the snow fell on top of him and he must have lost a boot. I felt his foot. It was still warm, but there was no pulse."

"I hated that camera," says Benegas, seeing it as responsible for his friend's death. "I never thought Sherpas cared about that sort of stuff." But Boucher notes just how significant that camera was in showing

Western climbers who their Sherpa partners really were. "Babu was cap-
turing the art of the mountains," she says. "Yes, Babu definitely wanted
to lead the people out of being mountain servants. But, when he died, he
wasn't out there trying to put up another rope line or carrying a load—
he was sort of in the moment just like anyone who loves the mountains,
finding the beauty in it."

Babu Chiri's early death meant he never got the chance to be the
kind of role model that he hoped. Quick as his star had risen, it fell, and
tragically, his name was rather quickly forgotten by the young Sherpas
whom he'd most wanted to influence. There was no one like him, in his
own generation, to carry the torch forward in terms of demonstrating
the possibility for Sherpas to take more ownership of the industry and
get more international recognition. However, there were people who did
pick up on his message about instituting more training opportunities
that would give Sherpa kids options.

Ironically, one of the people who was quickest to the task, and most
effective at it, was someone who had many friends in the guiding industry but could not exactly be called an advocate for it. Conrad Anker and
his wife, Jenny Lowe-Anker, founded the Khumbu Climbing Center
(KCC) in 2003. They built it in the village of Phortse, with Pete Athans
as one of the partners and Jon Krakauer on the board of directors. The
KCC was set up with the sole purpose of providing vocational training for high-altitude workers, and it became one of the first reputable, formal training structures in Nepal. "The goal, initially, was to give
something back to the Sherpa people, particularly in Phortse," Anker
explains.

From the start, the KCC was intended to kick off a virtuous cycle,
in which Sherpas who had trained there could become instructors
themselves and pass on what they'd learned, including rope-fixing skills.
Phunuru, who is from Phortse and had met Anker in 1999 as a teenager on the Simonson-led expedition where they found Mallory's body,

began training at KCC a year after it opened. In 2008, he became an instructor there. (While a small Western team still travels to KCC each season to help out, in 2019 the Ankers and their cofounders handed over full management of the organization to the Sherpa community.) As of 2023, approximately one thousand Nepali men and women have been trained at KCC, and the organization now oversees the formal instruction program for the Icefall Doctors.

Other Sherpas sought out different ways to help their countrymen receive training. A climber named Ang Norbu Sherpa started the rigorous, roughly five-year training program to get his International Federation of Mountain Guides Associations (IFMGA) certification in 1994 in France. When he returned to Nepal in the early 2000s, he recognized that Nepalis needed more training options and opportunities and became part of a movement to form the IFMGA-endorsed Nepal National Mountain Guide Association (NNMGA). In 2005, the NNMGA kicked off a run of high-level trainings. "We needed that professional education," Ang Norbu says. "These skills had always just been passed down from generation to generation. But we now know navigation, crevasse rescue, and a lot more."

The goal of the NNMGA was always accreditation from the IFMGA, and in 2012, Nepal was admitted as a full member. (It was given a special exemption for the skiing component because there is virtually no ski mountaineering in the Himalayas.) In the first year, it certified twenty-four guides. In 2018, Ang Norbu was named president of the IFMGA in Nepal. There are still fewer than eighty fully qualified Nepali IFMGA guides today—compared with the hundreds who hold a blue or red Book from the NMA—so the IFMGA membership appeared to many as largely a symbolic development. But it did go to show how motivated Sherpa mountaineers were to gain a level of proficiency equal to or, in some cases, higher than, their Western counterparts as the Everest industry grew and matured throughout the 2000s.

•   •   •

In the early 2000s, change was radiating out from Everest. The growth of the guiding industry and concurrent interest in Everest tourism created broader economic opportunities in the Solu-Khumbu. In a country where more than 50 percent of the population lived under the poverty line in 1995, the money was critical.

In the early 2000s, roughly seventy thousand people were visiting the Solu-Khumbu each year, accounting for the majority of Nepal's tourist revenue. Most of them arrived in the spring to make the ten-day hike from Tenzing-Hillary Airport in Lukla to the area just outside Everest base camp. Each day from about March to June, the well-sculpted trails and stone staircases among the villages would pop with the bright yellows, reds, and blues of Gore-Tex, technical fleece, and goose down jackets, the colors mirroring the red, yellow, and blue prayer flags draped over stupas of all sizes along the trail.

The bustling town of Namche Bazaar (population less than two thousand), considered a second home for many Everest guides, showcased the new prosperity of the region, with its charming narrow streets, bars, coffee shops, hotels, and internet cafés. Many of the businesses were started by Sherpas with savings they built up from working on Everest. "The Khumbu Valley is just so nurturing," says Burleson. "You could have pneumonia at Everest base camp on the south side—you could be dying up there—and if I take you down to eleven thousand feet in Namche Bazaar, eighty percent of the time, you'll be better in a few days."

Other, smaller villages farther along the trail, like Gorak Shep, a two-hour hike from base camp, went from being a jumble of yak corrals by which climbers would pitch tents and often pick up a stomach bug, to a comfortably maintained pit stop with lodges and hot meals. The money the families of the Solu-Khumbu Sherpa people made from tourism was often funneled into their children's education.

Another uplifting but little-known narrative that was playing out in the 1990s and early 2000s was the marked uptick in women Sherpa—or Sherpani—climbers and guides. Back in 1993, Pasang Lhamu had organized the first ever all-Sherpa Everest expedition (the same year that she tried to charge other climbers for completing the rope-fixing in the icefall and unintentionally gave Henry Todd the idea to do the same). Though she tragically died on the mountain after she summited—as did her husband during the same climb—she had successfully led four Sherpa men to the summit in the process who descended safely. Her story was a big deal in Nepal, and it inspired a younger generation of Sherpanis, including a young woman from the foothills beneath Lukla named Maya Sherpa. While Pasang Lhamu was the first Sherpani to show a love and talent for climbing the mountains, Maya was the first to actively pursue a career in guiding. And while the male Sherpas of her generation were mostly keeping their heads down, she was more similar in ambition to Babu Chiri.

"There were no climbers in my family," says Maya. "But my father and uncles were trekking guides. So, when I was young, I was not yet thinking about climbing mountains, but I always wanted to do something to change women's life in Nepal. In our society, the women are always behind. I was quite lucky because my father understood this—he was working with foreigners, so he could see there was no difference between men and women. I dreamed of traveling around the world and meeting different people. So I thought maybe it's a good idea to follow in my father's footsteps and then maybe travel for work."

Maya began working as a trekking guide in the early 2000s. She immediately stood out for her strength, speed, and charisma. She was outpacing many of her male counterparts, and was contacted by Dan Mazur, who offered to pay for and facilitate her training to work on more technical terrain, with the hope of then hiring her.

In 2003, just a couple weeks after finishing her training, Maya was working for Mazur's Summit Climb on an expedition to the challeng-ing mountain Ama Dablam. At the age of twenty-five, she was put in charge of Camille Kinney, who, at twenty, was hoping to become the youngest Australian to summit. "That was my first expedition, so I was happy, nervous, excited—everything at the same time," Maya says. "I was always thinking in my mind, 'This is quite a technical mountain.' I wasn't sure I could climb it. I started asking other Sherpas if they thought I could climb it. They said I would have no problem, but when I was alone inside the tent, I was just thinking, 'Don't cry, don't cry.'"

Maya not only summited Ama Dablam, she became the first Nepali woman to do so and then, shortly after, the first to summit Cho Oyu, an eight-thousander. "When I came back to Kathmandu there was a big celebration in our office. And the press was there. I was getting quite famous and I thought, 'Wow, I want more.'"

Maya then guided on Everest for Mazur for two seasons, by which point she met her husband, a Dutch Everest guide named Arnold Coster. The two later formed their own company. Now in her midfor-ties and having summited 8,000-meter peaks seven times—including Everest three times—Maya is a mentor to a new generation of Sherpani mountain guides.

One of those women is an outstanding climber named Dawa Yang-zum, who arrived on the scene in 2012, at the age of twenty-two. Like Maya, she had wanted to climb Everest since she was a kid. She'd gotten a college scholarship for endurance running and then started working as a trekking guide. But she knew from the beginning that climbing would be her career, and so she enrolled in a ten-day mountaineering course with the KCC. In 2011, she summited Ama Dablam. The following year, she was asked by Conrad Anker to join an Everest climb sponsored by the North Face, and she summited. After that, she immersed herself in guide training. In 2018 she became the first-ever woman Nepali to be IFMGA certified, and in 2019, the North Face added her to its sponsored-athlete team, right alongside superstars like Anker, Alex Honnold, and Jimmy Chin.

Interestingly, Western women guides and climbers faced a pecking-order challenge of their own, as they tried to prove themselves in a male-dominated industry. Lydia Bradey, the first woman and New Zealander in history to climb Everest without supplemental oxygen, in 1988, faced a stark double standard throughout the 1990s. "I was wild, I had dreadlocks, I slept around, and I was super driven—all those things make you an easy target if you're a woman," she says. "I'm so glad that social media didn't exist then."

Bradey stuck with it. She began guiding 8,000-meter peaks for Himex in 2004 and later on a regular basis for Adventure Consultants. She guided Everest for the first time in 2008 and went on to guide 8,000-meter peaks eight more times, with her last Everest summit in 2019.

Bradey is quick to point out that the title of first woman to successfully guide Everest—to get a client to the top—could in fact belong to Adele Pennington. Affectionately described as "nutty and tiny" by Bradey, Pennington was a British mountain guide who was on Everest with Bradey in 2008.

"When I was seven or eight my stepdad took me up Snowdon in Wales," Pennington remembers. "It was the best day of my life. And Everest was the only other mountain I had ever heard of, so I became a bit obsessed. I think I told the schoolteachers I wanted to climb Everest and they just thought I was a silly little girl. When I told my mum she said, 'A girl from Corby?! Forget it!'" Pennington, who idolized the British climber Alison Hargreaves, summited Ama Dablam in 1998, when she was twenty, and Cho Oyu, alone, in 2007. She summited Everest for her first time the following year, working for Jagged Globe under David Hamilton.

While sexist dinosaurs within the guide community were slowly going extinct, narcissistic, predominantly male Everest clients still presented a huge challenge for women guides. Pennington recalls that wolf whistles were routine in base camp, and her second time guiding on Everest was downright humiliating.

"In 2009, I went back to Everest for Jagged Globe as the big chief and it was a horrible experience," she remembers. "I had two assistant male guides and one of them had quite a bit of experience and was fairly well known. So the men in the team just treated *him* as leader. The entire time it felt like they were trying to break me. That trip actually made me decide I never, ever wanted to go back to Everest."

"As a woman, you always had to pull more than your weight," Heather Macdonald notes. "That said, the older American guides— Phil, Eric, George, Robert Link—were mentors, and I felt incredibly supported by them."

"It's a big difference," says Maya Sherpa. "Women have proved themselves. Nowadays they believe in us. But a few women really did the hard work to change the thinking. Now people won't underestimate or judge us in the future."

Both Sherpa and Sherpani guides were demonstrating a new sort of progress on Everest in the early 2000s, but the fact remained that the risks of high-altitude work were not shared equally, and when something terrible happened, they were disproportionately felt. Whereas Western mountaineers who perished on Everest typically died doing what they loved and in the name of that which was most important to them, a Sherpa's death was simply a workplace mishap and usually left a family with a token life insurance payout and zero earning power. The same year David Sharp died on Everest, an even more devastating death occurred on Ama Dablam, which few outside the Khumbu Valley ever heard about.

Mingma Nuru Sherpa was one of the elite climbing Sherpas getting steady work in the early 2000s. By 2006, he had worked on eleven

8,000-meter expeditions, and had summited Everest three times. Then he died in an avalanche on Ama Dablam working for Henry Todd. "He was a sirdar, very experienced," says his son Pasang Gyalzen Sherpa, who was only six when his father was killed but knows the story well. "In the night, when they were sleeping at Camp Two, the avalanche came and smashed them. My mother told me they tried to rescue him but his body was never found."

"I hadn't seen or heard from him for seven days," says Mingma Nuru's widow, Sita Phuti Sherpa. Like most climbing widows in the Khumbu Valley, she was suddenly faced with a unique financial hardship. Not only had her husband's income disappeared, the elaborate Buddhist funeral traditions that Sherpas conduct swallowed the $3,000 to $4,000 the government provided as a state-sponsored life insurance policy for families of those killed while working in the mountaineering sector. With a faith built around reincarnation, the way in which a family handles that passage from this life to the next is as much of a necessity as food and shelter. The funerals last for as long as a month and require the hiring and feeding of important lamas. It put Sita Phuti in debt.

She had to find a way out for herself and her children. A superb cook, she took out a $15,000 loan and opened Namaste Lodge and Restaurant in the village of Pangboche a year after her husband died. The two-story stone structure, with a large stone patio and blue roof, is one of the first buildings trekkers see upon entering the village. They come for lightly fried potatoes, tea, and a warm bed.

The business has enabled Sita Phuti to send her eldest and youngest children to school in Kathmandu. Pasang Gyalzen, her middle child, helps his mother run the lodge, though he too intends to go to school and wants to study electrical engineering. He says he would like to someday create hydropower in Pangboche and is happy to stay in the Khumbu for the rest of his life. "Kathmandu is nice for a few days, but I get fed up with it," he says.

Sita Phuti found a way to live off the same industry that stole her husband. It's a complex legacy, and not an uncommon one for the Sherpas of the Khumbu Valley. As more and more Sherpas took work in high-altitude mountaineering, more attention was drawn to what free will meant in an industry that was often the sole option for some of the poorest people within one of the world's poorest countries. Many Sherpas of the Khumbu felt they had no choice, which is why people often level accusations of exploitation at the guiding industry. But this is perhaps one of the most misunderstood pieces of the Sherpa story. Like so many Sherpas, Situ Phuti holds no ill will toward the Everest industry. She is representative of the members of her community who primarily feel gratitude that the money flowing in has enabled them to send their children to school or start a business. The mountaineering and trekking industries were the sole reason for their prosperity.

"I have no negative feelings, because Everest is the main business here," she says. But, then, she also admits to feeling scared whenever she knows an expedition team is going for a summit—fear over whether another Sherpa family will lose a father and husband. She says she prays a lot. She looks older than her forty-five years but is always smiling. Her laugh is a loud and joyful cackle that echoes through the thin walls of her lodge and, even when she's serious, she smiles. "When I hear they are going for the summit, I do a small puja," she says. "Is it good? Is it bad? I don't know—it is life."

Over time, even Sherry Ortner, who professed to being appalled by the mountaineering industry in her 1999 book, has come to terms somewhat with the economics of the industry. In 2022, she said, "The relationship seems dysfunctional, but in the same way capitalism is dysfunctional. It also shows exactly how capitalism can work for good."

15

FREE MOUNT EVEREST

By the mid-2000s, most everyone spending time at base camp on the south side agreed that it had gotten pretty crowded. Then in 2008, the population effectively doubled overnight.

Less than three months before the start of the 2008 spring season—when many outfitters were already in Nepal and Tibet gearing up to welcome clients, and client climbers were making sure they knew where their passport was—the Chinese government suddenly decided it wanted to put a torch on the summit of Everest as part of the hype leading into the 2008 Beijing Summer Olympics. To give them assurance that a naked streaker with FREE TIBET written on their body wouldn't blemish the buttoned-up vibe they were going for, they announced that no one would be allowed to begin climbing on the Tibet side before May 15—at which point most teams would normally have been preparing for their final summit pushes, if they had not summited already. For all intents and purposes, the north side's season was canceled.

Most of those on the north side managed to jump over to the south side within a matter of weeks and save their seasons. Phil Crampton's Altitude Junkies and Dan Mazur's Summit Climb, along with Kobler & Partner (owned by Kari Kobler, a Swiss guide) and 7 Summits Club (owned by Alex Abramov, a Russian guide)—all of which were major players by then, with large teams of clients and Sherpa staff—made the move. So did the young American guide Ryan Waters and his upstart company, Mountain Professionals. Most never went back to the north side. The year before the Olympics, there were at least ten guiding companies operating on the Tibet side; the year after, two returned. China's unexpected and disruptive show of muscle ended up cementing Nepal's reputation as the easier, more predictable, and more client-friendly side of the mountain.

The most notable company making the jump was Himex. Brice had always been proud of working on the north side, but he was furious with the last-minute interruption to his spring 2008 expedition (which also resulted in his Discovery Channel show having to take a break between its second and third seasons). He picked up his pleasure dome and moved it to the Nepal side for good. The south side camp was suddenly swelling with about eighteen different guided outfitters, ranging from the high end and finely tuned to the ragtag, plus whatever independent expeditions were on the mountain. Asian Trekking remained the only guiding company owned by Nepalis. The Nepal base camp population was pushing a thousand people.

The season was chaotic from start to finish. Though the south side was open, it turned out the Chinese government was so protective of its Olympic torch–bearing team that it wanted to prevent anyone from climbing even from the *Nepal* side during that period. They convinced the Nepalese government to post machine-gun-toting guards at base camp and Camp Two for the days when the Chinese climbers would be on the mountain. The Chinese also managed to impose a no-phone rule at the south side base camp—all phones had to be turned over for two weeks and could only be used in the presence of a guard. Some climbers and guides hung FREE EVEREST signs outside their tents. At one point, Chinese fighter jets flew over Everest's peak.

"Two thousand eight was wild," remembers Waters. "Suddenly, there are armed guards at Camp Two so no one can climb any higher for about a week. So what did people do? They had big parties. People were drinking, blasting music, going from one camp to the next, then ending up at Russell's dome for a big rave."

Heading off charges of base camp's reputation as a high-altitude frat house, he adds, "The partying back then felt pretty normal, though, for a group of people that simply knew they weren't going anywhere for four or five days because of the closure—which also happened often simply because of bad weather."

As Waters's story indicates, Brice and Himex found their footing in Nepal easily, picking up right where they'd left off in Tibet. "When I switched to the south side, I immediately was trying to figure out how to get the best radio reception and the best view of the climbers high on the mountain," says Brice. "We set up in a spot lower down on the glacier where we could actually see the summit through a telescope—there were people who had been coming to Everest for years who didn't even know you could see the summit from the base camp."

For some of the other guides and companies, there was more of a learning curve. "I'd never been to the south side before," says Crampton.

"I thought of the Nepal side as the place where AAI was charging sixty-five thousand dollars and Adventure Consultants was charging sixty thousand . . . I'm not even a certified guide. But when China closed the north, I still had clients, so I just thought, 'OK, let's try it.' And Oh. My. God . . . it was like night and day—the people are friendly, the climbing was easier, the weather was better, there's a constant supply of fresh vegetables and fresh meat . . . and the summit success rate was so much higher, because the route was so much easier.

"So, when I got up to Camp Two on the south side with my clients, I'm putting up my camp and there was a Western guide saying, 'Oh, no, you can't camp there.' I'm like, 'Why not?' He says, 'Well, we usually camp there—and by the way, shouldn't you be on the north side?' I just said, 'Well, you should fuck off. I've paid for my permit, I can do what I want.' I think the professional guides on the south side felt superior to us guys on the north—it was like a caste system."

Dan Mazur was also looked at warily by some of the south side's legacy guides, and sported a similarly unpolished attitude. Like Crampton, he was not a certified guide, but he was certainly an experienced mountaineer. Originally from Washington State, Mazur had been climbing in the Himalayas since 1991, which was also the first year he summited Everest. In the early 2000s, shortly after turning forty, he'd started Summit Climb to service a market of people like him—climbing bums who needed their expeditions organized but did not want to have their hands held. His trips cost about $30,000, and were for people who didn't care about fancy hotels in Kathmandu and gourmet meals at base camp, but just wanted the basics: access to Mazur's expertise and leadership (but not guiding), climbing Sherpas nearby as they ascended (though not necessarily side by side with them), rope-fixing prepared for them in advance, and basic food services and shelter provided. "To me, it's no different than choosing between flying first class and economy," Mazur says.

The model was a popular one, but those who ran fully guided, staffed, and resourced climbs, like Brice, Burleson, and Cotter, didn't like the looks of Mazur's setup. Interestingly, Simonson, who had long taken a similar approach that was barely tolerated by the pricier companies, didn't much like it either. He insisted there was no comparison between his trips and others in a similar price bracket. "It's all about contingencies and resources for emergencies," Simonson says. "We spent money on things like extra Sherpas, spare regulators, and extra oxygen up high. In my opinion, too many companies started cutting corners in those areas."

Other guides worried that Mazur didn't do nearly enough client vetting to ensure that he brought only the type of highly skilled and experienced climbers for whom his trips were best suited. As a result, his model relied on the climbers themselves needing to self-select and having an enormous amount of self-awareness—which can be in short supply among Everest clients. His nickname among the more traditional guides, "Danger Dan," reflected their concern, though Mazur thinks it's unwarranted.

"Dan was a thorn in many people's side," says Crampton. "I've known Dan now for twenty-five years, and I'm actually in the Dan Mazur fan club. I think he kind of takes pride in having the most basic, bare-bones, understaffed operation going. He thrives on it. And he doesn't give a shit what other people think. Though, I don't think Russell or Eric are big fans of Dan."

Mazur remained steadfast in his belief that people should have the free will to decide for themselves what type of expedition is right for them. And in the end, while his summit success rate was not as high as Himex's, for example, neither did he have an unusually high number of client fatalities, so his nickname was largely undeserved. That said, critics of the budget model argued that when these companies' clients needed rescuing—which some suggested happened too often—the better-equipped outfitters had to commit the resources and carry the operations out. Nonetheless, a lot of people who would not have otherwise been able to live out their Everest dream got the chance to do so by using Mazur's model.

Cotter believes that one of the reasons the model was so attractive was because Mazur hired Sherpa climbers for his expeditions with perhaps just one Western guide for the entire client group. "A lot of Westerners want to go back home and say, 'I climbed the mountain and I wasn't guided,'" Cotter says. "And since by then most Sherpas were not technically guides, the ego can suggest that the client made all the decisions themselves. But a lot of these people were complete basket cases and did need to be guided."

Mazur, on the other hand, points the finger back at those like Cotter who say that *he* is the one manufacturing a narrative of personal accomplishment on Everest.

"I've had very experienced people call and say they want less Sherpa assistance at a lower cost," he says. "I'd tell them we have a one-to-one ratio, which has been the requirement of the Nepalese government since 2016. They would say, 'But, the more expensive companies told me the same thing,' and I'd have to let them know that's just not true—I'm on that mountain every year and I see two, three, even four Sherpas per client. And they'd then ask, 'Well, why didn't they tell me that?' Because they didn't want you to feel like a total dweeb! It's like saying, 'Our clients are so weak they need one Sherpa for each arm and each leg.'"

As Greg Child claims, "I have yet to meet a person who was guided up Everest *admit* they were guided."

Yvon Chouinard just wishes that people who have been guided up Everest would stop calling themselves "climbers" and simply call themselves "clients." Or "hikers," even.

But few who went to Everest were interested in doing that. People wanted to imagine themselves summiting the tallest mountain in the world on their own steam. It was in part why in the 2000s, Everest clients got a reputation for being even more obnoxious, arrogant, and out of touch than they'd been in the 1990s. Unfortunately, there was some truth to it.

An oft repeated story you hear from veteran Everest guides is the one about the client who unboxed his new crampons for the first time at base camp and then put them on upside down—as in, sharp spikes digging into the sole of his boot instead of the icy ground they're meant to claw into. Only, it wasn't one client—it was several, each and every season.

"The bottom line is the clients coming to Everest were less focused on the actual climb and more focused on just the summit," says Benegas. "And they just thought, 'Oh, don't worry, my Sherpa will get me to the top,'" even if it's not what they would later tell their friends back home.

Alan Arnette is someone who heartily disagrees with all of this nay-saying about client climbers. At sixty-five, the Colorado native and former Hewlett-Packard executive is an authority on the matter of guides. He has joined ten separate guided Himalayan climbs—all but one on 8,000-meter peaks—and he has used five different guiding companies in the process. He climbed the Seven Summits using guides, and attempted Everest three times before summiting in 2011 with IMG. In the process, he attempted the mountain with more companies and a greater assortment of guides than anyone else on earth, and spent a cumulative nine months on the mountain, living cheek by jowl with dozens of other Everest clients during his expeditions. He's spent a half million dollars in the process.

"Anyone who reads my blog will find generous acknowledgment that I went on guided trips," he says.

"When I meet someone who has climbed Mount Everest with a guide, but never went on to climb anything else, I still have complete admiration for them. They set a really hard goal for themselves, they worked hard, they came back alive, perhaps they even summited. I'm not going to ask them how much oxygen they used or how many Sherpas they had, because, for them, none of that matters. All that matters is that they got something out of that experience. And just the fact that they're talking about it suggests that they are proud of their achievement."

After retiring from his day job in 2007, Arnette committed full-time to studying and writing about the high-altitude guiding industry for his personal, eponymous website, which has slowly accumulated over three million readers. Arnette became so connected over the years with the various guides, guide services, and Sherpas that he became like the Bob Costas of guided climbing. He even began providing regular reports for various news outlets and magazines, including *Outside*, during the climbing season. "I began to find a lot of satisfaction helping the common person get their story out," he says. "That's why you won't find stories on my website about pro climbers like Simone Moro or Ueli Steck. It's more Lisa in Atlanta, the sixty-two-year-old that wants to do the Seven Summits, or Latecia, the forty-two-year-old real estate agent from New Mexico, who wants to climb Everest."

He took his passion a step further when he began advertising his services as a "summit coach." For roughly a few thousand dollars, people can hire Arnette to help them through the entire process, from which boots to buy to which style of guided expedition suits them best, and which company to therefore choose.

Mark Horrell is another good-natured and self-deprecating former Everest client who provides more evidence that not everyone who wants to climb the mountain is a clueless, arrogant person. "I'm not a climber, but I was able to get up Everest—because it's not really a climb," says Horrell, who, through his own blog, has become a sort of British Alan Arnette. "But it was a ten-year journey that I'm proud of. I first went to Nepal in 2002 to do a bit of high-altitude trekking, then sort of gradually worked up, learned the skills, did my first eight-thousander in 2009, attempted a few more, then climbed Everest in 2012.

"The popular perception is that we are completely helpless if anything goes wrong. I don't think that's true, and I never really came across somebody like that in any of the guided expeditions that I've been on."

In 2010, 365 clients, Sherpa climbers, and independent climbers summited Everest and 0 clients or Sherpa climbers died. A thirteen-year-old American, an Indian teenager, and a twenty-two-year-old British woman summited—all setting age records for their countries.

A new generation of Sherpas working on Everest looked at these huge numbers of clients and saw an opportunity. Asian Trekking was still the only Nepali-owned guiding operation on the mountain. Though there were other sizable companies, like Thamserku Trekking, Beyul Travel & Trek, and, later, Himalayan Guides (not to be mistaken for Henry Todd's former guiding company, which ran its last trip on Everest in 2013), which were owned by business-savvy Nepalis and provided logistics to the Western guiding companies, they weren't marketing to clients directly, or packaging expeditions themselves, like Asian Trekking. Since its rocky start in 2006, Dawa Steven had led the company through the growing pains of its next few seasons, and it had emerged as one of the most profitable and influential on the mountain.

Many younger Sherpas began to feel frustrated with the way their upward mobility was determined by the otherwise entirely Western-owned companies. Often as a result of the money their parents had made in the Everest industry, these Sherpas had gotten educations in which they'd learned about things like class structure and nationalism. They'd also grown up in a country in which political, nationalistic, and identity-based violence was a daily reality. "The younger Nepalis working on Everest had grown up in a fairly chaotic, quasi–civil war environment," notes Freddie Wilkinson, a professional climber and journalist.

Nearly eighteen thousand Nepalis died in the Maoist conflict before the violence tapered off in 2006. (The Maoist party was ultimately integrated into the country's political system after winning a key election in 2008, though its reputation for violence stuck with it.)

"Nepali guides were butting heads against some Western climbers," Dawa Steven says. "In the old days, one of these guys might have said something disrespectful and Sherpas would have said, 'OK, sir.' This newer generation knew better. They had their own opinions, and we even began to feel like it was our territory—we were all of a sudden as equally qualified as these Western guides."

In the eyes of some younger Sherpas, it wasn't only the Westerners holding them back. To them, the previous generation of Sherpa climbers had been too docile and complacent. "I think Sherpas of my generation, who worked in the mountaineering industry, might think we have compromised too much," says professor Pasang Yangjee. "From [the younger Sherpas'] perspective, it's the total compromise—they're looking at the older generations and thinking, 'What were they thinking? Why didn't they ask for better pay? Why didn't they ask for more rights?' In some ways, that anger was directed toward the previous generation."

A few younger Sherpas began funneling that energy into starting their own businesses. In 2010, three brothers from the Makalu Valley—Mingma Sherpa, Chhang Dawa Sherpa, and Tashi Lakpa Sherpa—launched a company called Seven Summit Treks (SST). It was initially set up in the same way as the other Nepali logistics companies, but the brothers were always clear in announcing their intentions: they wanted to follow in the footsteps of Asian Trekking and offer fully guided Everest expeditions of their own as soon as possible. Because of their mountaineering résumés, people took them seriously.

The eldest brother, Mingma, had kicked off his high-altitude career in 2000, at age twenty-two, summiting both Manaslu and Cho Oyu while working for Nepal's largest back-end outfitter, Thamserku Trekking, and some independent expeditions. Then in 2004, he climbed Everest with his eighteen-year-old brother, Tashi Lakpa, while working for a Greek expedition. Tashi Lakpa continued to work on large numbers of successful Himalayan expeditions from there, while Mingma went on to become the first Nepali to climb all fourteen 8,000-meter peaks. The middle brother, Chhang Dawa, soon followed, becoming the second Nepali to complete them and also the youngest person in history to do so, at age thirty-two.

"I had lots of experience in the mountains and I had lots of contacts around the world," says Tashi Lakpa of the decision to start SST. He had led seven climbs on eight-thousanders by 2010, summiting Everest four times in the process. "Me and my two brothers, we were climbers—they had almost finished climbing all fourteen eight-thousand-meter mountains, and I had guided many, many expeditions. So we decided to work together and to open our company."

The brothers were indeed exceptional mountaineers, fast learners, and shrewd entrepreneurs. Tashi Lakpa, in particular, had been getting the same sort of intense on-the-job training as older Sherpas like Lakpa Rita had gotten, but there was a notable difference. He had done so while being hired out on expeditions by the Nepali-owned logistics company Thamserku Trekking, *not* while working for a Western outfit. That said, by 2010 there were enough experienced sirdars and even Sherpa lead guides on the mountain working for Western companies that a young Sherpa could also work for a company like AAI and apprentice entirely under Sherpas.

Two years after SST was founded, another company called Dreamers Destination emerged with the same aspiration to one day become a full guiding operation. The company was founded by four Sherpas, the most prominent of whom was Mingma Gyalje Sherpa, better known as Mingma G. His family had a long history in the mountains. "It wasn't my plan at all to go into the climbing business," says Mingma G. "But my father, my uncles, everyone in my family were high-altitude workers. I heard all their stories during my child-hood. After every season they would come home and talk about life on the mountain, about how hard they work, and also about how there were times they thought it was their last day. Fortunately, no one in my family was killed, but my father did end up losing eight fingers to frostbite back in 1983, working for an independent Japanese team. He had to have them amputated."

One of Mingma G.'s uncles invited him on a Manaslu climb in 2006, when he was twenty years old. One of the large Nepali logistics companies had been hired by foreign climbers to organize the opera-tions, and Mingma G.'s uncle was allowed to bring a few inexperi-enced workers. "I had such a good time climbing Manaslu with them," he remembers. "I made lots of new friends—it was the first time I was hanging out with foreign people. And I found that it was very dif-ferent from how people described it. So, after that, I got a little more addicted. Then I joined another expedition the same year and then again the next year. This time it was Everest and I summited for the first time."

In 2010, Mingma G. summited Everest for the second time, but learned a painful lesson in the process. "I had a really bad experi-ence," he remembers. "I was with a Western climber who was using the company I was working for, and two more senior Sherpas. The Westerner was climbing well and even summited. But then he started having a problem with his chest. We think he had a heart attack. But he was still alive so we began trying to get him down—we basically had to carry him. It was so hard. We were all putting in a lot of effort but it was not as quick as we wanted, and in the way we wanted. We spent all day and all night getting him down to Camp Four—and then he died right in front of his tent. It was such a pity. And it was because we didn't have the skills for rescue—we had no formal training."

Mingma G. became resolute in attaining the same technical skills as his Western counterparts. He signed up for basic mountaineering training through the NMA in 2010 and enrolled in his first IFMGA training in 2012, the same year he founded Dreamers Destination.

16

COLLAPSE

The spring 2012 season presented the first in a series of stress tests for the evolving Everest guiding industry. It was the twenty-year anniversary of the first paying clients being guided to the top and back down safely: an important milestone. But there was an ominous feeling around base camp as the outfitters and then clients arrived. It was unusually warm that year, with wildfires raging in the hills of the low country. The Icefall Doctors were fixing the ropes and ladders in T-shirts. It was also exceptionally dry, with not quite enough snowfall to glue things in place. As a result, giant blocks of glacial ice were melting and breaking free around the Khumbu Icefall.

The icefall was "very scary," says Freddie Wilkinson, who was at base camp reporting on the season for *Rock and Ice* magazine, while also participating in some acclimatization climbs with his good friend and fellow Mountain Hardwear–sponsored climber Ueli Steck.

"Just about every time we were going through the Khumbu Icefall the Sherpas were dodging falling blocks of ice," says Brice. "Day after day after day, the Sherpas were running for their lives." Brice was particularly worried about one block of ice and snow hanging right above the icefall route.

The trajectory of that route was a source of tension between the Sherpas and the Western guides. "For years, [the route] went up the middle and to the right a little," Dave Hahn says. "But in 2005 there was a small avalanche that killed three Sherpas—one from IMG and two from Alpine Ascents—so, moving it to the left was kind of in reaction to that. But it started going a little too far left each year." In 2012, it had moved very far left, high and tight against the wall of the west ridge, where many of the hanging snowfields were breaking free from the mountainside and plunging down and detonating on the icefall. Some Western guides asked the Sherpas to consider moving the route, but it didn't go over well. The Icefall Doctors said they knew how to do their job. After all, they were the ones who had to travel through the gantlet most often.

"Once the icefall became a way for the Sherpas to make money, we lost control of where the route went," says Burleson. "We were told to stay out of it."

The tension was compounded by the ever-greater number of clients—particularly inexperienced ones—who were bringing ever-growing loads of gear with them. That meant larger teams of load-carrying Sherpas were required to ferry the goods through the icefall to the higher camps.

An antsy Brice finally had enough. He took a look at the situation and did one of the hardest things an Everest operator can do—even harder than turning a client around near the summit. He canceled Himex's entire spring 2012 expedition. Brice was known to be the only company owner who would wake up at two a.m. every time his Sherpas were doing a rotation through the icefall to personally see them off. "It wasn't just a feeling," Brice told Wilkinson. "We take records of temperatures when the Sherpas leave for the icefall in the morning. Normally, it's about seven degrees. The last day our Sherpas went through, it was *thirty-two degrees.* It was like sending guys out to war—you don't know who is coming home."

While Brice felt the conditions had crossed the line between acceptable and unacceptable risk, it turned out that he was the only one who felt this way. "Russell came and told us he was pulling the plug—and he suggested we do the same," remembers Greg Vernovage, IMG's most senior Everest expedition leader. "A lot of teams look at Russell and think he's the be-all and end-all. But I just wasn't quite ready to do that. We stayed. And we got to the summit." IMG put a whopping forty-two people on the summit that season, to be exact.

The mass-casualty event Brice feared thankfully didn't happen, though he points out that just a few weeks after he backed out, a huge block of ice above Camp Three toppled and crushed three of Jagged Globe's tents, which would have killed fifteen people if they were full. It was pure luck nobody was in them. Yet, in the end, it turned out to be a surprisingly successful summit season for most teams on the mountain. In the spring of 1992, nine client climbers had summited from the Nepal side under the guidance of two companies. In the spring of 2012, nearly two hundred client climbers successfully summited Everest from the Nepal side on expeditions run by about sixteen different companies.

While some guides felt reassured—proud, even—by the fact that so many people were reaching the top and that the ominous feeling at the start of the season hadn't resulted in a high number of fatalities, others, like Brice, simply lived with the dread that their luck couldn't last forever. Weather remained a concern, but not nearly as much as the increasingly large crowds and the inexperience of those climbers. There were climbers and guides who reported running into large, poorly managed groups high on the mountain in 2012. Wilkinson's *Rock and Ice* article cited "reports of hundreds of climbers logjammed and poised for disaster."

With the intersecting tensions of large numbers of companies and clients, uncertain weather conditions, and ambitious young Sherpas frustrated with the status quo and with designs on carving out a different future, Wilkinson sensed a worrying dynamic that spring, even if he couldn't quite put his finger on it. In his article, he posited a question: Would 2012 be "a harbinger of a more dangerous chapter on the mountain's history?"

It was a prescient question.

Before Simone Moro, Ueli Steck, and Jonathan Griffith even made it back to base camp on April 27, 2013, news of their fight with the Sherpas was already one of the top stories around the world. Shaky cell phone footage taken of the standoff and the physical attacks in front of the Europeans' tents was must-see TV for the Everest junkies, a vivid manifestation of a type of instability on the mountain that was social instead of natural, but just as tectonic. "That fight was a dream come true for the media," says David Hamilton. "Not the fight itself, but that this is what it had come to, from the days of Hillary and Tenzing, it had just devolved from there. Just as everyone expected, rich Western climbers were at odds with Sherpas."

It was achingly obvious that this was about much more than the day itself. *Outside* published a Q&A with Tashi Riten Sherpa—the young IMG employee who had been involved in escalating the fight—in which he aired his grievances. "Sherpas have all along respected the foreign climbers. All of us respect them. The relation has been that of trust and friendship. But it got a bad name due to one person—Simone," Tashi Riten said.

The much more senior IMG rope-fixer, Mingma Tenzing, who had been angry but not aggressive at the time, reacted entirely differently. He was so devastated by seeing how fragile the relationship between the

Westerners and Sherpas had become that he retired after the 2013 season. It was a great loss not only to IMG but also to the Everest guiding industry in general, and it underscored the generational split visible to those looking closely between the younger and older Sherpa climbers.

Meanwhile, a number of Western guides felt that the hype over the incident was being wildly overblown in the media. "Once again, they were ignoring stories about all these people that are getting along great to tell the story of some asshole," Hamilton says. It's unclear in his account whether the asshole was one of the European climbers or one of the Sherpa rope-fixers.

Vernovage felt that the coverage had flattened the situation to a ridiculous proportion, turning the four hundred or so Sherpas on the mountain into a single entity: the Angry Sherpa Mob. "The angry mob is a falsehood," he says. "It was basically that fender-bender that everyone slows down for. I personally believe there were also quite a few Sherpas there that day that would have stopped it from going any further."

While the motivation for the industry's stakeholders, particularly the Western guides, to downplay the incident's severity was understandable, the media wasn't prepared to look away anytime soon. And they were landing some blows. In July 2013, *Outside*'s newest Everest correspondent, Grayson Schaffer, published the most thorough and damning report to date on the numbers of Sherpas who had died over the years while working in the industry. Sadly, there were four Sherpa deaths in the spring 2013 season alone to cite, two from falling in crevasses, and two from cardiac or cerebral events related to altitude. "A Sherpa working above Base Camp on Everest is nearly ten times more likely to die than a commercial fisherman," he wrote, "and more than three and a half times as likely to perish than an infantryman during the first four years of the Iraq war. As a dice roll for someone paying to reach the summit, the dangers of climbing can perhaps be rationalized. But as a workplace safety statistic, 1.2 percent mortality is outrageous." While Schaffer's math was rightfully criticized for being misleading and creating false equivalencies, it was impossible to argue with his assertion that Sherpa deaths "unfold each year in relative obscurity" and that "Western out-fitters, guides, and their clients rarely witness the true fallout." Sherpa families suffered out of sight.

And yet, neither the Westerners wanting to downplay what the fight revealed about the inner workings of Everest, nor the Sherpas hoping to draw attention to disparity in the industry, were ready to press pause on Everest and take stock. They all had families to support and taxes to pay. 547 total people ended up summiting from the Nepal side in 2013, up significantly over the previous year. After being let go from IMG, Tashi Riten joined up with Ryan Waters at Mountain Professionals. It would take something truly impossible to ignore, and beyond human control, for the industry to pause and reflect.

In the spring of 2014, Everest employees might have had a slight hangover from the year before, but they showed up to work as usual. Once again, the route through the icefall was set beneath the wall of the west ridge, far to the left of where it had been a decade earlier. At first light on April 18, approximately two hundred high-altitude workers began arriving at the foot of the icefall and making their way through it, carrying gear to cache at Camps One and Two. The majority of these workers were Sherpas, though men and women from other ethnic groups like the Gurung or Tamang, who were typically less experienced, were there as well.

The Nepali workers were ferrying loads for the fifty expeditions that were based on the Khumbu Glacier that season, and trying to trans-port as many creature comforts for them as physically possible. Moving along at different paces in small groups, the workers were spread out along the entire icefall as morning progressed.

The ever-efficient Brice sent nineteen Himex Sherpa workers through the icefall very early that morning. Brice was meticulous about radio communication with his team. "Our climbing Sherpas radioed us from Camp One letting us know that there was a problem with one of the ladders in the icefall and that we needed the Icefall Doctors to get on it," he remembers. The Himex Sherpas were skilled enough to improvise a safe way to cross and reached Camp One by sunrise. However, they knew that others behind them may be significantly slowed down or stopped altogether.

Indeed, a ladder spanning one of the larger crevasses had come loose. A little after five a.m., as groups of load-carriers arrived at that area from other companies, a bottleneck began to form. From what the expedition leaders and sirdars could gather, the load-carriers' plan was to sit and wait until the Icefall Doctors arrived. This was somewhat unusual, as, by then, many Sherpas either had the skill to fix the ladders themselves or the experience to know they should instead drop their loads and descend back down to the safety of base camp while the Icefall Doctors worked. Nonetheless the workers sat in the icefall, waiting. The sun rose. Temperatures crept up.

Ang Tshering Sherpa, a sixty-year-old longtime AAI Camp Two cook, who had just opened his own guesthouse in his home village of Thamo, was one of the people waiting. An experienced forty-year-old high-altitude worker named Dorje Khatri, who was from a lowland village called Taplejung and had almost exclusively worked on the Tibet side before 2014, also waited. So did a talented thirty-five-year-old Sherpa climber named Ang Kaji, who was a close friend of Conrad Anker's, having climbed with him several times. They were planning to go to Makalu together the following year.

The group waited for about ninety minutes. At six forty-five a.m., with the Icefall Doctors still not having arrived, a hanging block of ice the size of a fifty-foot ocean wave silently broke away from the wall above. "You don't necessarily hear them when they fall," says Hahn, who was asleep in base camp at the time. "But when they land, the sound is like thunder and the feeling is a lot like an earthquake."

The block smashed onto the icefall and exploded into a cloud of what was essentially freezing wet concrete, plummeting toward its upper section and becoming an avalanche that barreled toward the exact spot where the workers were sitting waiting for the ladder crossing to be repaired, pouring down on them and then setting around them. Thirteen of the high-altitude workers died almost instantly, either entombed in snow, torn apart, or crushed to death. Ang Tshering, Dorje Khatri, and Ang Kaji were all killed. Three more workers would later succumb to their injuries. Several others survived but were seriously hurt.

The following days were a chaotic blur of rescues, helicopter evacuations, and body recoveries. Mountain guides are particularly talented when dealing with trauma, but they say this was like nothing any of them had ever seen. Images of the mutilated corpses lingered hauntingly in their minds.

It was the single worst tragedy in a century of climbing on Everest—and all the victims were Nepali. Not a single Western guide or climber was hurt.

Anger and sadness welled up at base camp. "Many of those Sherpas who died were carrying Persian rugs, propane tanks, all kinds of useless junk that you don't need up at Camp Two," says Mazur. He is still raw about it to this day, believing the 2014 tragedy was a prime example of how the unnecessary comforts provided by luxury companies, especially higher on the mountain, can be deadlier than the low-cost operation he runs.

Another understandable cause of fury was the fact that the workers were reportedly carrying sizable loads for an NBC adventure-sports documentary production that many considered pointless. Dozens of plastic

Pelican cases holding delicate camera equipment were being shuttled through the icefall in the early days of the 2014 season, intended to capture an American wingsuit daredevil, Joby Ogwyn, become the first to "fly" off the summit of Everest. Ogwyn didn't help matters by announcing after the avalanche that he wanted to continue his attempt "in the name of the Sherpas."

"Americans are always dedicating something to someone," says Dawa Steven.

A four-day ban on climbing was put in place, which was eventually extended to seven days. Those who were on Everest that year remember witnessing the Sherpas initially gathering to discuss how they could possibly continue working in the guiding industry. This business was their livelihood, but they needed a voice. Power. Reforms. At the very least, they wanted larger insurance payouts to families if heads of household were killed or disabled working in the mountains. But they had been asking for this for years, as had many of their Western employers, including Brice. The payouts came from private insurance companies, which were required and regulated by the Nepali government, but Western guide owners were considered influential in helping to lobby for improvements to the scheme. Widows and families of those killed on Everest were still receiving only between $3,000 and $4,000.

The discussions among the Sherpas initially morphed into rather tame protest demonstrations. "Send stronger ladders!" someone would yell from the crowd; others would cheer in response. Nevertheless, Brice recalls a tense meeting in the SPCC tent between the local liaison officer and some of the Sherpas. "A brawl almost broke out," he says. Then, among a core group of younger Sherpas, including Pasang Tenzing Sherpa, a former Jagged Globe sirdar, an idea took root of how they might be able to finally exert even more meaningful pressure to demand change: a good, old-fashioned strike.

As with the 2013 conflict, not everyone was on board with the confrontational movement, especially among the older Sherpas. A strike would effectively end the climbing season, which would have grave financial consequences for many families throughout the Khumbu Valley and beyond. Some Sherpas felt the season should continue, not only for the livelihoods of the workforce, but for the simple fact that climbing mountains does not stop when people die. But a vocal few were adamant about the shutdown and continued rallying support among the hundreds of Sherpas and other Nepali workers at base camp that season. Even longtime sirdars like Himex's Phurba Tashi, who did not at first agree with the move to strike, eventually fell into line.

Some Western guides and media outlets once again seemed alarmed to have their preferred stereotype of the Sherpas as happy, smiling people thrown into doubt. "After the [2013] fight, the word 'militant' came to be associated with Sherpas," says Pasang Yangjee. "Even those of us on the outside of the mountaineering industry felt like we needed to reclaim our name."

"People were accusing them of being aggressive again," says Tenzing Norgay's eldest living son, Norbu Tenzing, who is vice president of the American Himalayan Foundation, based in San Francisco. "From the Western point of view, they thought, 'Oh, these people have changed, they're now demanding things.' What people forget is all they were doing was fighting for their rights—for the first time! Sherpas have a lot of pride." Though Western guides were unanimous in their support for higher insurance payouts to Sherpas killed or injured on the mountain, none were prepared to put their wallets and business reputations on the line by joining the strike in order to send a stronger message to the Nepali government. Brice, in trying to save the season, chartered a helicopter from base camp to Kathmandu to ask government officials to come and address the Sherpas' demands in person. He went so far as to request police or military security be positioned in Pheriche, a ten-minute helicopter ride from base camp, in case the meeting went badly. He was denied. Some saw Brice's actions as honorable; others saw them as tone deaf. After all, Brice was under financial pressure from having canceled his 2012 season. Some of his clients from 2012 were now back in 2014 and wanting their long-awaited shot at the top. Though Brice started to get some traction with the government, it wasn't enough to move the needle.

In the end, the Sherpas were resolute: they wanted to end the season and had the momentum to do it. They seized the tragic moment and used it as a wake-up call to show in no uncertain terms that guided climbing was impossible without them. If there were no Sherpas working, there was no Everest industry. Period.

The wounds of 2014—both physical and emotional—had only begun to heal when inexplicable tragedy struck once again.

On April 25, 2015, almost one year to the day after the Khumbu Icefall avalanche, Nepal was struck by a magnitude 7.8 earthquake. The quake triggered an avalanche off Pumori, right near Everest, and the thick cloud of ice and snow barreled straight through base camp, like an Arctic typhoon. Nineteen people were killed this time, ten of them Sherpas. The other nine were foreign climbers and trekkers, including Marisa Eve Girawong—Garrett Madison's girlfriend and the Madison Mountaineering expedition doctor—and a Google executive who had been working on bringing the company's "Street View" feature to Everest. Base camp was turned into a postapocalyptic wasteland of mangled tents and piles of rubble. The force of the blast hurled bodies far and wide; there was blood streaked across the glacier. It resembled a battlefield and, indeed, compounded the PTSD many guides and rescuers had been dealing with in the aftermath of the avalanche. For the second year in a row—and only the third time since 1953—the season was canceled.

Thankfully, there were few casualties in the Khumbu Valley outside

Everest base camp, but elsewhere, especially around Kathmandu, the damage was staggering. Ancient stone and brick buildings in the capital were reduced to rubble. Historic temples disappeared in seconds, as if demolished by dynamite. Entire villages needed to be rebuilt. In all, approximately nine thousand Nepalis were killed.

The earthquake was a breaking point, not just for Sherpas, but for the industry as a whole.

"2015 was . . . oof," says Vernovage—who was there again that year leading IMG's expeditions. "I wouldn't wish any human being to go through those two days at base camp. My hope is just that I was a better expedition leader because of those two years."

Hahn, the most respected guide on Everest at that point—the Western climber with the most summits and most experience on the mountain, who had been coming there for twenty years, who had helped dozens of client climbers achieve their dream of summiting—was done. He retired from guiding Everest after 2015. "Yeah, I got thrown off the horse," he says. "I went to Everest twenty-one times. I went to eight-thousand-meter peaks twenty-four times. At a certain point I was going to need to figure out how to stop. If not for the disasters, I don't know that I would've had the discipline or good sense to quit.

"I found myself doing a whole lot of defending against this idea that we were exploiting the Sherpas, which I didn't think was true," says Hahn. "But it was becoming a pretty tough argument to make with that avalanche death toll."

One of the hardest things for Hahn in 2015 was the feeling of helplessness, as he and hundreds of others were stuck at Camp One when the earthquake hit. "I remember sitting up at Camp One after the earthquake with the other guides, trying to figure out what we should do," says Hahn. "But it wasn't, 'What will six or eight of us do?' like it used to be, in which case, we probably all could have rappelled down the icefall. It was now, 'What will two hundred of us do?' That's a really different question. Maybe there's just not that much room for an industry on Everest. Things like avalanches have always happened on the mountain; there just were never five hundred people under them. And the torture for us was knowing—understanding what was happening at base camp via the radio—and not being able to help. We knew that our teammates—our friends—were going through living hell down there, and we were fine. But we were trapped. If you're an Everest guide or expedition leader, you're a control freak. I didn't feel like I could be in control anymore."

AAI's lead guide, David Morton, also quit. "Having Sherpas dying is just hard to watch over and over," he told *Outside* magazine. "At some point you're exacerbating it by participating in it."

Four straight years of conflict, stress, and loss, from 2012 to 2015, and unthinkable back-to-back tragedies in the previous two years, forced just about everyone to pause and reflect. It was impossible for Hahn, Morton, and others like them to justify the ever-growing industry on a mountain that had perhaps reached its limits for safety and success. The larger guided groups were simply too unwieldy and unpredictable. It seemed as if the goddess mother of earth, Sagarmatha, was giving her children a time-out.

It was right at this moment of reckoning, at the close of the canceled 2015 season, that two films about Everest were released. One was backward looking, the other forward looking, and their vast differences gave those paying attention to the mountain much to think about.

17

EVEREST THROUGH *a* LENS

Everest is photogenic. Film crews have always been drawn to it, whether to make awe-inspiring *Planet Earth*–style nature documentaries or pulse-quickening climbing movies. Some painted Everest as the tragic, overcrowded mess, some as the majestic natural wonder, some as the ultimate symbol of human triumph.

Two important Everest films had their major festival premieres two weeks apart in 2015, just months after the earthquake. They each presented a very different way of looking at the mountain, but both showed how art could be a powerful tool for better understanding Everest.

After making his trip to Everest in 2004 and putting a lot of thought into it, director Stephen Daldry had decided to bow out of the Hollywood-backed feature about the 1996 disaster. "There was something about the story that was both bizarre and heartbreaking," he says. "But after spending quite a lot of time—and, I have to say, quite a lot of the movie studio's money—I began to see it as a story of hubris. And I wasn't convinced that was a story that everybody wants to watch. It seemed insurmountable—and I couldn't find a way through the story that didn't somehow end up with hubris.

"It felt a little bit like we would always be looking at the characters in the story through a prism. Take the woman with the cappuccino machine, for example. Sandy Hill actually had a lot of experience. And I couldn't find a way for the film not to sort of feel like it was going to say, 'Well, that'll teach them.' It would not be a story about people behaving heroically. It would be a story about a load of people who shouldn't have been there in the first place."

Despite Daldry's exit, the producer Tim Bevan remained passionate about getting the film made. "After Daldry left the project, we had all these different versions of a script," he says. "Because the 1996 story is so sprawling, in terms of the number of characters, it actually just got too big, too long. In the end, we decided to make it more the Rob Hall story."

It was rumored that David Fincher was attached to the film for a time, but after nearly a decade of stops and starts on the project, Bevan finally connected with the up-and-coming director Baltasar Kormákur. Together they got the production underway in 2014.

Kormákur was a rugged outdoor type who felt a deep connection to the powerful forces of nature that he'd grown up with in Iceland. "[When] people were asking me how I prepared for the shoot I just said, 'By walking to school every morning,'" he quipped. He was determined to cast actors who were willing to travel outside their comfort zone and experience at least some of the discomfort and majesty of Everest as a team. Josh Brolin signed on to play Adventure Consultants client Beck Weathers; John Hawkes was cast as Doug Hansen; Jake Gyllenhaal emerged as the perfect Scott Fischer; Michael Kelly was set to play Jon Krakauer; and Jason Clarke was cast as Rob Hall.

In January 2014, the actors hiked sections of the route to base camp, with camera crews nearby, before taking sightseeing flights over the icefall and, in Clarke's case, into the Western Cwm. Not all of them were well prepared. "I had one actor crying, saying, 'I don't want to be doing this, can you let me off the movie?'" says Kormákur. "They couldn't have their assistants with them. But I wanted them on that journey and to at least touch the bottom of the mountain."

The New Zealand–born Clarke didn't have any such complaints. He had been trekking in the Himalayas before he was ever attached to the film and had climbed with guides on several lower peaks around the world. "When the actual event happened in 1996, I remember I was doing a play in Sydney," he says. "I went outside for a smoke—I think we were doing tech rehearsals—and it was on the news. This guy was up there on the mountain saying goodbye to his wife."

During preproduction, Clarke, Bevan, and Kormákur were invited by Jan Arnold to come to New Zealand and listen to the tape of her and Rob's final phone call, as Rob lay dying near the South Summit. Clarke was overwhelmed, analyzing every word, every pause, anything that might help him understand Rob.

"For a long time, I really wanted to know exactly what happened," says Clarke.

"I had a timeline, I read all the books, I interviewed everybody . . . Was there actually oxygen at the South Summit? Who's at fault? What went wrong? I got really obsessed with it. I read Rob's diaries to give me an idea of who the man was but also thought long and hard about what Rob's duty was in that situation, with regards to himself and the contract that passed between him and Doug. And it goes nowhere. The whole finger-pointing thing becomes pointless in the end. It was all about what happened in one single moment. I just tried to imagine it."

The moment Clarke is referring to is the one that remains the biggest mystery of the 1996 tragedy. Hall had summited but Hansen was still on his way up, way past the agreed-on turnaround time. Hall walked down to intercept Hansen but instead of telling Hansen to descend with him, decided instead to turn around and help him to the top. What exactly had caused Hall to make this crucial guiding mistake?

"This is the pivotal moment for me," says Kormákur. "Rob was a good man. He had been there with Doug before, he wanted him to summit. Doug was not like some top doctor that could pay for this every year. He had been saving and this was his life dream."

Clarke is of the mind that no one will ever know exactly what caused Hall to make the decision—the altitude, the competition with Fischer, the pressure of having a journalist along, the loyalty to his client and desire to get him to the top, or all of the above. In the end, for him, the film wasn't about sorting through facts and creating a perfectly accurate record of what happened. It was about a single look toward the summit, which is just forty feet above them, and then back to Hansen. It was perhaps the moment in the movie that baffled viewers most—as in horror films when a character steps over a dead body to investigate a darkened hallway instead of turning and running. "I just tried to give that moment enough so you know there's three or four scenarios running through Rob's head," Clarke says.

Having heard the tapes and read Hall's diaries, Clarke came to believe that *Hall* believed there was still hope, even when he and Hansen got stuck in bad weather. "I think Rob fully intended to make it down with Doug," says Clarke. "I've listened to those tapes, and it was put to Rob several times that perhaps he should leave Doug behind and save himself. But Rob still sounded strong and there was one comment he made: 'We're not at that point yet.'"

Most of the mountaineering footage involving the primary cast was filmed in the Italian Alps, but Bevan and Kormákur badly wanted to use as much real footage of Everest as possible, so Baltasar hired a climber and cinematographer from Colorado with Everest experience named Kent Harvey as a second-unit director. After working with the actors in the Alps, Harvey headed to Everest base camp in the spring of 2014.

The plan was to get footage all the way to the summit. But after the avalanche, it was clear that wasn't going to happen. "Considering this was a movie about Everest, there was surprisingly little shot on Everest," says Harvey. "In the end, what they created in the visual effects department was impressive."

In contemplating the fact that he was on the mountain to help film a re-creation of a major tragedy when another major tragedy struck, Harvey says that there's "a relevance there, but Hollywood doesn't give a shit and no matter what trauma happens on Everest there is still going to be a line of people the next year to go climb it."

Everest premiered at the Venice Film Festival on September 2, 2015. The film made $200 million, worldwide. Krakauer hated it and broke his self-imposed vow of silence on all things Everest to say so in an interview with a *Los Angeles Times* reporter. Harvey says he liked the film even though he knew the hard-core climbing community would never embrace it. Clarke was proud of it too, but when asked if he'd like to climb Everest himself someday, he said, "Nah, it's just too busy. And there are too many other beautiful mountains around."

That the Everest movie Hollywood finally made in 2015 was about the disaster of 1996 was telling, in much the same way it was telling that reporters still reached out to Jon Krakauer for comment about Everest, even though it had been nearly twenty years since he'd climbed it.

To many, the release of the film was proof of how little had changed on the mountain since one of its darkest days. The Sherpa and Western climbers who were actually on Everest in 2014 and 2015 knew better. Change was happening, and it was unstoppable.

It was at base camp in the spring of 2014 that Kent Harvey met Jennifer Peedom, an Australian filmmaker who was on the mountain that season to make a movie of her own. The two became friends, bonding over the challenge they both faced trying to do similar jobs. Peedom was also an experienced mountain filmmaker. She had been part of several documentary productions over the years, including having been one of the Discovery Channel producers who followed Brice around for the *Everest: Beyond the Limit* show.

"After I worked on the Discovery Channel series with Russell, I started seeing comments from Sherpas asking why their faces were so rarely seen in the show. They're wondering, 'Why aren't they showing the work we do?'" Taking the criticism to heart, Peedom made a short documentary about Sherpas for an Australian broadcaster. "I took it back to Nepal and showed it to some of these Sherpas I'd worked with and I immediately became folded into their lives—they were just so grateful that someone had chosen to take their point of view," she says. She then decided to make a feature-length documentary called *Sherpa.* "My original intention was to show how it really works, specifically the disproportionate risks that the Sherpa make in order to get a foreigner—even a semicompetent climber—up Everest. And after that fight in 2013, boy, we had no trouble financing the film."

Peedom decided to build her film around the seventeen-year friendship between Brice and Phurba Tashi but was clear from the start that the primary focus was "to follow an expedition from a Sherpa's point of view," as descriptions of the film put it. Brice agreed to be interviewed extensively for the movie and even agreed to help train a couple key Sherpa cameramen. "It was supposed to be about how great the relationship was, or so I was told," he says.

Brice and Phurba Tashi shared a bond with the mountain that perhaps went deeper than any other in their lives, including with their kin. "He loves the mountain more than his family," says Phurba Tashi's wife, tearfully, in an interview for the film. "What can I say," Phurba Tashi responds. "I like doing this work. I feel good doing this work." Brice was similarly enmeshed with Everest. Unlike other company owners, he continued to return each and every season to lead his enormous Himex teams. He spent so much time in Himalayan base camps throughout the year, many wondered if he even had a home to go back to.

In 2014, Phurba Tashi was forty-three years old and had summited Everest twenty-one times. He was aiming for his twenty-second that spring, which would be a new record. Brice was sixty-four years old and was by far the most experienced expedition leader on the mountain, if not in the world. Brice had led twenty-three Everest expeditions, and gotten approximately four hundred clients, guides, and Sherpas to the top. In all those expeditions, he had *zero* client deaths and *zero* climbing fatalities. (Two Sherpas had died, one from pulmonary edema and one from a stroke, likely brought on by altitude; both were considered unavoidable.) Brice was, without a doubt, one of the most influential pioneers of the guiding industry on Everest, and just about everything having to do with climbing the mountain had his fingerprints on it.

The year 2014 proved to be a fulcrum for the mountain, for Brice, and for the entire Western guiding industry, and Peedom's cameras were there to capture it all in real time. They were rolling the moment the block of ice fell onto the icefall: the raw footage shows an atomic bomb–like cloud of ice and snow engulfing the upper part of the glacier. They were rolling during the rescue operation, taking brutal images of dead Sherpas being removed from the impact zone by helicopter lines. And they were rolling as the Sherpa strike got underway.

"It's not workable for us," Brice said to the camera, when asked what he thought of the Sherpas' decision, unable to hide his frustration. "We can't have this happening every time there is an accident, every season. But I'm confident we'll recover the season if we act now."

Peedom then captured Brice boarding the helicopter to fly from base camp to Kathmandu to request an emergency meeting with the Ministry of Tourism about insurance payouts to Sherpas killed on the mountain. He convinced a team of government officials to return to base camp with him and attempt to address the Sherpas' grievances in a way that might save the season. But it wasn't enough, and Brice's decision comes off in the film as self-serving and missing the point in a moment of high emotion.

When the strike was underway but it still seemed to Brice there was a possibility of saving the season, he became visibly angry upon hearing rumors that some Sherpas were threatening violence toward any others that broke the strike and continued working. "These guys are ruining your reputation," Brice told his own Sherpa team, as shown in the documentary. He then told his clients, who were eagerly awaiting news about whether they might still be able to try to summit, "Effectively, what these militant Sherpas are saying is that if our Sherpas go through the icefall they'll beat them up. As far as I know our Sherpas want to climb but they fear for their life." This of course left the Himex clients angry with the Sherpas.

Phurba Tashi was later asked on camera whether there were any threats of violence. "No," he said, shaking his head.

"I had empathy for Russell's situation," Peedom says today. "Russell had a number of returning clients from the season that was canceled and they did not want to be canceled on again. One of Russell's clients was a very rich American lawyer—Russell knew he would probably be sued by him. I feel all the Western operators were working together on how to spin the narrative so that they wouldn't get sued by their clients . . . I do think Russell tried to create a villain—the Sherpa—as a way to protect himself."

Sherpa played on the major festival circuit and had its North American premiere on September 15, 2015, at the Toronto Film Festival. It was nominated for a number of major awards including Best Documentary Feature at the BAFTAs (often referred to as the British Oscars).

"You should see the hate mail I get from people watching that *Sherpa* movie," Brice says today. He's dismayed about how much he feels the documentary *didn't* show. "We were expecting to have an avalanche in the icefall at some stage," he says. "This is why I always insisted on radios for the Sherpas, so we could account for each and every one of them as they moved through different sections. We had placed big steel shovels for rescue at various points in the icefall, in case of an emergency. We had medical equipment at the beginning and in the middle of the icefall. That's why we were able to maneuver so quickly when it did happen—I don't think that documentary showed any of that."

He's right. Brice was without a doubt the most innovative expedition leader on Everest when it came to reducing risk and fatalities, and it's in large part because of his quick actions to mobilize rescue efforts in response to the avalanche, as well as the safety systems he had been a driving force in getting put into place over the years, that rescue and body recovery happened as quickly as it did. Brice took pride in that. And yet, when he talks in the film about recovering the Sherpas killed on the icefall, he sounds a little like an FAA inspector going into great detail about how a jet engine's fuel injectors work in addressing the families of people who have just died in a plane crash.

The film also didn't do much to demonstrate the efforts Himex made to reduce the amount of time its Sherpas and clients spent in the icefall. Himex's clients were the only ones who regularly acclimatized by climbing a nearby peak called Lobuche, instead of by going up to the first few camps on Everest. This meant not only they, but Himex's Sherpas, could make fewer laps through the icefall, as clients spending less time on the mountain needed less food and supplies at the higher camps. In the film, it is pointed out that while Brice's clients are away climbing Lobuche, the Himex Sherpas are still ferrying loads through the icefall to stock Camps One and Two, but it is not explained that this was a calculation by Brice that would reduce their total amount of time spent in the icefall.

Peedom says the studio cut ten minutes of footage explaining how Brice had been the only outfitter to cancel his 2012 season due to safety concerns, and regrets that this section of the film was lost, as it would have gone a long way to explain the pressure he was under in 2014. Yet the primary questions her film was interested in exploring were about the power dynamics on the mountain, and that's where her focus remained.

"I know Russell cares about Phurba Tashi and his family, and his whole Sherpa team," says Peedom. "I also know he's done more than most other operators to protect his team. But here's the thing: like a lot of these original Everest guide company owners, he's of a certain era—a *Westerner* of a certain era. They are very old school and can be very paternalistic. In their mind they are the good guys. And I don't necessarily dispute that."

"I just don't buy the whole downtrodden Sherpa thing," says Simonson, never having been someone to hold back how he feels—even when he knows he might have to apologize later. He says he never believed the Sherpas were really all that concerned with power imbalances so long as they could send their children to good schools and live a relatively easy life in a country where very few do. But the measuring stick of the power broker and the measuring stick of the aggrieved are two different instruments.

In truth, all major Western-owned Everest guide companies had long been making significant contributions to the Sherpa communities, including Simonson. He had always handed out cash directly to the families of IMG Sherpas who had died working on the mountain—something that many of the other owners did as well. Burleson had founded the Alpine Ascents Foundation in 1999 with the primary purpose of enabling better education in the rural mountain regions by raising money and funding school construction. The foundation built a preschool in Namche Bazaar. And two guides, Melissa Arnot and David Morton, created the Juniper

Fund in 2012 to provide support to people in Nepal who had lost a family member on an expedition.

But these philanthropic efforts were largely unknown or dismissed. Some Western owners were even accused of using their charitable foundations as a tax dodge. More to the point, the younger Sherpas noticed that while the Western operators mostly resisted the 2014 strike, Asian Trekking, along with the large Nepali-owned logistics companies, stood in solidarity with them. They also looked toward the newer company SST, which had been hoping to fulfill its promise and launch its first fully guided Everest expedition in the spring of 2014, but decided instead to join the strike and support the cancelation of the season.

Many young Sherpas decided that relying on the Westerners for systemic change was a fool's errand. Like Asian Trekking, SST, and Dreamers Destination, they would make their own future. In this way, Peedom's film ended up documenting not only a highly consequential tragedy on Everest, but also the fall of an icon and an era in flux. Brice's client rosters began to shrink after 2015, as did his enthusiasm for Everest. Time was being called not only on his stewardship, but also, in many ways, on that of IMG, AAI, Jagged Globe, and Adventure Consultants.

18

UNDER NEW MANAGEMENT

It was frustrating for the three brothers who started Seven Summit Treks to have their early days as entrepreneurs stymied by Everest's uncontrollable forces. They had a large roster of clients on Manaslu in 2013 and then hoped to make SST's guiding debut on Everest in 2014, but they were derailed by the avalanche, and again in 2015 by the earthquake. However, those back-to-back tragedies had also provoked change on the mountain that made room for new players like them. Many Western clients were holding off on pursuing their Everest dream in the wake of the consecutive mass-casualty events. As a result, Western guide companies' client rosters dwindled, some by as much as 50 percent, according to *Outside* magazine. Nepali and other Asian mountain guides felt empowered to stake out their patch in the industry, and even reimagine it on their terms. When SST arrived at Everest with five clients in the spring of 2016, it was to a south side base camp in which suddenly roughly half of the twenty-five companies were owned by non-Westerners, mostly from Nepal, but also from India, China, and Japan.

The spring of 2016 proved to be yet another record-setting season, with 449 people summiting from the Nepal side. At least half were Sherpa climbers and guides, and more than 180 of them were client climbers. Ninety percent of the people who summited were part of a guided expedition. The number of companies and climbers on the mountain was in part so high because the Nepal Ministry of Tourism had decided to honor permits from the 2014 and 2015 spring seasons. Base camp looked like Disney World on a summer day with a half-off promotion.

The expeditions offered by the Nepali- and Asian-owned companies were attracting a different clientele to the mountain, especially Indians and Chinese. The trips were typically more affordable, and the companies were good at providing a more culturally specific experience to their clients, in terms of food, atmosphere, and the languages spoken by their guides. "They actually have a different setup for Indians, a different setup for Chinese," says Debraj Dutta, an Indian mountaineer who summited Everest in 2016. A trip to Everest was an exciting status symbol to people in the emerging upper middle classes in these countries. Many of the Nepali-owned companies engaged in price wars with one another to drive the cost as low as possible, with some all-inclusive climbs coming in for as little as $18,000, while some Western companies were nearing the $100,000 mark. Nepali companies had a built-in advantage on cost, as they paid lower permit fees to the government for foreign clients than the Western companies, and zero permit fees for the local guides, saving them tens of thousands of dollars on each expedition.

The avalanche and the earthquake had more than just shaken the chess pieces of the guiding industry off the board. As if out of a script, the mountain underwent an unexpected physical transformation in tandem with its symbolic one. When guides returned to Everest in 2016, they noticed the Hillary Step looked different. The forty-foot-high section of solid limestone, located just two hundred feet below the summit, seemed shorter, but it was buried under so much snow that year that it was hard to tell. By 2017, however, there was no doubt about it: the iconic monument to the beekeeper from New Zealand was not broken, not shifted: it was gone. Once considered the crux of the summit push, requiring technical rock climbing in the death zone while wearing clunky mountaineering boots, the Hillary Step was now just an easy set of giant stairs, which allow the crowds to flow up and down more easily and reduce the chance of a bottleneck.

Legacy companies like Himex and AAI may have been feeling outmaneuvered by the Nepali upstarts, but many of the younger Western Everest guides and guide company owners felt their moment on the mountain had arrived, too. In 2016, Garrett Madison was at base camp with a whopping twenty-seven clients, mostly Westerners, for his company, Madison Mountaineering. While there were fewer Western clients coming to the mountain in total, there were also fewer companies they were choosing to climb with, and Madison Mountaineering was one of them. Madison had actually been approached by the SST brothers in 2012, when he was still working for AAI. "I remember meeting Mingma in a Kathmandu coffee shop," he says. "He was basically telling me I should come work with him, come climb all these eight-thousand-meter peaks. He was saying how Russell, and others who belonged to the old guard, shouldn't be doing this anymore—that he's too old, that we need to be doing this. He was quite aggressive. Tashi Lakpa was even more aggressive." While Madison was put off by what he felt were conspiratorial undertones to push out the older generation, and turned down the offer, he had no qualms about the opportunities that were now presenting themselves for him to gain market share.

Mike Hamill and Adrian Ballinger were two of the other ambitious and highly experienced young guides who were looking for a life of more than just bumming around the death zone for a paycheck. After more than ten years of regularly guiding for IMG on Everest, Hamill took a groundbreaking step and linked up in 2017 with a respected Nepali climber, businessman, and IFMGA-certified guide named Tendi Sherpa in a sort of exclusive in-country partnership (with Tendi's company TAG Nepal), and launched a sister guiding company, Climbing the Seven Summits (CTSS), with an eye, specifically, on the very high end of the market. Hamill was still working for IMG through 2017; then he brought CTSS's first batch of five Everest clients to the mountain in 2018. Ballinger's company, Alpenglow Expeditions, was on the north side of the mountain in 2017 with thirteen clients. Ryan Waters's Mountain Professionals was also on Everest that year, on the south side, with five clients.

Of the business ambitions and personal goals these young Western guides shared, Hamill says: "Me, Ryan, Garrett, and Adrian, we all knew we wanted to do more than just guide our whole lives. It was the only way to have a family and be home more."

"The new guides were much more media savvy and I think that's why they progressed so fast," says Brice. "Us old guys were more concerned about running the expeditions than about the media side."

For Brice, the trickiest potential competitor to contend with was Ballinger, because they had such history together. Ballinger had actually started Alpenglow in 2006, when he was just thirty, but he'd decided he wanted to learn his way around Himalayan guiding from the best before striking out on his own entirely. "I searched out Russell and I asked him if Alpenglow clients could join with Himex on their 2007 Cho Oyu climb," remembers Ballinger. "I had three clients of my own but they all paid Himex and Russ paid me as a guide. And Russell and I just totally clicked." Ballinger began working with Brice regularly, summiting Everest for his first time with Himex in 2009, then becoming Himex's lead guide on all 8,000-meter peaks.

Brice and Ballinger grew so close so quickly that they began to talk about succession opportunities. "We made plans for me to ultimately buy Himex," Ballinger says. But the two began to diverge in the way they envisioned running the company. During the warm 2012 season, it was the weather that concerned Brice and caused him to cancel Himex's climbs, but it was the size of the expeditions that concerned Ballinger. "We had thirty-nine clients, between Everest and Lhotse," he remembers. "The company had grown to a size where we kind of lost the ability to be fluid or responsive to the mountain."

By the end of 2012, Ballinger's buyout of Himex had stalled. It seemed the famously fastidious Brice was not prepared to give up control after all. "We had already been struggling with the big picture of me even wanting to change things," Ballinger remembers. "How was I going to own the business if I couldn't even change what brand of ketchup we bring to base camp?"

In addition to the four Americans, an Austrian guide who had spent years bringing clients up mountains in Pakistan soon began making waves on Everest. In 2016, at the age of thirty, Lukas Furtenbach decided to go all in on the world's highest mountain with his company Furtenbach Adventures. That year, he arrived on the south side with a half dozen clients from across Europe. "When we first arrived on the scene, everyone hated us," Furtenbach says. "The Western operators hated us because they thought that we are taking their clients. And the Nepali companies hated us because I was openly criticizing them in public."

By 2016 and 2017, the fact was clear: the old Big Five was losing its dominance. Members of the younger generation of Sherpas and Western guides were beginning to run impressive Everest expeditions under their own banners. It wasn't easy for an old-timer like Brice to take. "I do think they sort of kicked us teachers in the teeth," he says.

For Brice, seeing the younger guides and Sherpas come in and reinvent the industry was like seeing a house that he had lovingly remodeled and raised children in for thirty years get bought just for the lot and torn down. "I think we experienced the best part of climbing history on Everest," he says, wistfully. "In those early days we didn't know anything—but we had a pretty good time there."

After 2015, Brice's client roster diminished each year. He held on until 2020, when he officially stopped running guided expeditions on Everest and quietly exited from the industry as a whole. He had run fifty commercial trips on 8,000-meter peaks, with not a single client fatality.

"I spent forty-odd years going to Nepal twice a year. I needed to get away from that and rest my body and rest my mind," Brice says. "Those last years in base camp were kind of sad. They weren't fun like they used to be. There was tension between companies and I just wasn't seeing the camaraderie anymore."

An Austrian guide named Stephan Keck purchased Himex, though his lack of success in running it has, understandably, only added to Brice's bitterness. "Stephan had worked for me as one of my guides and he showed an interest in buying the company," says Brice, who explains they struck a deal in which Keck got the company for a low price but would pay Brice a 10 percent share of future profits. "I'm not sure he has even operated any trips under the Himex name—he has never paid me anything since. Effectively, I have never made anything out of Himex."

Yet one recent, pleasant memory stands out to Brice. "On my last trip to Nepal, in 2019, Phurba [Tashi] and I went looking for a new route on Lobuche Peak," he recalls. "It was just he and I and we were wandering around the foothills together for two days, me trying to keep up with him, which is impossible. That was great, to spend that time just wandering around, going up to five and a half thousand meters, just looking for a new way to climb the mountain." Nothing could ever erase what the Himalayas, and his dear friend Phurba Tashi, meant to him.

• • •

SST had only five clients in 2016, its first year on Everest, while Asian Trekking had twenty-one. However, thanks to their refinement of a highly flexible business model, SST's numbers rose dramatically year over year. While Asian Trekking and many of the other Asian-owned companies were primarily focused on affordability, SST began offering tiered rates and service in 2017. IMG had long done something of this kind in general terms, but the variations among its expedition tiers were minuscule compared with what SST started doing. SST's offerings ranged from a no-frills climb at around $25,000 that included simple infrastructure and minimal Sherpa support—not unlike the Summit Climb model, for which Dan Mazur charged $35,000—to "VVIP packages" running up to $300,000, the most expensive ever marketed on Everest, by far. These over-the-top trips included huge quantities of oxygen, several Sherpa guides who would accompany clients all the way to the summit, and even midexpedition getaways to Kathmandu, in which clients would be whisked away from base camp by helicopter and dropped in the capital for twenty-four hours of R&R in a five-star hotel.

The founders saw no shame in calling it how they saw it about who they were trying to attract with the package. It was not just for wealthy people, but wealthy people whom other companies might see as too big of a risk to bring to Everest. SST's marketing material for its top-end climb states, "If you have a strong economic background to compensate for your old age and fear of risks, you can sign up for the VVIP Mount Everest Expedition."

"There are so many people who have the very big dream to climb Everest," says cofounder Tashi Lakpa, in defense of his company's less rigorous vetting process. "And that's why we have so many different services. If someone has full skills in climbing, but doesn't have money, we have a package for them. If you do have lots of money, but no experience, we also have a package for them. We are climbers and we know the feelings and understand financial situations."

SST's tiered offerings were a huge success. In 2019, SST had 100 clients on Everest and Lhotse—the majority of whom summited— and 250 across all mountains on its menu. It was honored that year by the government for being the largest taxpayer in the trekking and expedition industry (despite the fact that it was also dealing with a scandal over one of its employees having been caught pocketing permit fees the year before instead of paying the government). It was bringing huge numbers of clients to other mountains in the Himalayas as well. Part of its business plan relied on diversification, and SST offered guided trips on more 8,000-meter peaks than anyone else.

As many of the companies that preceded it had learned previously, however, moving fast and breaking things often exposes cracks in the model and brings out the critics. Some Western guides were concerned that SST was recruiting poorer Nepalis from lowland ethnic groups such as the Rai and Tamang to fill menial roles like load-carrying. Mike Roberts, an Adventure Consultants guide who has summited Everest nine times between 2002 and 2017, says that these new porters were paid far less than they typically had been in the past. "The hardest part of that for me is when people put the exploitation on the Westerners, not realizing it became a real problem within the Nepali-run trips," Roberts says. Meanwhile, Sherpas with limited climbing experience were being rapidly elevated into higher positions, including as leaders of the more affordable expeditions at SST and other companies. This was seen as potentially dangerous.

Guides who were expressing safety concerns about the scale at which SST was operating pointed to some legitimately worrying numbers, especially in 2019. On Everest, there were nine total deaths that spring; two of them were SST clients. Across all Himalayan peaks in

Nepal, there were eighteen total deaths, five of which were on SST expeditions—four clients, and one Sherpa climber.

"Close calls happened all the time on Everest," says Hahn. "But close calls could usually be dealt with quickly because of really good guides and really good Sherpas. Some of the newer operators, when they had a close call, it would often spiral down into a disaster."

"The Sherpa-run companies had a lot of problems in the beginning," says Waters. "And a lot of it could be attributed to them not quite being up to the task yet. Then, with all those inexperienced clients, it was a bad combination."

"At one point, whenever there was a fatality, people just assumed it was Seven Summit Treks," says Crampton.

When Western guides discussed the early failings of companies like SST, as they had with Asian Trekking ten years prior, the colonialist undertones were hard to ignore. Begrudging any kind of success for the Nepalis, who were becoming bigger players in the Everest guiding industry every year, was often dismissed as ivory-tower elitism, if not worse. Yet, some of this criticism was also coming from other Nepalis—and not unfairly.

By 2018, it had come to light that SST was at the heart of what many were calling the rescue scam, in which, as owners of a helicopter company, the SST founder-brothers could organize and mount a rescue on a mountain and then charge whatever they wanted, after the fact—sometimes up to $40,000. The easiest way to recoup this money was to simply bill the various travel insurance companies that trekkers and climbers often use. The government of Nepal even launched an investigation—and confirmed fraud among up to fifteen different trekking companies—and the controversy was widely reported in the international press. Travel insurance company Global Rescue refused to pay some claims in light of the facts. Most insurance companies now require pre-authorization for rescue expenses.

Tashi Lakpa himself admits that his and his brothers' company should have done better up through 2019. "I probably had some ego at that time," he says. "The Western guides, they owned the company *and* they did the operations, and I was thinking that I could do this, too."

SST eventually launched a subsidiary company called 14 Peaks Expedition, some say to provide distance from the controversies. Meanwhile, former SST employees broke away to form Pioneer Adventure and 8K Expeditions, which have grown exponentially in the last few years but are seen as well behind SST in safety standards.

That said, with the exception of Himex and its zero client climbing fatalities, it's not as though other companies were avoiding client deaths altogether. Everyone had to deal with at least one client fatality over their years in business. IMG has had at least three since its inaugural trip in 1994; AAI has had at least two. But the longest-tenured guides on the mountain pointed out that it was still crucial to look at the specifics of *how* clients were dying. People like Simonson would argue that the circumstances of an IMG client fatality—as a result of random altitude problems, collapses in the icefall, or strokes, for example—are an important distinction and were far different from the way SST's clients were succumbing to exhaustion on summit day. That term—"exhaustion"—is what was officially recorded as the cause of death for both SST clients who perished on Everest in 2019. To many, this indicated bad client management—a cardinal sin in the guiding world.

Others pointed to overcrowding. One of the SST Everest client fatalities was the American Donald Cash. He died on May 22, a date that became infamous when a startling photograph taken by a Nepali climber named Nirmal Purja spread on social media. The image showed a river of approximately two hundred climbers standing single file in the death zone, stuck on a knife-edge just below the Hillary Step. Cash got stuck in the traffic jam there with his Sherpas for more than two hours on his way down from the summit, fainted, and was unable to be revived. Everest was the final peak in his quest to complete the Seven Summits.

The photo of the "conga line" was picked up in magazines and by cable news organizations, which seemed gleeful in declaring it evidence of all that was wrong with the guiding industry. "The rumor that you had to stand in line to get to the summit of Everest was no longer a rumor to the public," said David Hamilton. "And here was the photographic proof."

Hamilton refers to it as a "rumor" because the good news was that this type of bottleneck was a very rare phenomenon that happened only when all teams made a break for the summit during the first viable weather window. Historically, there are anywhere from seven to fifteen summit windows each spring season. In 2019, there were only three, hence the bottleneck. Three hundred and seventy people summited on May 22—a massive number for a single day. Yet, even then, only two people died—Cash and Anjali Kulkarni, a climber from India. While tragic on a human level, when looked at statistically, this was not at all an unusually high death-to-summit ratio on Everest.

Stepping even further back, the death-to-summit ratio at this point in Everest's history was more impressive than ever. In the 1980s, it was upward of 12 percent (18 deaths to 142 people summiting). In the 2010s, it was about 1 percent, after removing the 30 deaths from the mass-casualty events of 2014 and 2015 (46 deaths to 4,289 people summiting). And only *half* of those were among clients and Sherpas working for guiding companies—the rest were from independent climbs—despite the fact that guided expeditions accounted for roughly 90 percent of the people on the mountain, bringing the likelihood of losing your life as a client of a guided group to an exceedingly low number.

It is exactly these seemingly impressive statistics that have motivated guides like Tim Mosedale to wonder if they should call it quits. He's been guiding in the Himalayas since 2003 and has summited Everest eight times. Wiry, with large sideburns, thick hoop earrings, and eyeglasses, he is one of a few independent guides with a steady enough clientele to be able to show up each year and easily slot into the infrastructure of a larger guided group, usually a Nepali-based company. He simply pays a set fee for him and his handful of clients to operate on the fringe.

"I'm afraid that recording deaths as a percentage is not a great marker," he explains. "Every death counts—that person was a father, mother, brother, sister, son, uncle, whatever. Every death is a big deal."

American client climbers seem to have taken a different lesson from the statistics. Fewer Americans have been coming to Everest in recent years, and many guides say it is exactly the appearance of Everest as being not dangerous *enough* that is keeping them away. As hard as it still is to summit the mountain, in actuality, it no longer carries the reputation of being the sort of death-defying accomplishment that once allowed American climbers to dine out on the story for the rest of their lives.

Mosedale remains passionate about helping client climbers achieve their dreams in the mountains and seasoned enough to accept death on Everest—just not avoidable deaths. Of the companies like SST, Mosedale says, "The number of people that they're putting on the summit—even clients that a Western guide might say shouldn't be there—is impressive. But people are dying who shouldn't be dying, because either they shouldn't be there in the first place, or there wasn't enough oxygen available to them up high, or there were no high-altitude medications nearby. I just find that really sad, particularly for the families—because it's avoidable. And, in the case of people being accepted onto expeditions who shouldn't be, I find that morally reprehensible. If any Western company had the fatalities that a couple of the Nepali companies have had over the years, their license to operate would be revoked."

(Mosedale is referring to the license required to guide on other popular mountains such as Mont Blanc that is not in fact required on Everest.)

Others point out that many of the Nepali companies, and SST in particular, have done incredible work to improve their practices and have become very safe operators. Especially with the rise of the breakaway companies like Pioneer and 8K, SST has been striving to distinguish itself from the Nepali-owned upstarts and prove it is a top company that is safe and reliable.

"The guys at SST do a pretty amazing job now," says Ben Jones, who began working for AAI on Everest in 2011 and is now AAI's lead Everest guide. He says he once decried the incompetence of SST and other local companies, but spoke too soon. "It's definitely not fair anymore to say they're always killing people," he says. "And I was guilty of thinking that in the beginning too, but I think they've proved themselves. Just a few years ago I think I was going on about the lack of communication between the Nepali and the Western companies, how since they were running the whole show, they thought there was no need for them to deal with us. But, in just a couple years, that has totally changed.

"They're sort of retaking the mountain, in some ways," he says of SST, getting philosophical about it. "I guess that could potentially affect my job and career. But I'm still super happy for them."

"I can't think of any people more deserving than the Sherpas to take over," says Hahn. "Many of them have come up through the system, learned everything they could from Western guides, they put in their time—they absolutely should be running this business now."

Despite lingering issues, for the first time in a long time, Norbu Tenzing of the American Himalayan Foundation is upbeat about what he is seeing on Everest—guardedly optimistic, as he puts it. "It's taken over a hundred years for Sherpas to take some control of the narrative," he says. "Now we have to be responsible stewards, whether it's the garbage, environmental issues, or just taking care of each other."

One telling indication for Norbu Tenzing is how many Nepalis have started climbing in the past few years for the sheer joy of it. "I hear about whole groups of Sherpas going to climb eight-thousand-meter peaks just because they want to," he says. "Because they're passionate, and now because they have a group of guides and friends who are just as enthusiastic and just as highly trained, as motivated, and just as ambitious."

Mingma G. was himself one of those mountaineers. He was an ardent climber, as he proved when he embarked on a personal expedition in 2015 in which he made a first ascent of the extremely technical west face of Mount Chobuje. He was also evolving as a businessman. The company he'd started in 2012, Dreamers Destination, hit a rough patch financially and had to dissolve before Mingma G. was able to take any of his own clients to the peak. But he'd led seven other Himalayan expeditions, five of them on 8,000-meter peaks, and as soon as Dreamers Destination folded, he immediately founded a new company, Imagine Nepal, while his former partners went on to create guiding companies of their own (one as a partner at Pioneer Adventure). In 2018, Imagine Nepal had clients on Everest for the first time—eight of them. His business was off to the races.

Still, Mingma G. fantasized about making a name for himself as a climber with his personal first ascents and by breaking records. One climb, in particular, that he fixed his mind on was so audacious it would have reverberations far beyond his own reputation: a winter ascent of K2. It had never been accomplished.

However, it turned out another young hotshot climber, Nirmal Purja—the same climber who took the 2019 conga line photo—had the same idea. Both Nepalis shared a vision for pushing the edge, and for pursuing claims of Himalayan mountaineering supremacy for their country once and for all.

19

The HIMALAYAN
FAME GAME

In the span of four years, from 2016 to 2019, a Nepali ex-soldier who initially went to the Himalayas with friends for fun and to test himself became the most famous mountaineer in the world. Today, Nirmal Purja, more often known as Nimsdai (*dai* meaning "brother" in Nepalese, used as a term of endearment), or just Nims, has become the figurehead for Nepali empowerment, accomplishment, and business success on Everest and beyond. Whether that's entirely deserving, and an entirely accurate assessment, is another matter.

Born in 1983, Nims passed one of the toughest military selection processes in the world at the age of twenty to join the Gurkhas, the famed two-hundred-year-old army battalion made up of Nepalis (as well as Indians, in other regiments) who fight for the British Army. Nims was from a resource-strapped family in a small village in southern Nepal far away from the mountains, and for a kid like him this was a way out of poverty and into status, purpose, and good pay. He loved the work, and he was good at it, too. So good, in fact, that in 2009, he became the first Gurkha ever to be accepted into the British

Royal Navy's Special Boat Service (SBS), a unit akin to the US Navy SEALs.

He took that same never-quit spirit to the mountains. With no prior alpine climbing experience, he summited Lobuche East in 2012 during some time off, with the help of a mentor named Dorje Khatri. In 2014, he climbed his first eight-thousander, Dhaulagiri, during a British Army expedition. (Dorje Khatri was killed that year on Everest by the avalanche in the Khumbu Icefall.) In 2016, when Everest reopened, Nims reached the top of the world with SST's co-owner Chhang Dawa. He returned the following year with a British military expedition, this time helping to fix the ropes and summiting Everest twice in the same season. Within five days of his second ascent, he also summited Lhotse and Makalu. Three eight-thousanders in five days was a world record (though not one many climbers were really chasing or took notice of at the time).

Then, in 2018, the thirty-five-year-old made an announcement that shocked the climbing world: he would be attempting to climb all fourteen eight-thousand-meter peaks in *seven months*. The existing record, held by Kim Chang-ho, a South Korean climber, was *seven years, 310 days*. Still a relative unknown and still considered extremely inexperienced as a high-altitude mountaineer, Nims resigned from the British military, sacrificed his pension, and embarked on his adventure.

Nims was taking a page right out of the Rob Hall–Gary Ball playbook. Just as Hall and Ball announced their Seven-Summits-in-seven-months plan on the verge of launching Adventure Consultants in 1990, Nims made his announcement as a precursor to the launch of his own guiding company, Elite Expeditions. (He would drop hints about its launch on social media throughout his endeavor.)

Much like Hall's and Ball's Seven Summits speed record, Nims's project to race to the top of the fourteen peaks would be as much a matter of precise logistical execution and teamwork as climbing expertise and individual strength. To that end, Nims hired SST to handle the operations, recognizing that full-service and ingenious logistical support when it came to permitting, transportation, gear, and so on—of a type rarely before seen—would be the only way to pull off his mission. He would also not be undertaking the project alone. He assembled a dream team of Sherpa climbers and rope-fixers, including Mingma David Sherpa, who was another former apprentice of Dorje Khatri's.

On April 23, 2019, Nims and his team summited Annapurna, which is typically ranked among the top three most dangerous eight-thousanders, with K2 and Nanga Parbat. "Project Possible," as Nims was dubbing the endeavor, was underway.

A savvy user of social media, Nims filmed the entire expedition with the help of his team. On May 22, Nims had his camera ready as he neared the summit of Everest—the fourth peak on his itinerary—and snapped what became one of the most famous photos in Everest's history: the conga line of climbers on the overcrowded summit ridge. He touched the top of Everest, then scaled Lhotse within the same day. He then summited Makalu only two days later.

When he reached the top of Shishapangma on October 29, 2019, he'd completed his mission ahead of schedule. Nims had scaled all fourteen eight-thousanders in six months and six days.

While he had shattered a meaningful climbing record, he had also broken just about every unspoken aesthetic climbing rule in accomplishing his goal, which ruffled the feathers of a lot of hard-core alpinists. With the help of SST and his Sherpa team, he'd had scores of people fixing routes ahead of him; he had sometimes used helicopters to get to his next base camp as quickly as possible; and he'd had abundant oxygen on hand.

"What he has done is quite extraordinary, but it isn't mountaineering. Real mountaineering is exploratory—finding new routes up to big peaks . . . I don't see this as a major event," said Chris Bonington.

"The fact that he used supplementary oxygen detracts from the feat. He also used fixed ropes. It isn't exactly alpinism, as I understand it," said Stephen Venables, who had originated new routes on Everest.

"We don't support this kind of gimmick. If you have twenty people supporting you, of course you can achieve this," said the head of the Indian Mountaineering Foundation, Amit Chowdhuary.

Notably, the standard-bearer of the pure climbing aesthetic and first person to summit all fourteen eight-thousanders, Reinhold Messner himself, was complimentary of Nims, praising his "great capacity for economic management, leadership, logistics organization. And obviously, exceptional physical resistance."

So was just about the rest of the world, whether the people were climbers or not. Nims's public profile skyrocketed. When he started his project in April 2019, he had 45,000 followers on Instagram. After he took the photo that went viral on Everest, the count jumped to 75,000. By the time he summited Shishapangma in October 2019—completing Project Possible—he had 186,000. He soon lined up book and film deals, and officially announced the launch of his guide company, cofounded with his friend and partner Mingma David, which they called Elite Exped for short. The Nims brand was about to go nuclear.

Then the pandemic hit. Everest was shut down in 2020 on both the Nepal and Tibet sides. Nims and Mingma David, like all other guide company owners, had to put Elite Exped into hibernation mode—in their case, before it could really get started.

Nims had other goals on which he could train his formidable attention in the time being. In September 2019, Mingma G. had officially announced that he planned to make the first-ever ascent of K2 in winter. There had been eight previous such attempts by some of the boldest mountaineers in the world, and none had succeeded. Plus, no Nepali had ever claimed a first ascent—in summer or winter—of an 8,000-meter peak. Mingma G.'s announcement had gotten little notice, but when the ever-savvy Nims made the same public proclamation soon after, it was huge news. Perhaps in the wake of completing Project Possible, he saw it as all he could do to top himself. It was also the perfect way to supercharge his personal brand, and his climbing résumé, during the pandemic.

Nims assembled a team of strong climbers, mostly vets of Project Possible, including Mingma David. Mingma G. arrived on K2 in December 2020; Nims and his team arrived about a week later. By the time Nims's expedition reached Camp Two, Mingma G.'s team had already begun fixing the route to Camp Four. At Camp Three, Nims proposed to Mingma G. that they join forces, summit as one team, and jointly claim the ascent for Nepal.

On January 16, 2021, Nims, Mingma G., and their entire teams reached the summit together while singing the Nepali national anthem, then descended safely. To punctuate the point, Nims later revealed he had climbed without oxygen. (Some high-profile climbers doubted him, but no evidence has emerged that he was lying.)

It was a profound moment. Nims and Mingma G., having tossed rivalry aside to become good friends, had conquered what many believed to be the last great challenge left in the world of high-altitude mountaineering. In doing so, Nims in particular not only quieted most of the critics who questioned his skill, but also unleashed one of the greatest moments of national pride in Nepal's history. His fame in the country ratcheted up to a level previously known only by Tenzing Norgay.

In the spring of 2021, the Nepal side of Everest was open again. With the pandemic still underway, there was some debate about whether it was responsible to bring tourism back to an area where medical care wasn't easy to come by. Guy Cotter was particularly critical of the idea. However, a quorum—which included the majority of Sherpas—landed

on the other side, arguing that the cancelations to date had been financially devastating enough, and it was time to get back to work. (Many
companies, including Asian Trekking, IMG, AAI, and Adventure Consultants, had continued to pay their Sherpa teams wages in 2020, despite
never running a trip.) Clients started to return. COVID numbers and
COVID-related fatalities in the Khumbu *did* rise somewhat as a result,
but the climbing continued.

Elite Exped staked out its place on the Khumbu Glacier. The company brought eight clients to base camp in the spring of 2021. Six of
them summited. The combination of Nims's fame with the now proven
success of Elite Exped turned him into the most disruptive force in the
Everest industry. As such, it's fitting that Nims's company became the
final piece in the creation of the *new* Big Five. Elite Exped—along with
SST; Mingma G.'s Imagine; a company called 8K Expeditions founded
by three reputable guides and logistics experts, Lakpa Sherpa, Pemba
Sherpa, and Lakpa Thendu Sherpa; and, of course, the oldest of the five,
Asian Trekking—quickly solidified their positions as the most influential guiding companies on Everest. The days of Western dominance
were well and truly over.

In November 2021, Nims's autobiography, *Beyond Possible*, was published in the United Kingdom and was a bestseller. That same month,
a documentary made from the footage he and his team had shot during Project Possible, called *14 Peaks: Nothing Is Impossible*, was released
on Netflix. It was produced in collaboration with Red Bull, one of
Nims's new sponsors, as well as Jimmy Chin, whose affiliation significantly upped the movie's credibility. The documentary was a hit, reaching number seven in the overall global Netflix rankings. The following
spring, 2022, Elite Expeditions had sixteen Everest clients. All but one
summited.

The popularity of *14 Peaks* was another watershed moment in the
guiding industry. Just as with Dick Bass and his *Seven Summits* book,

many clients who otherwise wouldn't have imagined themselves capable of reaching the top of a more challenging eight-thousander than Everest were inspired by the videos of Nims and his team seemingly walking to the top of each one. So were other guides, who watched footage of Project Possible's crack Sherpas fixing the mountains ahead of each climb. Once again, phones were ringing off the hook at the guide companies—only this time with clients interested in Manaslu, Makalu, Kangchenjunga, Dhaulagiri, and even K2, instead of the Seven Summits. The type of recreational mountaineers who once had put Everest atop their bucket list could now consider putting all fourteen eight-thousanders on it. In 2012, the Chinese unexpectedly closed access to Cho Oyu at the last minute, which is why guiding companies began replacing their Cho Oyu offering with Manaslu, also considered one of the easiest eight-thousanders. "People got sick of the Chinese closing mountains in Tibet," recalls Madison.

The companies answering the majority of the calls were the same ones that had risen to the top of the heap on Everest. Nims's fame had galvanized the notion that it was the Nepalis who were the ultimate experts in the logistics and rope-fixing prowess necessary to make climbing these eight-thousanders efficient and client friendly. Elite Exped and the other Nepali-owned powerhouses began promoting themselves not only as Seven Summit companies, but as eight-thousander companies.

Most Western guides, however, ranged from hesitant to horrified at the idea of guiding on the scariest eight-thousanders—perhaps most of all, K2.

K2 is far more complex than Everest, far more deadly, and its margin for error is far smaller. It not only requires climbing in the death zone, but it is steep, technical, and riddled with objective hazards, namely an inescapable funnel for collapsing ice and snow called "the Bottleneck." Many of the world's greatest mountaineers have perished on K2, including Alison Hargreaves, Rick Allen, and Rolf Bae. In total, roughly a quarter of the people who have attempted it have died trying. Fewer than four hundred people have climbed K2 since its first ascent in 1954—which is approximately the same number of people who now summit Everest every year. Guiding on K2 *had* been successfully accomplished as early as 2004, but it was still an extremely rare occurrence.

However, long before Nims's Project Possible, there *were* Western guides looking at the mountain and believing it could be done more regularly. In 2006, Alan Arnette was attempting Broad Peak, which has stunning views of K2. Arnette remembers being awed and terrified by the neighboring mountain's size and steep faces. Then, in 2013, Arnette was on Manaslu with Phil Crampton as his guide, and one evening, Crampton shocked Arnette by suggesting he consider attempting it one day. "You're not getting any younger," Crampton blurted. To Arnette it sounded ridiculous—he was as intimidated by K2's mythology as anyone. "*You gotta be kidding me,*" he remembers thinking. "It's just this massive, unrelenting mountain." However, the encouragement from a well-respected guide like Crampton got Arnette daydreaming.

Soon after, Arnette was entering a challenging phase in his life—going through a messy divorce, but also meeting someone new whom he ended up marrying—and the idea of trying K2 came back to his mind. Climbing mountains was a way of sorting things out for him. "My life was a bit of a mixing bowl of emotions," he says. "I was fifty-seven, I had done all the Seven Summits except Denali, climbed Everest and Lhotse, got to high camp on Manaslu without supplemental oxygen—I felt ready. I felt confident."

Arnette learned that Garrett Madison was planning a K2 climb in 2014, and joined the trip as a paying client. "My mind was in exactly the right spot for that climb," says Arnette. "Garrett comes along, with his pedigree guiding these big mountains. I've got my guardian angel Kami

Sherpa. The stars aligned." The trip was a success. Madison, Arnette, and Kami all summited.

That didn't make Arnette an instant convert to the idea that K2 could be regularly guided. "I wrote an article for my website, in 2016, that laid out the ten reasons K2 will never become the new Everest," he recalls with a hearty laugh. "I was wrong about eight of the ten.

"In 2022, we saw the codification, if you will, of the formula of how you can take virtually anybody to the top of any eight-thousand-meter mountain," Arnette explains. "And it's pretty straightforward now: you send a team of seven to ten very strong, experienced Sherpas to put in the fixed lines from base camp to the summit. They plow the boot track while they're at it. They put in camps; stock them with oxygen, food, and fuel; then come back down. The clients show up at base camp, often by helicopter—they may have preacclimatized by doing a six-thousand-meter trekking peak. Then they bring in a fresh group of Sherpas to guide the climb itself, and begin giving clients unusually high flow rates of oxygen, starting at unusually low elevations."

Clients like Arnette are proving that with the right mentality and the right support, things that were once unthinkable for relatively experienced high-altitude mountaineers are now possible for relatively inexperienced ones. As an example, Arnette points to the client climber Rebecca Ferry. Becks, as she's known to everyone except the tax collector, is a mother of five teenagers. She lives in a cottage tucked into a stretch of rolling hills in southwest England known as the Cotswolds, and, at forty-five, is slight but athletic.

In 2019, she was competing in a trail running race in the Khumbu Valley, and when she finished she decided to join her friend who was trekking on one of Nepal's more accessible 6,000-meter peaks. Ferry, her friend, and their two Sherpa guides set their alarms for well before dawn. Ferry emerged from her tent, shone her headlamp on the snow in front of her, and began walking upward.

It's long been said that the satisfaction of mountaineering is in retrospect—that all the pleasure comes from having climbed and not from the climbing itself. Not for Ferry. "As soon as I set off, I was like, 'I love this,'" she remembers. "I'm walking up in the dark and even though it's just stepping, it felt like endurance running. Then the sun began to rise. I just remember looking around, thinking, 'Oh my God, this is amazing—this is . . . Wow.'

"And then I was passing people who were obviously suffering from the altitude. My Sherpa, Kagi, kept asking if I was feeling okay. I felt great. And it was the first time I'd been above fifteen thousand feet."

The following year, in December 2020, Ferry hired a British mountain guide, Jon Gupta, and a Nepali guide, Lhakpa Wangchu Sherpa, to help her summit the more technical Ama Dablam. It was midpandemic and also winter, so they basically had the mountain to themselves the entire way up.

To Ferry, Gupta was like a driving instructor with a second steering wheel and a second set of working brakes. With a good mountain guide by her side—someone with all the tools necessary to manage a worst-case scenario—the possibilities felt endless. Six months after climbing Ama Dablam, Ferry summited Everest and Lhotse with Gupta. But she always told him that it was K2 she was really after. By 2021, Gupta didn't think it was a ridiculous notion at all. That year, Ferry summited K2 with him—using Madison Mountaineering's base camp infrastructure—and attempted three other 8,000-meter peaks over the span of four months.

Ferry perfectly represents the modern Everest guiding industry, in the sense that it is no longer the Everest guiding industry at all—it is the 8,000-meter-peak guiding industry. Thanks in large part to SST and Nims, what was once considered an inconceivable, almost certainly fatal mountaineering ambition is now the new Ironman triathlon: maybe not for everybody—not even possible for many—but surprisingly accessible for hundreds of men and women around the world who simply enjoy biting off something huge and chewing until it's been swallowed.

Nims's boundless belief in himself is perhaps matched only by his boundless self-promotion. This has made him a love/hate figure in the mountaineering world. In the run-up to the 2022 spring season, he released his own line of down suits, the Ultimate Nimsdai Summit Suit, and partnered with the American outdoor gear manufacturer Osprey to launch the Mutant Nimsdai 90 backpack. These were just two additions to his growing line of eponymous merchandise.

"I'm the fucking face of these people, bro," he said about his Sherpa team to journalist Grayson Schaffer for a piece in *GQ*, but with the implication that he means Nepalis in general. "You'll see it everywhere in Kathmandu. I'm their hope now." This is not an unusual tenor of comment from Nims, who is known for his NFL-wide-receiver-level showboating and off-the-cuff catchphrases, such as "Your extreme is my normality." He wastes no time congratulating himself on social media for his accomplishments—though he is also fiercely protective of his image and declined to be interviewed for this book, citing his busy schedule. It's all part of his brand. At the same time, he's known as a friendly and caring guide who pays his employees well and wants to give back. "Some people respect Nims, some are jealous of Nims, a lot of people respect him but won't admit it," says Mingma G. "But it's actually because of the negative people around him that he'll do more and do bigger things—possibly something we never imagined. For Nims, it's almost like the negativity makes him more powerful."

On a crisp afternoon in April 2022, Nims was at an outdoor table at the Namche Bazaar coffee shop Sherpa Barista. Inside, young employees were getting a break after a busy few hours of delivering chocolate cake and cappuccinos, with the shiny espresso machine hissing away in the background. Near the pastry counter was a table stacked with copies of Nims's memoir, *Beyond Possible*. Nims sat with his private Everest client for the season, the princess of Qatar, Asma al-Thani. (Nims reportedly charges $1 million for private, one-on-one guiding.) Eventually, he got up from his table and came into Sherpa Barista to stand beside his books and make an Instagram post that would reach his followers, which by then numbered two million. His assistant/cameraman hit Record.

"Hi everyone, Nimsdai here again. Right now I am in Namche Bazaar, and I'm going sign a hundred copies of—*bestselling* copies of—*Beyond Possible*, and a hundred percent will go to the Nimsdai Foundation. Fifty percent of that will go to building a shelter for the porters and the other fifty will go toward the big mountain cleanup project."

"That felt authentic," Nims said. An Indian trekker lingered nearby, clearly starstruck and pointing his own camera at Nims.

"Hey buddy, how are you doing?" Nims asked him, mildly irritated.

"I'm, uh, kind of impressed," the Indian man replied. "I just want to say congratulations to you. Do you mind if I take a picture with you?"

"Sure," Nims replied. "Not now, though, because I'm working."

As he finished signing books, Sherpa Barista began to fill up with another wave of trekkers stopping in to refuel. Nims shook a few hands and then ducked out the side door, joining the princess as they got up and continued on their way.

A group of six British trekkers walked straight up to the counter and grabbed a stack of books at fifty dollars a pop. "We met him earlier today up at the Everest View hotel," one of them said. "Legend."

A month later, Princess al-Thani became the first Qatari woman to summit Everest. Less than three weeks after that, she and Nims were standing on the top of Denali together. (Al-Thani was going for the "Explorer's Grand Slam" of climbing the Seven Summits plus reaching the North and South Poles, and now seems to be going for all fourteen eight-thousanders.) Nims had to withstand plenty of sneering for the

hefty payday and free press that came with guiding the princess. However, another facet of Nims's reputation is that he's the first person to
jump to the rescue of climbers in trouble, whether they're part of Elite
Exped or not. In the fall of 2022, he proved this to be true once again
during a difficult climbing season on Manaslu.

Manaslu was fast becoming the second most popular peak to climb
in the new era of eight-thousander guided climbing. The eighth-tallest
mountain in the world has two stunningly sharp pyramids at the top,
but gentle slopes below, making it relatively accessible and a popular
stepping stone to Everest.

Manaslu base camp was buzzing in the fall of 2022. In addition to
Elite Exped, a large number of other guiding outfits were there, including SST, Asian Trekking, Imagine, IMG, CTSS, Summit Climb, and an
Indian-owned company called Transcend Adventures. In total, roughly
four hundred people were going to be attempting to climb the mountain.

Also in base camp was Hilaree Nelson, an American professional
climber and freeskier, with her pro-skier husband, Jim Morrison.
They planned to climb independently and then make the first-ever ski
descent from the summit. On September 26 they dashed to the top in
dicey weather amid intermittent heavy snowfall. On the ski down, Nelson was caught in a small avalanche and was swept over a 5,000-foot
face. Morrison tried desperately but could not find her. Thirteen other
climbers were injured that same day, and one Sherpa guide was killed in
a separate avalanche.

Nelson was a longtime North Face–sponsored teammate and friend
of Conrad Anker's and Jimmy Chin's. When Chin learned of the accident he was devastated, not only for the death of one of his closest
friends, but for the grief of Morrison, and of Nelson's two teenage sons
from a previous marriage. Morrison, uncertain of what to do, traveled to
a village down valley. Meanwhile, Chin phoned Nims.

Only days earlier, a fire had broken out at Elite Exped's Kathmandu headquarters that had killed two of Nims's own dear friends and employees, reportedly caused by the explosion of highly flammable oxygen bottles stored in the office. Nevertheless, Nims rallied his team at Manaslu base camp and essentially took control of all movement up and down the mountain. He coordinated multiple fast and light search teams, which were able to find and retrieve Nelson's body. The event remained tragic, but the quick closure was a minor miracle for Morrison, Chin, and many others in the climbing community.

"I feel like I'm indebted to him forever for that," Chin says. "He did not need to be involved in that. He and his team hung it way out there for me. To have him come through in that moment, to meet with Jim to make a plan in the midst of one of the most chaotic moments in his own life, was pretty striking—and he wouldn't take any money for any of it."

Whatever one makes of Nims—selfless hero or egotistical embellisher, empire builder or fallible man destined to crash and burn—he is unquestionably the face of Everest and the broader Himalayan climbing industry at the moment. Largely by choice, he's carrying the weight of representing Nepal.

20

#BROTHERHOOD

On Nims's Instagram feed, and the feed of just about every other Nepali guide and guide company owner today, you get a sense of the camaraderie that now exists between them and the Western guides and climbers.

Perhaps most telling of all was a picture posted by SST's co-owner Tashi Lakpa in April 2022. It was of him out to dinner with Simone Moro, who had returned to his job piloting helicopters in the Khumbu, where he'd resolidified bonds with his Sherpa friends. With my besties in Kathmandu, he wrote. #Brotherhood.

Of course, it wasn't always that way. The years of the conflict on the Lhotse Face, the avalanche, and the earthquake were tense. "Maybe Sherpas saw an opportunity to push the Western leaders out," Dawa Steven reflects. "They were probably thinking, 'Hey, this is a Sherpa mountain, and it should be Sherpas running any industry that happens on it.'" Dawa Steven says he isn't sure the "nationalistic rhetoric" was the right approach.

Garrett Madison was bothered by it. He believed that Sherpas getting ownership of Everest guiding companies made sense, but he felt they were too eager to cut Western guides out. He once worried that Sherpas might be "trying to figure out how to monopolize the mountain, once and for all, like maybe even get some government mandate saying no Western operators allowed."

Lukas Furtenbach has his own concerns about the outlook of his business. "The Nepali companies have taken over I would say ninety to ninety-five percent of the market in the last ten years," he explains. "The only reason why my company exists is because we are doing something that the Sherpas can't copy—yet." He's referring to an innovative expedition type that Furtenbach Adventures offers called "Flash Expeditions," which significantly speed up the length of an Everest climb for clients willing to pay a premium. "The Sherpas are not there yet," he says of this expedition type, but he predicts they will be very soon. "I give us maybe five to ten years and then we are gone." Though there's melancholy in Furtenbach's outlook, he also says, "I do see this as an important and right development. It is their mountain. We are guests in this country."

For his part, Madison has come to see things differently, and more optimistically, in 2023 than he did a few years ago. "A rising tide lifts all boats," he told *GQ* when asked if he was worried about Nims and his company Elite Exped taking over the Himalayan guiding industry.

For most guides, Western and Sherpa alike, that appears to be the feeling in Everest base camp today, that integration and cooperation, not elimination, is the way forward. Sherpa guide company owners like Mingma G. are able to hold difficult truths about the history of their industry in balance with respect and appreciation for the Westerners who were integral components of building it.

"I have huge respect for Russell Brice—for me, he's the most important person in the guiding era," Mingma G. says. "No accidents, no deaths at all, during his whole career. And if the route is not in good condition, he'll just shut it down. He doesn't care. And he doesn't only care about the clients either. He'll say his whole team is important.

There are a lot of companies who will tell you to just keep pushing, and keep pushing the clients.

"It is obviously a give-and-take relationship but, let's be honest, we are in this position because of our foreign friends. This relationship is nearly a century old—there is a lot of respect."

Phunuru feels the respect as well. Over at IMG, where he's been for twenty-three years, he is as integral to the company's Everest expeditions as Simonson. "I'm totally happy. I've had a lot of offers, too, from other companies—to guide, to become a partner—but IMG has been really good to me," he says. "I've worked for them—and with Westerners—since I was fifteen. Half my life. I was given a lot of opportunities with Eric and I really trust him. I'm one of only two or three Sherpas working the international programs for guide companies. Maybe I could make more money if I owned a business but it's not even about money for me."

Phunuru is particularly proud of his and Simonson's effort to bring more Sherpani guides into the IMG family. Phunuru says they aim to have ten women guides working in the Himalayas soon. Reflecting on the industry he helped shape, he says, "There has been so much change. These Sherpa teams are fixing the entire mountain, from the bottom of the icefall to the summit. There are Sherpa guides making, like, $35K in a season. The Sherpas are one hundred percent involved now. And the next generation will be excellent climbers."

Phunuru's friend Tashi Riten is a great example of the evolution. When he parted ways with IMG after the 2013 conflict, Ryan Waters hired him at Mountain Professionals, where he's since become the company's highest-ranking guide in the Himalayas. Waters was aware of Tashi Riten's reputation as opinionated and outspoken when they partnered up, but he says it hasn't been an issue in the least. The two have a great working relationship that was ten years strong already in 2023 and looks poised to last for the long term.

"I feel like all that stuff is in the past," says Waters. "I only know him as this soft-spoken, excellent guide. Clients love him. And I've had lots of people try to hire him away from me."

"He's a great person, very humble," Tashi Riten says of Waters.

Though Phunuru and Tashi Riten are both optimistic about the future of Himalayan guiding, there is one technical point they argue over: certification requirements. The matter is currently at the heart of a slow-burning and, as of 2023, unresolved supreme court battle in Nepal that is pitting the NNMGA (Nepal's arm of the IFMGA) against the NMA (the government-backed nonprofit that provides certification through its color-coded book system).

Tashi Riten is a fully certified IFMGA guide, and he would like the IFMGA certification to be recognized as the country's highest qualification. Though this would likely give IFMGA-certified guides a leg up in getting the best-paid jobs, Tashi Riten's motivation largely comes down to safety. His grandfather was killed by an avalanche on Manaslu in 1972, and his father, who also worked in the mountaineering field, never got over it. Tashi Riten believes most Sherpa deaths and injuries are still the result of inadequate training. "My family, my mother, they don't like me working on Everest," he says. "You might have a neighbor that works in the mountains—they leave and their family has no idea if they will come back. That is because people don't understand what a difference the training makes."

Phunuru agrees that safety is essential but thinks getting the certification is no substitute for decades of experience in the field. "I don't believe IFMGA certification automatically makes you a better guide. That's total bullshit," he says. Phunuru accepts that the NMA's red, blue, and black books are imperfect too, and largely symbolic. Yet, to him, any way to log experience in the places it counts most—high up on the biggest mountains in the world—is a better indicator of safety than a formalized training process. "Many of the younger IFMGA

guides do not even have very much eight-thousand-meter experience,"
he points out.

If the court case remains in stalemate, there may be a compromise.
The latest development is talk of a grandfathering system, whereby experienced NMA guides are able to earn IFMGA certification through a
series of simple assessments. Yet to be honest, Phunuru says he wouldn't
bother to go through that. He's not only one of the most sought-after
guides on Everest, but IMG clients also request him as a private guide on
several of the other Seven Summits, such as Aconcagua, Kilimanjaro, and
Denali, which don't require IFMGA certification anyway. "I've climbed
Denali five times," he says. "That's the most ascents for a Nepali."

With the help of a drone—of which there are many flying around the
Khumbu Valley these days, creating slick content for guiding company ad
campaigns—one can truly experience the full scale and sprawl of Everest
base camp. Clients, guides, and staff are constantly moving among the
brightly colored tents and expedition compounds, which are larger than
ever. There are now a dozen Brice-style domes on the Khumbu Glacier,
each with a big-screen TV surrounded by beanbags. Elite Exped has a
merch stand in its communal dome—basically a souvenir shop like you
might find in the office of a whitewater rafting company—where you can
buy logo tees, water bottles, and ball caps. The thrum of helicopter traffic
is persistent. Beyond base camp, in the lowest and flattest section of the
icefall, guides set up mini climbing camps on thirty-foot-tall fins of ice
to get clients acquainted with the various unfamiliar shiny metal things
hanging from their brand-spanking-new harnesses.

Over at Elite Exped's section of base camp, stylish and attractive
client teams full of selfie-loving, Nims-adoring extroverts enjoy rum-
fueled nightclub-style dance parties. "Next day if you can't operate,
that's your fuckup," Nims told the journalist Grayson Schaffer. Around

camp, the Elite Exped teams are often referred to as "Nimsfluencers." They also get access to one of the most skilled Sherpa guide teams on the mountain. Elite Exped charges only $45,000 for what it calls a "standard" guided climb, or $100,000 for those wishing to climb on an accelerated schedule.

While far more low-key than Nims, Mingma G. at Imagine Nepal and the three brothers from SST are not exactly camera shy either. Neither is Lakpa Rita's younger brother Kami Rita (not to be mistaken for Alan Arnette's regular climbing partner Kami Sherpa), who showcases impressive Instagram and social media skills for Khangri Experience, the company he and Lakpa Rita founded in 2022, and who also still guides for SST. Even more impressive are his climbing skills—Kami Rita holds the record for most Everest summits with twenty-eight as of the end of the spring 2023 season.

Dawa Steven, on the other hand, keeps a low profile these days. Since 2012, he's located Asian Trekking's tents down glacier, because there were too many people in the heart of base camp treating him like a camp counselor, asking him to mediate disagreements, organize rescues, and answer banal questions from clients of other groups. "Everest base camp started to feel more like a city than a village," he says. "That's when I guess you could say I chose to live in the suburbs."

Regardless of where they set down their tents, collectively, the Nepali guide companies are in charge. All signs point toward that being the case henceforth. From a business standpoint, they're working at a scale that is beyond what the Western guides either can or have the risk tolerance to copy. They also have stronger connections within the Nepali government, more direct access to people in power, and, thus, more influence. Western operators will often roll their eyes when they find out the Nepalis have figured out a "workaround" for a seemingly unsolvable problem. But this is the way of things.

Rope-fixing, not only in the icefall but all the way to the summit, is now entirely in the hands of Sherpas and is finished impressively early each season. When negotiations about things like helicopter traffic in the Khumbu Valley and the ethics of using helicopters to shuttle supplies to Camp Two in order to reduce time in the icefall are underway, Western guides are barely a part of the conversation.

"I went to the rope-fixing meeting in 2022 and I was the only Westerner there," says Ryan Waters.

"Tashi Riten would have gone but he was on the mountain with clients so I went instead. And they weren't talking about rope-fixing at all—because that's pretty straightforward these days—it was all about how to make guiding on Everest better. There were reps from each of the guiding companies, reps from the Himalayan Rescue Association, from the Ministry of Tourism—and it was all about making the mountain cleaner, about improving the MOT liaison officer system. But now, instead of, say, Russell complaining about something—which never seemed to land quite right—you have a hundred Sherpas complaining, and they have the real power in this country.

"The joke between all of us Western guides is that these base camp meetings had turned into a social hour for us," says AAI guide Ben Jones. "Because we'd show up and it was the Nepalis who were actually figuring out all the logistics and making things happen. We felt like we were kind of in control for a while. Not anymore . . . But they've been doing a phenomenal job."

Indeed, 2022 was a historically successful year on Everest. Some 670 people summited during the spring season alone—all from the Nepal side, as the Chinese side remained closed as a result of the pandemic. Only three people died over the course of the year, two Nepalis and one Russian, none of them above Camp Two. It was the second-lowest death-to-summits ratio in Everest history, after 2008. The remarkable achievement was a sharp rebuke to guiding industry critics who claimed overcrowding would lead to fatal disasters—and to anyone who still doubted the strength of Nepali-owned guide companies. It was a statement of how far the industry had come.

The spring of 2023, however, brought a series of events that reminded everyone how quickly things change on Everest. Tragedy struck before most clients had even arrived at base camp. On April 12, 2023, three of Mingma G.'s most experienced Sherpa support climbers at Imagine Nepal—Tenjing Sherpa, Lakpa Sherpa, and Badure Sherpa—were killed in the Khumbu Icefall when several towers of ice collapsed on them. Two weeks later, a sixty-nine-year-old American doctor named Jonathan Sugarman, who was climbing with IMG, died suddenly of heart failure at Camp Two. Then on May 16, Phurba Sherpa, who was part of a Nepal Army cleanup expedition (and is not to be confused with Phurba Tashi Sherpa), died of an unknown altitude illness on the Lhotse Face.

Five deaths so early in the season were a concerning number, but accidents—especially non-climbing deaths like Sugarman's—are chalked up as the price of doing business on Everest, and it was easy to focus on the wins. On the same day that Phurba Sherpa died, SST congratulated a team of Chinese climbers on being the first people to summit that season. Shortly thereafter, they posted to social media about Norwegian climber Kristin Harila, whose expedition they were providing logistical support to, successfully summiting Everest and Lhotse in her quest to break Nims's record for the fastest time to climb all fourteen eight-thousanders. "Let's cheer her on," said the post. (That July, Harila, thirty-seven, did in fact break the record, summiting all fourteen eight-thousanders in three months and one day.)

But slowly, the death toll continued climbing. Between May 17 and May 25, nine more climbers died or went missing between the South Col and the summit, seven of whom were clients of guided expeditions.

(The other two were a Sherpa guide of one of the climbers who went missing in the death zone and a Hungarian climber who was receiving logistical support from SST). All of the missing were eventually declared dead.

Meanwhile there had been another death at base camp, of a fifty-nine-year-old Indian woman named Suzanne Jesus; a sudden death of a Sherpa cook named Ang Kami Sherpa at Camp Two; and Garrett Madison lost a climber, very unexpectedly, just below Camp Four, when sixty-three-year-old South African doctor Pieter Swart died on his way down from the South Col to Camp Two after abandoning his summit bid. "I think it really surprised him—caught him off guard—as it did all of us," says Madison, who insists Swart had been going strong and that his deterioration was so unexpected and rapid that he believes it was unpreventable.

Just like that, the 2023 spring season closed with another record on Everest: it was officially the deadliest season in the mountain's history, with seventeen lives lost.

Because news of the 2023 Everest deaths was received by the press and the public in a trickle over the course of six weeks and not in the torrent of a single mass-casualty event, it didn't trigger the hysteria seen in previous years marked by a high number of deaths. Furthermore, the varying circumstances of each of the fatalities made it more difficult to find a single story to summarize them.

Yet those within the industry needed to make sense of the season. It was a remarkably cold spring, with hundreds of climbers getting frostbite, and there was a wicked virus that ravaged base camp and sent many people home, including guides and Sherpas whose expertise was needed on the mountain, and whose absence perhaps unbalanced the preferred guide-to-client ratios in certain cases. In this way, the season presented unique challenges. However, taking a closer look at the circumstances of the seven client deaths that occurred above 8,000 meters revealed a more familiar concern: they were all under the supervision of

Nepali-owned guiding companies. These included SST and one of its subsidiary companies called 14 Peaks; Pioneer Adventure; 8K Expeditions; Himalayan Traverse Adventure; and Asian Trekking. Distressed industry players, including many Western guides, worried the fatalities were the result of less diligent client vetting and an influx of less experienced climbing employees being allowed by these Nepali-owned companies to guide in the death zone.

"Seventeen deaths was incredibly surprising and disheartening, to be honest," says Mike Hamill. "I don't know the full backstory on all the deaths but there were an awful lot of people just disappearing." Adrian Ballinger goes a step further, pointing the finger at what he sees as shoddy operators, and saying he's "furious at the companies allowing this level of incompetence." Other Western guides who asked not to be named called the mishaps "criminal."

The Nepali company owners did not brush aside the losses. SST cofounder Tashi Lakpa said that the 2023 season was "so difficult" and "such sad news for mountaineering." Most of the Nepali operators expressed their commitment to avoid being overrepresented in the unwanted columns of the record books in future seasons, and their success in previous seasons on Everest has proven that they are more than capable of doing so. However, some Westerners expect that there will continue to be higher numbers of client deaths on Nepali-run expeditions. This is not because of negligence or callousness on the part of the Nepalis, but because of a cultural difference in their business models, in their way of conceptualizing their duty of care to their clients, and often, in their clients' preference to assess their own readiness to climb and make their own decisions about whether to turn around or not high on the mountain.

"A lot of the newer Nepali companies have been very frank and open about how they feel they are, in many cases, in the business of logistics—that your safety is your responsibility," says Hamill. Whereas most of the

Western guides believe it's their duty to scrupulously vet their clients before bringing them to Everest, and then force them to abandon their climbs if they're in danger on the mountain, many Nepali guides tend toward a belief that it's the client's job to be aware of the dangers, and their right to take the risks if they choose. Though Garret Madison takes client vetting and safety very seriously, he doesn't disagree with the underlying logic that responsibility in the mountains is a two-way street. "The whole thing about mountaineering in general is the importance of choosing your climbing partners carefully," he says. "You and your group have to be able to get yourself out of what you get into. The best thing client climbers can do is choose a team they want to be with up high."

Relevant as cultural and business-philosophy explanations may be, the 2023 spring season underscored the complexities of the contemporary Everest guiding industry, showcasing its continued failures and its successes. The Nepali-owned companies control the mountain, dominate its statistics, care about its future, and will be the chief architects of shaping it. They have poured time, money, and soul into building their skills and their businesses, and while they will take stock of spring 2023, they will continue to be open about celebrating their astonishing victories, as they were that season.

On May 19, Phunuru Sherpa posted a heroic summit shot wearing his trademark green down suit, with a shout-out to his sponsor Everest Outfit. Tashi Lakpa congratulated his seventeen-year-old son for summiting both Everest and Lhotse in the span of ten hours. Mingma G. praised his Imagine employee Sona Sherpa for summiting Everest three times in spring 2023 alone, once while fixing ropes and twice more with clients. And on May 24, Kami Rita made his record-setting twenty-eighth summit, which led Nims to Instagram to congratulate his "brother," writing, "I'm so proud of you and what you have achieved—you are an inspiration to Nepal and the whole climbing community."

Most resonant of all, and the news that got the most attention of the 2023 season, was the story of a startlingly improbable rescue. Gelje Sherpa, a thirty-year-old guide working for SST, spotted a nearly dead fifty-eight-year-old Malaysian climber named Ravichandran Tharumalingam stranded in the death zone. Tharumalingam, who had attempted Everest before, was climbing unguided under the logistics umbrella of SST subsidiary 14 Peaks. Gelje abandoned his own summit bid with a client, and in a superhuman effort, wrapped the stricken Tharumalingam in insulating foam, strapped him to his back, and spent six hours carrying him all the way down to Camp Three, where he was picked up by a helicopter. Tharumalingam made a full recovery.

The Sherpa operators on Everest still feel good about the future, and so do the handful of Westerners that have weathered the upheaval of the past ten years and remain on the Khumbu Glacier. Mountain Professionals, for example, excels at making its trips feel like the sort of boutique experience many Westerners of means are seeking these days. While Waters brings only moderate numbers of clients to the mountain each year, going after the higher end of the Western market is working for him. In 2023 he had four clients, and also successfully guided the fourth blind person to the summit.

Madison Mountaineering is operating on a larger scale. Garrett Madison has now summited Everest thirteen times—the third-most for any westerner—and within days of wrapping up both his 2022 and 2023 Everest climbs, he was hopping over to Pakistan to run what's become his annual guided expedition on K2. Madison has now guided clients on K2 eight times, the most for any guiding company in the world, and summited three times himself (a record for Westerners). His is one of the most dynamic companies on Everest, helped by his pragmatic outlook.

EVEREST, INC.   289

"Climbing Everest with a guide is an adventure travel activity. It's mountain tourism," Madison says of what he does. But that doesn't mean he's cynical about it, or about his clients. "These are all just people who have this amazing goal but also know that they don't necessarily have what it takes to climb Everest on their own." Like all the guides who have witnessed the evolution of Everest clientele over the years, he has simply moved on from the notion that less capable means less deserving.

Tucked low and out of sight, between two small rises in the Khumbu's moraine, is Madison's former employer, AAI. Todd Burleson's company charged $70,000 for its 2023 Everest expedition, and it remains one of the most consistently reliable outfitters on the mountain, despite having a shrinking share of the market. AAI had only three clients in 2022 and five in 2023. While Burleson isn't on Everest himself much these days, he is still quite particular about who he'll hire to guide and which types of clients he'll allow to join his teams. "I know other companies are running more clients," he admits. "We just come from a very conservative background. I certainly don't see K2 on our agenda."

"It will be interesting to see if we're able to continue getting enough people to make the Everest expeditions worthwhile," says AAI guide Ben Jones.

Mike Hamill's CTSS is offering a tiered model in the vein of SST. However, for its higher-priced options, CTSS is attracting a wealthy American clientele that SST still struggles to access. Photos of CTSS's private luxury domes, with large windows, shag carpeting, beds, and down comforters, went viral in 2021. In 2022, CTSS had twenty-nine Everest clients, the most for any Western guiding company, and in 2023 they were up to more than fifty clients, according to Hamill. No matter what tier they're at, Hamill and his in-country partner, Tendi, do their best to give their clients a good experience, because they believe it means they're more likely to get up and down Everest safely. "I know there's this old idea that you have to suffer on Everest, and that you can't have any of these amenities," he says. "Like at Camp Two: you really suffer a lot up there and we think we can make it more comfortable. It's our job to provide this for our clients, because it makes them climb better and stronger."

Due to New Zealand's strict policies during the pandemic, Adventure Consultants was away from Everest for three straight years, up through 2022. Guy Cotter and his group finally returned for the spring 2023 season, with seven clients. Cotter feels good about the future of the company. "I personally think that there will always be people who don't want to go on a trip that feels like it's being led by a boy band," Cotter says, taking a not-so-subtle dig at the flashy Nepali guides like Nims. "That said, I don't have the intention to build Adventure Consultants back up to where it was. We used to run thirty-three different expeditions a year—we had a New Zealand operation, a Chamonix operation, a couple dozen staff in the office—and we plan on running fewer trips, with a much smaller administration crew. We'll still run all the Seven Summits, though."

In early 2022, the sixty-nine-year-old George Dunn and seventy-one-year-old Phil Ershler cashed out and made the sixty-seven-year-old Eric Simonson the sole owner of IMG. Simonson is the rare Western elder statesman who seems as excited about running guided Everest climbs in 2023 as he did in the 1990s, despite an uncertain future for his company. In the 2023 spring season IMG had just five clients—down from eight the previous year—who paid $49,500 for IMG's "classic" Everest expedition. (Options for extra guidance and oxygen bumped up the price tag to $67,500). Mingma G. likes to joke that IMG's base camp, which sits below the scrum, low on the glacier, right where it's been for decades, looks a little too much like it did in the 1990s. Jokes aside, it's the low client numbers that have rattled the typically stubborn Simonson enough to make him start opening his mind to change. "I've been thinking a lot about reinventing what people want to pay for," he says. "But where you put your price point becomes a philosophical question about who you want your client to be. The world keeps changing and we need to adapt."

Over on the north side, Adrian Ballinger's Alpenglow hasn't been able to run Everest expeditions since 2019 due to China's lingering refusal to grant tourist visas as a result of the pandemic. But Alpenglow has been operational elsewhere, and the time away from Everest hasn't dampened Ballinger's excitement for innovation, particularly around what he calls the "Rapid Ascent Climb." Ballinger was in fact first to market the technologically assisted, sped-up style of approaching an Everest climb, which is similar to Furtenbach Adventures' Flash Expedition. Clients who fork over $98,000 for Alpenglow's Rapid Ascent climb, or $110,000 for a Furtenbach Flash Expedition, can knock one to two weeks off the typical Everest itinerary. The packages include what might be the most high-end technological assistance yet seen on Everest: preacclimatizing at home.

Before you leave for one of these climbs, something resembling a deflated bouncy castle shows up on your doorstep, with instructions on how to inflate it around your bed. This creates a hyperbaric chamber, in which you can control oxygen levels and sleep in an environment mimicking, say, 15,000 feet of elevation for a week. "It's actually a whole system," Ballinger explains. "It's not just the hyperbaric chambers. Our entire system is built around being able to move quickly." Alpenglow's approach is meant to cater to clients whose biggest barrier for entry is not skill or cost but time. Like a lot of his clients, Ballinger—who is a father to a two-year-old boy—wants to spend more time with family and friends, and to have big adventures on a tighter schedule.

Some of the old guard have been distrustful that Flash Expeditions and Rapid Ascents truly work, and don't mince words about it. "Eric Simonson said it's snake oil. Russell Brice said it's bullshit," says

Furtenbach. Yet, Ballinger and Furtenbach are proving the effectiveness of their speedy climbs, having both successfully run several shortened Everest expeditions. Ballinger had multiple successful Rapid Ascent summits on eight-thousanders, including on Everest before China closed access to the mountain in 2020, and Furtenbach has had up to ten Flash clients on Everest's south side, most of whom have summited within three weeks. Furtenbach sees constant reinvention as a necessity for survival. "The old companies are losing their share of the market and their clients to the Nepali companies because they didn't change the product. They are still trying to sell the same product as it has been in the eighties or nineties."

Ballinger, similarly, has no qualms about turning his back on tradition. "Look, we also don't take boats to India anymore, before trekking across the mountains to get to the Khumbu Valley," he says. "Even things like weather forecasting have shortened the length of all our expeditions, because we now only leave base camp when the weather's good. Personally, I think the coolest stuff that's happening in climbing and mountaineering has a lot to do with efficiency. People are moving faster up El Capitan. People are chasing FKTs [fastest known times] on mountains like Aconcagua and Denali. I think the cutting edge of the sport has a lot to do with efficiency, and I love efficiency. I don't expect everyone to agree with me but I feel pretty good about it."

Hamill agrees that reinvention is the way forward. "The old guard didn't really need to innovate anymore, because they had a steady stream of clients," he says. "But this industry needed to be shaken up. It hasn't changed in a generation. I think we can do things better and more efficiently. Me, Madison, Ballinger, we're competing against each other on that front."

Changes in the way rotations are done are also speeding up the experience. "It's kind of a new phenomenon," Jones says. "There are clients just doing one rotation and then summiting after that. We used to always sleep at Camp Three without oxygen during our second rotation, and then come down one last time before the summit push. No one does that anymore. I think it's only a matter of time before people will literally show up, put on oxygen in base camp, and climb to the summit and back in a week. Maybe it will be in a full space suit from SpaceX or something, and you just walk right up to the top."

Everest will probably forever be criticized for not being the most attractive of the 8,000-meter peaks, for being uninteresting to climb—for being *easy*, even. But it's important to note that most of those who have actually climbed it—including many who you'd think would look down their nose at Everest—feel different.

Conrad Anker doesn't necessarily understand why so many people still want to climb Everest, but he's beyond thrilled that the guiding industry is beginning to lift Nepal the way it should. "There is only one Everest," he says. "And it's really for the country of Nepal. Nepal does not have a cricket team to play against Pakistan or India, but they are very proud of Everest. There is a statue in Kathmandu for the first woman to climb Everest. There's an Everest summiteers association. Some of the top Sherpas endorse things like cement or bottled water. It's a big deal. Back in 2006, I went to an orphanage and this kid knew all the Sherpas who had multiple ascents. He said to me, 'I'm going to become a climber.' This is Nepal's greatness."

Simone Moro will always feel awed by Everest, particularly the way the mountain's top eight hundred feet pushes mountaineers. "The high camp, where you sleep, is about the same height as the summit of lower eight-thousand-meter peaks. You only spend a few minutes on these summits—you spend the *night* at that altitude on Everest. At that altitude your speed is around two hundred feet per hour, even with oxygen—much slower without. This means a difference of nearly four hours going up and at least one hour going down. A five-hour difference. It's huge at that altitude. Everest will remain Everest, especially for anyone who wants to climb without oxygen—there are still less than one hundred people in history who have done this."

Moro's climbing partner, Ueli Steck, shared a similar sentiment. Steck recovered from his 2013 experience and returned to Everest in 2017 to attempt a very similar route to the one he and Moro had wanted to climb together. Sadly, Steck ended up dying on an acclimatization foray up Nuptse. Before meeting that tragic end, he explained to *Outside* magazine what had drawn him back to Everest. "Of course, I climbed Everest without oxygen but it's not the end of the story for me. The summit itself is not what counts. It's how you got there, what did you climb. And there are really great opportunities to climb on this mountain. It's a beautiful place."

Perhaps the most unexpected expression of reverence came from Jon Krakauer. "Despite what people tell you, it was beautiful," he said of his summit day, while promoting *Into Thin Air* in 1997. "It was one of the most beautiful mornings of climbing I've ever had."

Whatever faults some people see in it, the tallest mountain in the world can't help but have a profound effect on anyone who climbs it. Yet climbing it is one thing. That there are men and women who choose to help others get up Everest year after year—sometimes twice a year—is something that has been harder to understand ever since Todd Burleson placed his ad in *Outside* magazine in 1989.

Yes, it's a job, and particularly for Sherpas, the astonishing economic boon their work has given not only them and their families but also their wider communities would be reason enough to do it. Yet whether they are Sherpa or Western or otherwise, very few guides would say the money is their motivation. They talk, instead, about the intoxication of getting people to the top.

GLOSSARY of KEY PLAYERS

Alex Abramov: Founder of guiding company 7 Summits Club. (Russia)

Conrad Anker: Professional alpinist and North Face athlete; member of the 1999 expedition on Everest that discovered the body of George Mallory. (United States)

Alan Arnette: Everest and K2 summiteer, journalist, and chronicler of guided Himalayan climbing. (United States)

Jan Arnold: Physician and spouse of Rob Hall. (New Zealand)

Melissa Arnot: Former Rainier Mountaineering Inc (RMI) guide, peacemaker during the 2013 conflict, and one of just nine women in history to summit Everest without oxygen. (United States)

Peter Athans: Had more attempts on Everest in the 1980s and early 1990s than any Western climber; Alpine Ascents International (AAI) Everest guide in the 1990s. (United States)

Gary Ball: Cofounder of guiding company Adventure Consultants. Grew up climbing with Nick Banks, Russell Brice, and Bill King. Ball died in 1993 on Dhaulagiri. (New Zealand)

Adrian Ballinger: Founder of guiding company Alpenglow Expeditions. Formerly the lead guide on all 8,000-meter peaks for Russell Brice's company Himalayan Experience (Himex). (United States/United Kingdom)

Nick Banks: Attempted Everest in 1977 and summited in 1979, becoming the second New Zealander in history to do so after Edmund Hillary. Guided on Everest for Jagged Globe. (New Zealand)

Dick Bass: Wealthy Snowbird Ski Resort owner and recreational mountaineer, who summited Everest in 1985, becoming the first person in history to complete the Seven Summits. (United States)

Steve Bell: Cofounder of guiding company Himalayan Kingdoms and, later, founder of Jagged Globe. (United Kingdom)

Willie Benegas: Cofounder with his brother of guiding company Benegas Brothers Expeditions. Formerly guided for Mountain Madness. Close friend of Babu Chiri Sherpa. (Argentina)

Wally Berg: Early AAI guide on Everest; later founded Berg Adventures. (United States)

Tim Bevan: Founder of Working Title Films, which produced the 2015 film *Everest.* (New Zealand)

Chris Bonington: Pioneering climber and mountaineer; a member of the same 1985 expedition in which Dick Bass summited. (United Kingdom)

Anatoli Boukreev: Prolific 8,000-meter mountaineer; guide for Henry Todd's Himalayan Guides in 1995 and Scott Fischer's Mountain Madness in 1996; killed while climbing Annapurna in 1997. (Kazakhstan)

Louis Bowen: Investment banker who was part of the first group of client climbers ever to reach the summit of Everest as part of a guided expedition, in May 1992, with AAI. (United States)

Lydia Bradey: First woman in history to summit Everest without oxygen in 1988; went on to guide Everest and other 8,000-meter peaks for Himex and Adventure Consultants. (New Zealand)

David Breashears: Mountaineer and filmmaker who accompanied Dick Bass on his 1985 climb, assisted in the rescue operation during the disaster of 1996, and made the *Everest* IMAX film, which was released in 1998. (United States)

Russell Brice: Founder of guiding company Himalayan Experience (Himex). (New Zealand)

Andy Broom: Cofounder of guiding company Out There Trekking (OTT). (United Kingdom)

Mark Bryant: Editor-in-chief of *Outside* magazine between 1990 and 1999. (United States)

Todd Burleson: Founder of Alpine Ascents International (AAI). First person to advertise a guided Everest climb. (United States.)

Greg Child: Climber and writer who summited Everest in 1995 and wrote about it in *Outside* magazine. (Australia/United States)

Jimmy Chin: Professional climber, North Face athlete, and award-winning filmmaker of *Meru* and *Free Solo*. (United States)

Yvon Chouinard: Early rock climbing pioneer, champion of minimum-impact climbing, founder of Patagonia clothing and gear company. (United States)

Jason Clarke: Actor who portrayed Rob Hall in the 2015 film *Everest*. (New Zealand)

Guy Cotter: Early Adventure Consultants guide on Everest, now owner of the company. (New Zealand)

Phil Crampton: Founder of guiding company Altitude Junkies. (United States/United Kingdom)

Stephen Daldry: Film director, attached to the Working Title *Everest* film early on but eventually left the project. (United Kingdom)

Mark Dekeyser: Weather forecaster for the Royal Meteorological Institute of Belgium and part-time Everest weather forecaster. (Belgium)

George Dunn: Cofounder of International Mountain Guides (IMG). (United States)

Phil Ershler: Cofounder of IMG. (United States)

Michael Fagan: Seattle-based amateur meteorologist and one of the first to sell weather forecasts to the Everest guiding industry in the late 1990s. (United States)

Kevin Fedarko: Journalist and contributor to *Outside* magazine. (United States)

Rebecca "Becks" Ferry: Semiprofessional runner, stay-at-home mom, 8,000-meter mountaineer, who has summited three 8,000-meter peaks: Everest, K2, and Lhotse (twice), with the help of guides. (United Kingdom)

Frank Fischbeck: Hong Kong–based businessman, who summited Denali with guide Vern Tejas in 1986 and was part of the 1992 AAI guided Everest climb but did not reach the summit. (South Africa)

Scott Fischer: Cofounder of guiding company Mountain Madness; killed on Everest in 1996. (United States)

Lukas Furtenbach: Founder of guiding company Furtenbach Adventures and owner of Everest Oxygen, the most widely used supplier on Everest today. (Austria)

Ray Genet: Pioneering Denali guide; founder of guiding company Genet Expeditions; died while climbing on Everest in 1979 with Nick Banks and Hannelore Schmatz. (Switzerland/United States)

Dunham Gooding: Founder of guiding service and climbing school American Alpine Institute in Washington State. (United States)

Mike Gordon: One of the four first client climbers ever to sign up for a guided Everest expedition, which was with AAI in 1990; Gordon returned to attempt Everest three times with AAI. (United States)

Jonathan Griffith: Climber and photographer accompanying Ueli Steck and Simone Moro during their 2013 climb that sparked a row with Sherpa workers. (United Kingdom)

Peter Habeler: One of the superstar mountaineers recruited to work as a guide during the first guided ascent of Everest in 1990. (Austria)

Peter Hackett: Doctor, Everest summiteer, and one of the world's leading altitude experts. (United States)

Eric Hagerman: *Outside* correspondent, who wrote about Babu Chiri Sherpa in 2001. (United States)

Dave Hahn: Longtime RMI guide, and IMG Everest guide, who held the record for ascents by a Westerner (fifteen) until 2022 (the record was broken by Brit Kenton Cool). Hahn was also part of the 1999 search for George Mallory's body. (United States)

Rob Hall: Cofounder of Adventure Consultants; died while guiding clients on Everest in 1996. (New Zealand)

Mike Hamill: Founder of guiding company Climbing the Seven Summits (CTSS). Former guide for IMG and RMI. (United States)

David Hamilton: Lead Everest guide for Jagged Globe between 1999 and 2019. (United Kingdom)

Doug Hansen: Mailman from Seattle and client climber who attempted Shisha-pangma with IMG in 1993, attempted Everest with Adventure Consultants in 1995, and died trying again in 1996. (United States)

Kent Harvey: Climber and cameraman who was on Everest during the 2014 avalanche, shooting footage for the 2015 film *Everest*. (United States)

Elizabeth Hawley: Kathmandu-based reporter and founder of the Himalayan Database, who began cataloging climbs in the 1960s to create what has become the most extensive and accurate record of Himalayan expeditions in the world. (United States)

Nick Heil: *Outside* magazine contributor and author of the book *Dark Summit*, an exposé on the circumstances of David Sharp's death and other events of the 2006 spring climbing season on Everest. (United States)

Sandy Hill: Made three attempts of Everest, including one guided AAI climb, one as a member of a David Breashears expedition, and one as part of the fateful guided Mountain Madness climb of 1996, in which she summited and became the second woman to complete the Seven Summits. (United States)

Edmund Hillary: First person to summit Everest (with Tenzing Norgay Sherpa). Later knighted for his accomplishments. (New Zealand)

Marty Hoey: Early RMI guide, first woman to guide on Denali, joined the 1982 Lou Whittaker Everest expedition alongside Dick Bass, but was killed after falling during the climb. (United States)

Skip Horner: Veteran guide first hired by the organizers of a 1989 Everest expedition, then hired again by AAI for the world's first guided

Everest attempt, and for a third time during AAI's first successful guided climb in 1992. Horner (along with Vern Tejas) was also the first in history to guide all of the Seven Summits. (United States)

Mark Horrell: Everest summiteer, writer, and chronicler of the Everest guiding business. (United Kingdom)

Bob John: IBM executive and one of the four people who signed up for the first-ever guided ascent of Everest, offered by AAI in 1990. (United States)

Harry Johnson: Bought guiding company Genet Expeditions after Ray Genet's death. Transformed it into one of the first Seven Summits guiding companies. (United States)

Ben Jones: AAI Everest guide since 2011. (United States)

Nick Kekus: OTT's lead Everest guide in the early 1990s. (United Kingdom)

Keith Kerr: Hong Kong–based businessman, who was part of the first group of client climbers ever to reach the summit of Everest as part of a guided expedition, in May of 1992, with AAI. (United Kingdom)

Dorje Khatri: Early mentor of Nirmal Purja and Mingma David; killed in the avalanche of 2014. (Nepal)

Kari Kobler: Veteran guide and founder of guiding company Kobler & Partner. (Switzerland)

Baltasar Kormákur: Director of the 2015 *Everest* film. (Iceland)

Jon Krakauer: Writer and climber who joined Adventure Consultants' 1996 guided Everest climb while on assignment for *Outside* magazine and wrote the bestselling 1997 book *Into Thin Air*. (United States)

Simon Lowe: Climber and managing director of Jagged Globe. (United Kingdom)

Heather Macdonald: Early RMI and IMG guide, one of the earliest women to guide on 8,000-meter peaks, including Everest. (United States)

Garrett Madison: Former lead Everest guide for AAI; founder of Madison Mountaineering; holds the third-most Everest ascents for a Western climber (thirteen). (United States)

George Mallory: Earliest Everest explorer, involved in several attempts in the early twentieth century; died above 8,000 meters on the north side, along with fellow climber Sandy Irvine, in 1924. (United Kingdom)

Dan Mazur: Climber and founder of guiding company Summit Climb. (United States)

Reinhold Messner: First person to climb Everest without oxygen, in 1978, and solo, in 1980. Considered by many to be the greatest mountaineer of all time. Vocal critic of the Everest guiding industry. (Austria)

Mark Miller: Cofounder of guiding company Out There Trekking (OTT); Miller was killed in a plane crash near Kathmandu in 1992. (United Kingdom)

Simone Moro: Professional alpinist and sponsored North Face athlete, who was at the center of the 2013 conflict between Western and Sherpa climbers. Works as a helicopter rescue pilot in the Khumbu Valley. (Italy)

Tim Mosedale: Independent Everest guide with seven ascents. (United Kingdom)

Bernard Muller: Pioneering 8,000-meter mountaineer and independent guide in the late 1980s and early 1990s. (France)

Arne Naess Jr.: Shipping magnate and leader of the 1985 Everest expeditions that included Chris Bonington, Dick Bass, and David Breashears; died in a climbing accident in South Africa in 2004. (Norway)

Larry Nielson: Member of the 1982 and 1983 Everest expeditions that Dick Bass was a part of; became the first American to summit Everest without oxygen in 1983. (United States)

Sherry Ortner: Anthropologist and author of seminal articles and books about Sherpa culture, in particular as it relates to the mountaineering industry on Everest in the 1980s and 1990s. (United States)

Jennifer Peedom: Australian filmmaker and director of the 2015 documentary *Sherpa*, who was on the mountain filming in 2014, the year of the catastrophic avalanche. (Australia)

Adele Pennington: Everest guide for Jagged Globe and one of the first women to guide on Everest. (United Kingdom)

Mike Perry: Founder of guiding company High Country Expeditions, one of the first to guide on 7,000-meter peaks in the Himalayas. (New Zealand)

Peter Potterfield: Founding editor-in-chief of MountainZone.com in 1996, the first as-it-happens online newsfeed of Himalayan climbing and global adventure; sponsor of the 1999 Mallory search expedition. (United States)

Nirmal "Nims" Purja: Cofounder of guiding company Elite Expeditions (Elite Exped). International celebrity with more than two million Instagram followers. Leader of the "Project Possible" mission in which he set a new record for scaling the fourteen 8,000-meter peaks. (Nepal)

Rick Ridgeway: Renowned climber and regular chaperone of Dick Bass and Frank Wells during their quest to climb the Seven Summits; cowrote their book *Seven Summits*, recounting their four-year adventure. (United States)

Mike Roberts: Veteran guide for Adventure Consultants between 2004 and 2019. (New Zealand)

David Rosenthal: Former publisher at Random House and important collaborator on Jon Krakauer's book *Into Thin Air*. (United States)

Grayson Schaffer: Journalist and former editor at *Outside* magazine; current correspondent. (United States)

Gerhard Schmatz: Climber, lawyer, and spouse of Hannelore. Leader of the Everest expedition in 1979 that included Nick Banks and Ray Genet. (Germany)

Hannelore Schmatz: Climber and spouse of Gerhard. First woman to die on Everest, in 1979, which happened after she summited. (Germany)

David Sharp: Client climber who died high on Everest, while climbing as a client of company Asian Trekking, sparking controversy over guiding industry ethics. (United Kingdom)

Ang Dorjee Sherpa: Longtime sirdar for Adventure Consultants, who has been with the company since their first successful guided climb in 1992. (Nepal)

Ang Jangbu Sherpa: Early high-altitude worker for IMG, who went on to found Beyul Treks, which has grown to become one of the largest back-end logistics companies in Nepal, and still works with IMG. (Nepal)

Ang Norbu Sherpa: IFMGA-certified guide and president of Nepal's NNMGA. (Nepal)

Ang Rita Sherpa: High-altitude worker on several early Everest expeditions, including Dick Bass's and David Breashears's 1985 climb; longtime friend of Breashears; record holder for most ascents of Everest without oxygen (ten); died in 2020. (Nepal)

Ang Tshering Sherpa: Purchased trekking company Asian Trekking in 1982 and grew it significantly; the first Nepali-owned company to offer a guided climb, in 2006; father of Dawa Steven Sherpa. (Nepal)

Apa Sherpa: Early Everest record holder, the first to reach twenty summits in 2010; prolific high-altitude worker on various guided and independent expeditions; regular guide for Asian Trekking. (Nepal)

Babu Chiri Sherpa: Sirdar for OTT with ten ascents, before his death near Camp Two in 2001. (Nepal)

Chhang Dawa Sherpa: Cofounder of Seven Summit Treks (SST), along with his two brothers, Mingma and Tashi Lakpa; formerly an employee of Nepal's largest trekking logistics company, Thamserku Trekking. (Nepal)

Dawa Steven Sherpa: CEO of Asian Trekking, the company owned by his father, Ang Tshering Sherpa. Expanded Asian Trekking from a logistics company to be a full-fledged guiding company in 2006, and went on to purchase oxygen system manufacturer Topout. (Nepal)

Dawa Yangzum Sherpa: IFMGA guide and North Face athlete, the first woman from Nepal to achieve either title. (Nepal)

Jamling Tenzing Norgay Sherpa: Eldest son of Tenzing Norgay, the first person to climb Everest; member of the *Everest* IMAX filming team. (Nepal)

Kami Rita Sherpa: Younger brother of AAI sirdar Lakpa Rita; guide for Seven Summit Treks, 14 Peaks Expedition, and his own trekking company, Khangri Experience; current Everest summit record holder with twenty-eight ascents. (Nepal)

Lakpa Rita Sherpa: Longtime sirdar for AAI, who has been with the company since 1992; lives in Washington State and now co-owns and leads treks for Khangri Experience with his brother, Kami Rita. (Nepal)

Lopsang Jangbu Sherpa: Scott Fischer's Mountain Madness sirdar during the fateful spring 1996 climb; died on Everest in the fall of 1996. (Nepal)

Maya Sherpa: Pioneering woman guide in the Himalayas and on Everest, often for Dan Mazur's Summit Climb; the wife of Dutch Everest guide Arnold Coster. (Nepal)

Mingma David Sherpa: Cofounder of guiding company Elite Expeditions (Elite Exped). Summited K2 in winter with Nims and Mingma G. Member of the "Project Possible" climbing team. (Nepal)

Mingma Gyalje Sherpa (Mingma G.): Founder of guiding company Imagine Nepal (formerly Dreamers Destination). Summited K2 in winter and has summited Everest eight times. (Nepal)

Mingma Sherpa: Cofounder of SST, along with his two brothers, Tashi Lakpa and Chhang Dawa; formerly an employee of Nepal's largest trekking logistics company, Thamserku Trekking. (Nepal)

Nawang Gombu Sherpa: Climbing partner of Jim Whittaker in 1963, during the first American ascent of Everest; worked as a guide in Washington State for Jim's brother Lou's company RMI. (Nepal)

Norbu Tenzing Sherpa: Son of Tenzing Norgay, the first person to climb Everest; vice president of the American Himalayan Foundation, based in San Francsisco. (Nepal)

Pasang Lhamu Sherpa: The first Nepalese woman to summit Everest, in 1993, on her third attempt, but she died on the descent. (Nepal)

Pasang Yangjee Sherpa: Khumbu Valley–born anthropologist and professor of lifeways in indigenous Asia at the University of British Columbia in Vancouver. (Nepal)

Phunuru Sherpa: Longtime sirdar and guide for IMG on mountains all over the world, including Everest, Denali, Vinson, and Kilimanjaro; has worked for IMG since 1999. (Nepal)

Phurba Tashi Sherpa: Longtime sirdar for Himex, since retired, who has made twenty-one ascents of Everest. (Nepal)

Sungdare Sherpa: Climbing partner of Hannelore Schmatz on Everest in 1979. (Nepal)

Tashi Lakpa Sherpa: Cofounder of SST, along with his two brothers, Chhang Dawa and Mingma; formerly an employee of Nepal's largest trekking logistics company, Thamserku Trekking. (Nepal)

Tashi Riten Sherpa: High-altitude worker involved in the 2013 conflict between Western and Sherpa climbers while employed by IMG; has since gained IFMGA certification and become the lead guide on Everest for Mountain Professionals. (Nepal)

Tendi Sherpa: Owner of TAG Nepal trekking agency, and business partner of Mike Hamill of CTSS. IFMGA-certified guide with fourteen Everest summits as of 2023. (Nepal)

Tenzing Norgay Sherpa: First person to summit Everest (with Edmund Hillary); among the most famous Nepalis in history. (Nepal/India)

Tsering Gyaltsen Sherpa: Creator of the highest Wi-Fi hot spot in the world, Everest Link.

Anil Sigdel: Nepal-born political scientist and the founder of Washington, DC–based nonprofit think tank Nepal Matters for America. (Nepal)

Eric Simonson: Early RMI guide; cofounder of International Mountain Guides (IMG) with fellow RMI guides George Dunn and Phil Ershler. (United States)

Ueli Steck: Professional alpinist at the center of the 2013 conflict between Western and Sherpa climbers; died in 2017 on Nuptse, near Everest. (Switzerland)

Terry "Mugs" Stump: Early mentor of Conrad Anker; died while guiding on Denali in 1992, after falling in a crevasse. (United States)

Vern Tejas: Early Denali guide for Genet Expeditions; went on to guide several AAI Everest climbs, including the first successful guided climb in 1992, when he and fellow guide Skip Horner also became the first people to guide all of the Seven Summits successfully. (United States)

Jon Tinker: Became co-owner and lead Everest guide of OTT after Mark Miller's death in 1992. (United Kingdom)

Henry Todd: Founder of guiding company Himalayan Guides (not to be confused with the Nepali logistics company of the same name). Early importer to Everest of aluminum ladders and the Russian-made Poisk oxygen system. (United Kingdom)

Greg Vernovage: IMG Everest expedition leader between 2010 and 2019. (United States)

Ed Viesturs: Professional mountaineer who dabbled in guiding on Everest in the 1990s, working for Adventure Consultants, but turned his focus to becoming the first American to summit all fourteen of the 8,000-meter peaks, which he did in 2005; still occasionally guides on Rainier for RMI. (United States)

Jaime Viñals: First Guatemalan to climb the Seven Summits after attempting Everest twice with Himex and Jagged Globe, as a client in 1994 and 1999, respectively, before succeeding on his third guided attempt with Himex in 2001. (Guatemala)

Ryan Waters: Former RMI guide, founder of guiding company Mountain Professionals. (United States)

Frank Wells: Former president of Warner Bros. and Disney, who linked up with Dick Bass in the 1980s, in a quest to become the first to climb the Seven Summits; Wells had to quit the project in 1984, with Everest still to climb. (United States)

Brad Wetzler: Senior editor at *Outside* magazine in the 1990s, who worked closely with editor-in-chief Mark Bryant on Jon Krakauer's explosive story about the 1996 disaster, published in the magazine in the fall of that same year. (United States)

Jim Whittaker: Twin brother of Lou. First American to summit Everest, in 1963. Longtime CEO of outdoor retail company REI. (United States)

Lou Whittaker: Twin brother of Jim, founder of guiding company Rainier Mountaineering Inc (RMI) in 1969, based near Mount Rainier in Washington State. (United States)

Peter Whittaker: Lou Whittaker's son, who was working as a guide for RMI by age sixteen in 1974, summited Everest in 2009, and currently manages RMI. (United States)

Jim Wickwire: Veteran Seattle-based mountaineer who was part of several early Himalayan expeditions in the 1980s, including the 1982 Everest climb with Dick Bass that killed Marty Hoey. (United States)

Freddie Wilkinson: Climber, sponsored Mountain Hardwear athlete, and journalist, who has reported on Everest and mountaineering extensively. (United States)

Martín Zabaleta: Veteran Himalayan climber and guide, who worked for AAI on the first but unsuccessful guided ascent attempt of Everest in 1990. (Spain)

ACKNOWLEDGMENTS

First and foremost, I'd like to acknowledge every man and woman who has lost their life while making a living on Mount Everest. The Everest guiding industry brought unimaginable prosperity to Nepal's Sherpa population, but the cost has been similarly unimaginable. Sherpa guides, porters, and high-altitude workers deserve a book in which they are heroes and not victims. Western Everest guides, meanwhile, deserve a book in which they are shown as well-intentioned but human, and not as villains.

Understanding the modern guiding industry on Everest—and its future—required me to do an immense amount of learning and listening, and would not have been possible without the participation of Sherpas and other Nepalis. They include: the brilliant Khumbu-born-BC-based anthropologist Pasang Yangjee Sherpa; Nepalese political scientist Anil Sigdel; longtime vice president of the San Francisco–based American Himalayan Foundation, Norbu Tenzing Sherpa; three of Everest's longest-serving high-altitude workers and guides, Apa Sherpa, Phunuru Sherpa, and Lakpa Rita Sherpa; my invaluable in-country Nepalese contacts, Rajan Bhattarai and Iswari and Bhola Paudel; and my trekking partner in the Khumbu Valley, Sudip Rai.

I am also grateful for the memories and details provided by guide company owners, including Eric Simonson, Russell Brice, Steve Bell, Guy Cotter, and Todd Burleson, which were equally vital to this account. Though they represent a small handful of the hundred or so people I interviewed for the book, they feature heavily and were extremely generous with their time, as well as with background research and fact-checking. Thank you as well to the many other Western climbers and guides who offered up important historical insight, including Yvon Chouinard, Conrad Anker, Dave Hahn, Wally Berg, David Hamilton, Willie Benegas, Dan Mazur, Heather Macdonald, Peter Whittaker, Jimmy Chin, Simone Moro, Robert Anderson, and Alan Arnette.

Just like Dick Bass, my own journey with Everest, at least when it came to this book, began with David Breashears. Thank you, David— there is not a single living person that I can think of with more experience, insight, institutional understanding, and opinions about Everest, spanning four decades and especially regarding the dawn of the guiding era.

The editors and writers of *Outside* magazine, meanwhile, have probably been the most thorough and faithful chroniclers of the guiding era on Everest, and I would like to thank them for their stellar reporting, which I was fortunate to have on hand as research material, and occasionally narrative material.

My agent, Danielle Svetcov, came into my life at just the right time, when I needed a boost of enthusiasm, creativity, and perspective on why there might be room in the world for yet another Everest book. Danielle is my dream collaborator.

My editor at Gallery, Max Meltzer, meanwhile, did a masterful job distilling this story into a narrative that feels very different from anything else out there about the world's most famous—and controversial—

mountain. Max's equal reverence for storytelling and mountaineering history is baked into every line in this book. I also want to thank everyone else at Gallery, including publisher Jennifer Bergstrom, associate publisher Jennifer Long, editorial director Aimee Bell, publicity director Sally Marvin, publicist Sydney Morris, associate publicist Cassidy Sattler, marketing director Bianca Ducasse, managing editor Caroline Pallotta, production editor Jonathan Evans, and designer Jaime Putorti, who threw themselves into the making and publication of this book.

I probably never would have even considered trying to climb mountains for fun or to make a living as a journalist if it weren't for my late mother, Sherry. My father, Fred, meanwhile, is as sharp as ever and I felt lucky to have had such a reliable reader and sounding board throughout the writing process. The notion of writing a book also feels much less preposterous when the most avid reader you've known throughout your life happens to be your stepmother, and the owner of the local independent bookstore for forty years happens to be your stepfather. Thank you, Vicki and Michael.

My deepest gratitude goes to my wife, Amy, and our two daughters, Autumn and Isla. Living with a writer, especially one who works from home, can be strange—we're always there but somehow still never around. Always know that the loud and messy life happening right outside my office door was just what I needed, as essential to my process as my morning cup of coffee.

NOTE on SOURCES

The backbone of this book was built from the interviews I conducted, many of them with men and women who have been intimately involved with the guiding industry on Mount Everest for its entire existence. The book is full of direct quotes from these interviews. It's also full of material that was not directly quoted, but that helped me paint a faithful, accurate, and vivid picture—the detailed memories, descriptions, and stories people shared. Among the more than 120 people I interviewed were multiple sources who were not quoted in the book—and in some cases, not even mentioned—but who provided further clarity to a complex narrative and verified the most obscure details. I double-checked and cross-referenced every detail, chronology, and rumor with multiple sources, whenever possible.

Many books that have preceded this one were also invaluable sources, and I now own a much more extensive Everest library than when I started this project. Dick Bass and Frank Wells's story in *Seven Summits*, as chronicled by Rick Ridgeway, was indispensable. It not only became my primary reference for Bass and Wells's Seven Summits journey, but

it also informed subsequent original interviews I conducted with Ridgeway and two of Bass's four children, Jim and Barbara, among others.
Another well-worn reference book in my collection is Walt Unsworth's
Everest: A Mountaineering History, considered the definitive record of
Everest expeditions between 1922 and 1999. I also regularly referred
to books like Jon Krakauer's *Into Thin Air* and Anatoli Boukreev's *The
Climb* (especially when writing about the 1996 tragedy), as well as the
autobiographies of important figures in Everest's history, such as those
of Tenzing Norgay Sherpa, Lou Whittaker, David Breashears, Chris
Bonington, Reinhold Messner, and Nirmal Purja (a.k.a. Nimsdai).

Another incredibly important chronicler of the guiding era on
Everest—and a key reference in my reporting—has been *Outside* magazine. For forty years, *Outside* has been covering climbing on Everest
in more depth than any other publication. With access to the print
archives, I not only studied *Outside*'s coverage of Everest between 1985
and 2023, but also referenced or quoted the magazine multiple times
and interviewed reporters who wrote some of the more seminal features.

Last but not least, my accuracy handrail throughout the process
was something called the Himalayan Database—without which I'm
not even sure a book like this would be possible. It was started by a
young Kathmandu-based American reporter named Elizabeth Hawley in the 1960s. Though not a mountaineer herself, Hawley immersed
herself in the world of Himalayan climbing, first ascents, controversies, and tragedies. Soon she found herself recording each and every
expedition—across all high peaks of the Himalayas—and Everest
guides and climbers became meticulous in liaising with Hawley in the
name of keeping the most accurate records on every ascent, death, near
miss, or milestone, as they continue to do today. Hawley died in 2018,
but equally dedicated stewards have taken over, and their records can
now be accessed as an online database.

As a result, just as I was able to go to the World Bank's website for accurate social and economic statistics about Nepal, by typing just a few keywords into the Himalayan Database, I was able to confirm things like whether a particular Sherpa climber was part of particular expedition, who the other expedition members were, how many people summited, and whether there were any fatalities and what caused them. Almost all stats in the book are sourced from the Himalayan Database (and then double-checked with people involved, when possible). Everyone I spoke to expressed a great reverence for Hawley's work that I too now share. The ability to access so many layers of detail so quickly freed up my time and energy for finding the great stories behind the numbers.

INDEX

ABOUT *the* AUTHOR

Will Cockrell has spent more than twenty years as a senior editor, writer, and consultant for national magazines including *Men's Journal*, *Outside*, *Men's Fitness*, and *GQ*. His work has been awarded by the American Society of Magazine Editors and Professional Publishers Association UK. A former outdoor guide, Cockrell has covered Everest throughout his career, and has visited Everest base camp in Nepal. He lives with his family in Los Angeles, California. Find more at his website, WillCockrell.com.